MAN INTO WOLF

MAN INTO WOLF

AN ANTHROPOLOGICAL INTERPRETATION
OF SADISM, MASOCHISM, AND
LYCANTHROPY

*a lecture
delivered at·a meeting
of the Royal Society of Medicine
by*

ROBERT EISLER

with an introduction by

SIR DAVID K. HENDERSON
F.R.C.P. (Ed. and Lon.), F.R.S.E.

GREENWOOD PRESS, PUBLISHERS
NEW YORK

ʾΕστιν γάρ τις ἡδονή λύπη συγγενής. ['For there is a kind of pleasure that is akin to pain.']—Metrodôrus, quoted by Seneca, *Epistulae ad Lucilium* (*Epist*. xcix. 26)

. . . *curae sua cuique voluptas*
Haec quoque ab alterius grata dolore venit. ['Each man is concerned with his own pleasure; and that is sweet which springs from another's pain.']—Ovid, *Ars amatoria*, I. 749 s.

Animal prius est homine. ['The animal is prior to man.']— Boethius, *Arithmetica*, I. i. p. 10

Quisque suos patimur manes. ['Each man suffers his own spirit.']— Virgil, *Aeneid*, VI. 743

'As to the diseases of the body the physician is now in command. The microbes which cause the acute infections are in full retreat. That retreat might before long become a rout.

'I can tell you no such tale of triumph when we have tried to follow the working of the mind and its many aberrations. In this field our innocence is disconcerting. In consequence of this gap in our knowledge, we have not acquired the art of living together, either at home, where there is a threat of civil discord, or abroad, where there is the menace of war. This is the crucial problem which confronts society in our time.'—Lord Moran, President of the Royal College of Physicians, speaking in Canterbury Cathedral, 25 June 1949. *The Observer*, 26 June 1949.

CONTENTS

INTRODUCTION

BY PROFESSOR SIR DAVID K. HENDERSON
F.R.C.P. (Ed. and Lon.), F.R.S.E.

IT is a great privilege and honour to be invited to write a fore-word to Dr. Robert Eisler's book dealing with 'An Anthropological Interpretation of Sadism, Masochism and Lycanthropy'. I was fortunate enough to be the Chairman of the Psychiatric Section of the Royal Society of Medicine when Dr. Eisler lectured to the Section on this topic. I was enthralled and amazed by the arresting manner in which he presented his material, by the depth of his knowledge, and by his modesty. He conveyed a message to his audience, and he made me realize, as I had never fully done before, how much psychiatrists, lawyers and judges, schoolmasters, and ministers of religion might profit by a far greater knowledge of anthropological data, and their application to human development.

This, then, is a book which is long overdue, but there is some satisfaction in the thought that, at last, it has been undertaken by a man whose scholarly and cultural interests have developed over many years, and covered a wide variety of topics. At one time or another in his career he has interested himself in such subjects as physics, archaeology, the history of art, the history of religion, astrology, and ancient manuscripts, any one of which might be thought sufficient for any man. But Eisler has advanced much further than that, because his publications in the form of books and lectures have received recognition all over the world. Furthermore, he has taken part in and addressed important Congresses; he has lectured at the Sorbonne on religious, social and economic problems, and has even addressed the British Parliamentary Finance Committee, and the U.S. Congress Committee on the Gold Reserve Act of 1934.

It may be said, then, that Eisler is a man of many-sided interests who has added something new to whatever has engaged his attention. But his main object has always been to effect a greater understanding of his fellow-man in the hope of bettering humanity's lot socially and economically.

The problem he has set himself in this book is to study and sift the evidence in relation to the question how anthropology may make a worthwhile contribution to the art of living. It has been a pleasure and an education to read, now, what was previously the spoken word, and to sit again at the feet of one who is so truly a master of his subject. The suggestions which he makes are directed particularly to an understanding of crimes of violence, and to the mass extermination of mankind which occurs in war-time. Much, however, of what he says is capable of application to an even wider range of behaviour disorders affecting both children and adults.

This book is presented in a rather unusual manner. In the first place we have the lecture itself; then those explanations and annotations which a reader might demand are supplied in the most lavish and comprehensive manner. They constitute a mine of information which should satisfy the anxious spirit of the most curious.

In analysing the basic factors leading to sadism and masochism Dr. Eisler draws attention to what he describes as 'a feeble sympathetic resonance', the lack of emotional response, the insanity affecting altruistic feeling which forms so large a part of the constitution some of us describe as the psychopathic personality. This, however, according to Eisler, is not simply a throw-back to primeval savagery, for, as he shows, primitive man in his primeval forest was not a killer but rather a peaceful creature—*le bon sauvage*. In confirmation of this fact the author mentions numerous small tribes who have never as yet heard of or encountered war. Killing and being killed has been a developmental process whereby the carnivorous, predatory packs, the ancestors of the hunting and game-seeking tribes, have preyed on the vegetarian, frugivorous, peace-loving herds. Eisler elaborates his theme by utilizing Jung's conception of archetypal race memories. Such memories may be not only ancestral, but may occur even in the sub-human animal strata of the collective unconscious. Confirmation of such a view may receive considerable support from an interpretation of a particular person's dream life. The development of these ideas leads Eisler, in conclusion, to ask the question which is in all our minds: 'Must war go on?' He is hopeful that, if his thesis of man as essentially a peace-loving, non-jealous, non-fighting being can be accepted, the wolf's mask can be discarded, and the world return to a state of innocence. How such a transformation can be effected is a larger question altogether, but the information contained in this book helps to focus the issue, gives us much food for thought, and sends out a challenge which we must all strive to answer. The elucidation and understanding of the anthropological factors here so skilfully unfolded and collected make a great contribution towards a return to that saner, safer and better world so much to be desired. This book, therefore, is one not for the scientist alone, but for everyone interested in human betterment. A man who, in addition to all his scientific attainments, served as an officer in the Austrian 59th Infantry Regiment during the first World War, and suffered the indignities and brutalities of Dachau and Buchenwald in the year before the second World War, is well qualified to give a stirring and stimulating message to mankind.

Since the above Introduction was written, it was with profound regret I noted that on 17 December 1949 Dr. Robert Eisler had passed away. Everyone will deeply regret that he did not live to see the publication of his book, to which he had given so much work and thought.

AUTHOR'S FOREWORD

THE aim of this book is wider than its title would lead the reader to expect. It attempts to suggest the possibility of a historical, or rather prehistorical, evolutionist derivation of all crimes of violence, from the individual attack on life known as murder or manslaughter to the collective organized killing which we call war. The author has tried to show that the mute witness of the fossil archaeological remains of prehistory—the period before articulated human thought found the means of permanent expression in word and writing—can be made intelligible on the basis of Jung's theory of archetypal ideas surviving in the ancestral subconscious strata of the human mind and revealing themselves all over the world in the legends, myths and rites of historic man as well as in the fleeting dreams and lasting delusions of contemporary humanity.

If this is true, an introductory chapter of fundamental importance can be lifted from the realm of the myths or legends concerning the 'Fall of Man' into the range of the authentic history of humanity. If it is not, the author would like to say with Macaulay*: 'If I am in the wrong, my errors may set the minds of others at work, and may be the means of bringing both them and me to a knowledge of the truth.'

If Professor Jung is right in assuming, on the basis of his wide experience as an analyst, that the memory of a contemporary human being contains a basic, unconscious, ancestral layer or system of archetypal, mnemonic engrams, discussed in our Appendix I, it is obvious that the psychiatrist needs the help of the historian and prehistorian of religions, myths, legends and superstitions. A practical example of this will be found in Appendix V. Indeed, Professor Jung, a son of the manse, has been the first to recognize this imperative need and to organize, for the purpose of meeting it, the annual *Eranos* Conferences at

Ascona between the members of his school and the Zürich Psychological Club on the one hand, and a number of specialists in the various linguistic branches of the history of religion and of anthropology on the other. In these discussions the present writer had the honour of participating by giving a number of lectures in August 1935. He wishes to thank Professor Jung for what he learnt from him on the occasion of that first fortunate meeting and ever since.

To facilitate the critic's task, this book has deliberately been arranged in an unusual way. It starts with the text of the author's address to the Psychiatric Section of the Royal Society of Medicine, reproduced as exactly as the speaker can remember words not written down in advance. To this text, which contains the new thesis in all essential details, the author has added, in the form of notes, the whole factual material on which his statements were based. A lecturer addressing a learned audience is expected to answer all questions and counter all objections raised in the customary discussion following the lecture. The reader of the lecture as published in book form may be expected to feel the same need for supplementary information and justification as the original audience. To supply this, a bracketed reference number has been added to every word or sentence that could possibly suggest a question or raise an objection in the reader's mind. Every time the specialist in another branch of learning or the educated layman feels inclined to ask 'Why do you say this?' or 'How do we know that?', 'Who is this man?' or 'What on earth is that?', this reference number should guide him not only to the required bibliographical or biographical references, but in many cases to a shorter or longer monographic treatment of a subsidiary problem not adequately dealt with in the existing literature† on all the various subjects touched upon in the lecture itself, which can only now for the first time be seen in their proper connexion.

It was inevitable that these elaborations of every single point raised by the lecturer should be found to occupy in all much more space than the thesis itself. There should be no harm in this disproportion. It is hoped that these notes or excursuses may prove as readable as the main text for those who want to dig down to the empirical rock-bottom of the factual foundations upon which the author has based his anthropo-sociological explanation of what must be admitted to be the most paradoxical feature of the human mind: the attempt to obtain some sort of satisfaction, *prima facie* incomprehensible, from the suffering of pain or the infliction of it on other sentient beings.

It would, no doubt, have been possible to insert many or all of the subsidiary papers which are here printed as notes into an expanded text of the lecture and thus convert it into a more orthodox book. This, however, would not have made the main thesis either clearer or more convincing, but rather the contrary. The many trees to be looked at more closely would have obscured rather than shown the way through the wood. A chapter of 'Conclusions' would necessarily have had to be added at the end, instead of the straightforward presentation of the problem and its solution which the reader now finds at the beginning, its proper place. Instead of wading through the book to these conclusions, the reader would naturally have started to read the book from the tail end. As it is now arranged, he will be able to begin at the beginning, and after a few dozen pages, having read the gist of it, decide whether or not he wants to go on into the greater detail of the notes. Surely this is both a more logical and a more practical arrangement than hiding the skeleton of the structure in the mass of documentation and leaving it to the reader to disentangle, by a system of marking and underlining in red and blue the main lines of thought.

Himself a voracious reader, the author knows a good deal about the art of skipping, so necessary to those who have to study voluminous books for their own special purposes. In the preface to a previous large book §—μέγα βιβλίον, μέγα κακόν— (the greater the book the greater the evil)—he supplied a special guide for expert skippers. From the numerous reviews he was able to see how exactly and willingly these directions had been followed. This time he has decided to go one better: here is a fat book where there is no need to skip any pages in order to get rapidly through what the author has to say. Less than an hour's reading will enable even a plodding student to assimilate a lecture delivered in no more than that time. If this hour's reading is found illuminating, as the lecturer trusts it will be, the large amount of carefully sifted material which follows the main thesis should satisfy the most exacting appetite for corroboratory evidence. Such evidence will not be required and need not be looked into by those who reject the thesis *a limine*, and would not be rendered convincing to them by any amount of further argument.

Quotations in foreign languages other than Greek have been printed in Roman letters, not only to save expense, but also to avoid the unnecessary pedantry of using unfamiliar type in a book intended for the general reader as well as for the various specialists interested in the subject.

I am well aware of the fact that many people will feel inclined to protest against such a subject being treated at all, let alone in all its gruesome details.

In a recent book on *Mental Abnormality* the distinguished author, Dr. Millais Culpin, late Professor of Medical Psychology in the University of London, has devoted little more than a dozen lines to the problem of sadism and masochism. 'The germ of these aberrations', he says, 'lies in all of us, and I have more than once had the opportunity of noting the effect that publicity given to their manifestations has in stimulating a tendency towards either perversion.' Considering the important part played by imitation (see notes *103, 104*) in the origins of lycanthropy, no-one would feel inclined to question the truth of this statement. Publicity in the sensation-mongering Press is, however, a very different thing from ventilating the problem in a scientific publication, even if it is destined for a wider public than the professions concerned with the adequate psychiatric, social and political treatment of the phenomena in question.

Also it should not be forgotten that there is such a thing as the 'abreaction' of a-social, nay criminal, tendencies by imaginary activities. For reasons explained below (pp. 25–6) mild sadistic or masochistic propensities can be completely satisfied by gazing spellbound at such films as *No Orchids for Miss Blandish* or reading such novels as those of de Sade and Sacher-Masoch (see notes *1, 2*). If these imaginative outlets are blocked, persons subject to such cravings will not be helped in overcoming them, but will probably resort to far less innocuous ways of finding satisfaction.

Even in the Victorian age (1892) the American translator of

Krafft-Ebing's *Psychopathia Sexualis*, Dr. Charles Gilbert Chaddock of Philadelphia, discussing in his preface 'the baneful influence possibly exerted by such publications', admits that 'the appearance of the seventh edition' (there is now a twenty-fourth!) 'could not be accounted for, were its circulation confined to scientific readers' and that a morbid 'interest on the part of the public is accountable for a part of the wide circulation of the book', yet concludes with these words: 'But in spite of this disadvantage the injury done by implanting knowledge of sexual pathology in unqualified persons is not to be compared with the good accomplished'.

Nowadays, when the therapeutic efforts of the psychiatrist are mainly aimed at giving the patient as much understanding of his own state of mind and as much help in unravelling the complicated knots into which it may have tied itself as possible, it sounds strange to hear 'the implanting of knowledge of sexual pathology in unqualified' minds described as a 'disadvantage'. It may still be true that 'he who increaseth knowledge, increaseth sorrow', but it does not follow that for the lay mind 'ignorance is bliss' or, for the matter of that, equal to in-nocence (note *240*). On the contrary, the author would at all times be willing to underwrite the words of Ben Jonson:

'I know no disease of the soul but ignorance:...a pernicious evil, the darkener of man's life, the disturber of his reason and common confounder of truth'.

R. E.

London, 28 October 1948

Note. The figures in brackets in the text pages and the signs * † § in this foreword refer to the notes on pp. 53 ff. below.

MAN INTO WOLF

AN ANTHROPOLOGICAL INTERPRETATION
OF SADISM, MASOCHISM, AND
LYCANTHROPY

MAN INTO WOLF

AN ANTHROPOLOGICAL INTERPRETATION
OF SADISM, MASOCHISM, AND
LYCANTHROPY

THERE is a copious literature—probably greater than I am aware of—on the syndrome of psychological phenomena named after the two famous or, if you prefer, notorious novelists who described them in their works from their own unfortunate experiences: the Marquis Donatien Alphonse François de Sade [1] and the Chevalier Leopold de Sacher-Masoch [2].

The very fact that these phenomena are generally described as 'unnatural' or 'perverse' [3] is sufficient evidence of the failure of psychology—which is, after all, a discipline of natural science —to understand and explain them. If there are any 'laws of nature' [4], no human activity can 'pervert' or run counter to them.

As a matter of fact, the paradox of the widespread desire to suffer pain—for which I introduced [5] in 1904 the term *algobulia* to distinguish it from Offner's and von Schrenck-Notzing's concept of *algolagnia* [6], that is, sexual excitement or gratification obtained by suffering pain [7]—exists only for the naïve hedonist who believes that all human, indeed all animal, behaviour is aimed at obtaining a maximum of pleasure and a minimum of pain, or even asserts that the desire for pleasure and the fear of pain are the main motives of all our actions [8].

'Why', says St. Augustine [9], 'does man want to see (on the stage) mournful scenes full of misery which he would not himself care to live through in reality? And yet the spectator wants to be dolefully affected, nay the pain itself is what he relishes. Is not that a lamentable madness? [*10*] . . . Is it, then, that tears and pains are loved? Yet every human being strives for pleasure!'

The truth of the matter is that the hedonistic theory of motivation is equivalent to the absurd belief of a person so deluded as to think that the power which drives motor vehicles through our streets or stops them at the crossings is provided by the rays emanating from the red and green traffic-lights. If we [*11*] adopt Münsterberg's [*12*] and William James's [*13*] more plausible view that emotions are complexes of somatic sensations, resulting from the motor and vasomotor, 'volitional' or 'conative' reactions of our body to its environment, pleasure and pain are seen to be nothing but the signals—green or red as it were—informing us of the positive or negative measure of our organism's adaptation to its spatio-temporal environment or to the particular constituent parts of it; in other words, of the 'utility' or 'disutility' of every 'thing' relevant to our survival and to the free or hampered expansion of our lives.

If pleasure and pain are such plus or minus signals conveyed to us by our somatic sensations, there must be some sort of sense-organ—presumably the sympathetic nervous system—for receiving and conveying this vitally necessary information to the reacting centre. In the absence of stimuli this sense-organ would be subject to atrophy and degeneration, just as the eyes of the little reptile *Proteus anguineus Laur.* living in the dark underground caves and subterranean rivers of the Carso have become blind through absence of light.

Because a sense-organ degenerates by atrophy in the absence of the specific stimuli to which it reacts, every sense-organ may be said to stand in need of functional exercise, no less than every muscle of our body. Since it is as vitally necessary for an organism to experience pain as to enjoy pleasure, perhaps even more vital for it to be aware of dissatisfaction than of satisfaction, to be speedily informed of a lack of adaptation rather than of its perfected achievement [*14*], which it has to retain, quite possibly, by mere inaction [*15*]—the organs for sensing pain need a minimum of stimulation just as much as do those for sensing pleasure. If an individual or a society is well enough adapted to its environment to feel moderately happy in this world—as Athens seems to have been in the days when she gave birth to the incomparable majesty of Greek tragedy, or Elizabethan England in the time of Shakespeare and his rivals—the need for experiencing, by 'sympathy', the sufferings of their less fortunate fellow-creatures will be imperiously felt by a number of wealthy and happy citizens large enough to support the production of 'tragic' drama, and to accept works of art which present or recall subjects having a painful connotation. Nor is high tragedy, the spectacle of 'great suffering nobly borne', the only means of satisfying the need to stimulate our organs of pain-perception. The crowds attracted by the piteous, often sordid spectacle of real catastrophe or witnessing the horrors of bull-fights, boxing matches, or the gladiatorial performances of the ancient Roman circus; the girl so well known to me years ago, who followed every funeral she could, just to have a good cry in sympathy with the bereaved; the other, now a major poet in my native language [16], who in her young days, remembering Andersen's tale of *The Princess on the Pea* [17], 'put pebbles into her shoes so as to feel a bodily pain to balance her mental suffering' and who 'in these years loved nothing so much as pain'; or the insensitive hysteric who burns the back of her hands with glowing cigarette-stubs or match-ends, all bear witness to a felt need for experiencing pain—not, of course, exceeding a certain varying limit of intensity [18]. This limit can be raised to an astonishing height in cases where the desire for self-torture is reinforced by the strong mystical motives at the bottom of the various forms of religious asceticism [18].

The phenomena of algobulia will thus be seen to fall naturally and easily into a well-known general pattern of appreciation applying to all our somatic and external sensations.

Everyone knows that our food and drink may be 'not sweet [sour, salt, bitter] enough', or '*too* sweet' (cloying), 'too sour, too bitter, too salt'. A graph (p. 26), its abscissa denoting the intensity of the sensation, its ordinate its 'positive' or 'negative' appreciation, will show a curve of typical shape: the dissatisfaction caused by a faint stimulus difficult to perceive diminishes and is gradually converted into growing satisfaction, which soon reverses its direction and turns again into increasing dissatisfaction when the intensity of the stimulus passes its optimum strength. The formula is known to apply to all sensations of colour, sound, pressure, friction, or warmth, to kinesthetic perceptions of movement (that is of difference of position in space-time), to all smells and to all tastes.

It is necessary to know this pattern of values or appreciation in order to understand the sadist and the masochist. The sadist, including the murderer of the Neville Heath [19] type, is obviously a person of feeble sympathetic resonance—this being the general description of the 'a-social' individual—able to enjoy the most horrible real sufferings inflicted on others [20] just as some of us can enjoy on the stage the fictitious pain of King Oedipus piercing his own eyes, because those sufferings are sufficiently toned down through their defective transmission to the torturer's consciousness to remain just below the limit of

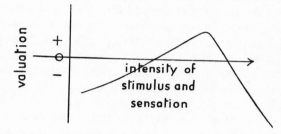

toleration, at or very near the highest point of 'ecstasy' that can be attained by algobulia. The masochist, too, is a person of subnormal emotional sensitivity whose need for emotional stimulation of a painful character cannot be fulfilled by the normal sympathy with the real, let alone the fictitious, sufferings of others, and must therefore be assuaged by a strong dose of pain directly inflicted upon his or her own organism [21].

While these considerations yield, no doubt, a measure of general understanding of the algobulic phenomena under review, they fail to explain the particular erotic side of the syndrome known to the sexologist as *algolagnia*. It is, of course, arguable that the adrenal internal secretions and the general tingling excitement caused by 'the lover's pinch which hurts but is desired' [22] or Penthesileia's blood-sucking bites [23] and scratchings are likely to irradiate into the specific sexual sphere and thus to excite an otherwise sluggish and unrespon-sive temperament. But it is by no means clear why such an indirect approach to the sexual through a general excitement should be more effective than the direct stimulation of the erogenous zones by the most expert caresses. It is not clear why the insult should not provoke an equally hostile reaction, rather than a loving and submissive response.

On the side of the active partner, the sadist who cannot become erotically excited otherwise than by inflicting cruelty of less or greater intensity on the object of his ruthless desires, there remains the paradox of the close, indeed necessary associa-tion between cruelty—the very word is derived from the Latin *cruor* = 'blood,' and means 'blood lust' [24], culminating in murder and mutilation—and love, which is, according to St. Thomas, quoting Aristotle [25], 'the desire to do good' to the person who is the object of this emotion, *i.e.* 'benevolence'. Nor can the general theory account for such peculiar features as von Sacher-Masoch's 'domineering lady in the fur'—so alluringly represented by Rubens in the famous portrait of his second wife, the fair and rosy Hélène Fourment, in a dark fur but otherwise nude [26]; or by Titian's portrait of his nude 'Bella' wrapped in a fur but baring one of her breasts [27], or for the fact that the type of Hercules with his club and lion's pelt is preferred by many a fair Deianeira to the charming and gentle Adonis [28]. Finally, the characteristic gruesome cannibalistic features [29] of sadistic murder remain entirely unexplained.

This is why psychopathologists have in the last resort turned to explaining sadism as an atavistic [30] throwback to primeval savagery [31], a theory extended by C. Lombroso [32] to all crimes of violence. The flaw in this argument is that it implies a total misrepresentation of the state of human evolution to which the term 'savagery' is properly applied. The word 'savage', from French *sauvage*, Italian *selvaggio*, Latin *silvaticus*, derived from *silva*, means nothing but a 'wood-dweller'. Now primitive man in the primeval virgin forest is most certainly not a killing, cruel, murderous or war-making animal; quite the reverse [33].

The Eskimo, the Yahgans of Tierra del Fuego, and numerous small tribes in the jungle recesses of India, Ceylon, the Malay Peninsula, Sumatra, Borneo, New Guinea and the Philippines live to this day in complete ignorance of war. Professor L. T. Hobhouse [34] enumerates twelve such timid, kindly and peaceful tribes. Sir Arthur Keith [35] has added twenty-four more, and estimates that they still number in all about half a million persons. Some of them do not even hunt or kill animals. Sir Arthur Keith [36] and Professor E. A. Hooton of Harvard [37] have tried to deny that they are representative samples of the original peaceful *bon sauvage* of Rousseau and the ancient traditions of a Golden Age [38]:

> *At vetus illa aetas cui fecimus aureae nomen*
> *Fructibus arboreis et quas humus educat herbas*
> *Fortunata fuit nec polluit ora cruore.* [39]

['But that ancient age which we call the age of gold was content with the fruits of trees and the crops that spring forth from the soil, and did not defile the mouth with blood.']

Both these distinguished authors have, however, conveniently overlooked the fact that our Primate ape ancestors were beyond any doubt perfectly innocuous frugivorous 'savages' or 'silvan' animals swinging from tree to tree in the primeval virgin forest.

With very few exceptions [40], all monkeys and apes eat nothing but fruit, seeds, tender shoots and leaves. The chimpanzee is sometimes said [41] to devour occasionally a small bird, lizard or insect, but Dr. G. M. Vevers, formerly superintendent of the London Zoological Gardens, assures me [42] that he has never seen a chimpanzee eating meat, although he has often seen one catch a sparrow or rat intruding in its cage, play with the captured animal for a while and then throw it away.

If modern man—*Neo-anthropus insipiens damnatus* [*Jacksi*] [43] —can correctly be described biologically, with William James [44], as 'the most formidable of all the beasts of prey and, indeed the only one that preys systematically on its own species' [45] and if, on the contrary, like the monkeys and great apes, the primitive fruit-collecting and root-grubbing peaceful pygmy of the jungle is properly characterized by Plato [46], and other ancient philosophers [47] as 'man the tame, unarmed' [48] animal', relying for his defence against attack only on his superior intelligence [49], there must have occurred at some time in the course of evolution a radical change in the human diet or *modus vivendi*, a mutation, as de Vries called these sudden, irrevocable alterations, such as is remembered in mankind's widespread traditions of a 'Fall' or 'original sin' [*38*], with permanently disastrous consequences.

In other words, *Pithecanthropus frugivorus*, the arboreal fruit-picking man who could find enough succulent or hard-shelled fruits, berries, leaf-buds, young shoots and sprouts all the year round only in the tropical and subtropical forest-belt, is the legendary 'good savage' of the primeval Golden [*50*] Age, living on acorns [*51*] and at peace with the other animals, like *Adam*, that is 'Man' in the 'garden of the desert' [*52*], the oasis of the date-palm growers, and like the hairy Engidu eating herbs with the animals and drinking water at their pool in the Babylonian Gilgamesh epic [*53*].

Just as the Malays call the great anthropoid apes living in the jungles of Borneo and Sumatra *Orang-utan*, 'Wood-men', so the Romans named the aboriginal primitive inhabitants of the Italian forests—in historical times, rather the ghosts, which were believed to survive, of these by then extinct wood-dwellers— 'Silvani'. Another name for these wood-people was *Fauni*, from 'favere' [*54*], *i.e.* the 'favouring', good spirits. Thus we encounter here also the notion of the *bon sauvage*, the harmless and kind wood-dweller, and by no means that of a primeval, predatory and cruel, bloodthirsty [*25*], a-social brute, a *bête humaine* [*55*], a type to which the modern sadist murderer could represent an 'atavist' throwback.

That man was from the beginning a social [*56*] or gregarious animal was emphasized by Aristotle in a famous passage of his *Zoology* [*57*]. Everyone knows that he distinguishes gregarious animals (ἀγέλαῖα ζῷα) from the dispersed (σποραδικά) and solitary (μοναδικά). Among the gregarious creatures (ἀγελαῖα) he singles out civic or urban animals (πολίτικα ζῷα) [*58*]—which work in collaboration, such as bees, wasps, ants or men [*59*].

The gregarious nature of *Homo sapiens socialis* [*60*] proves that he cannot be descended from an ancestor similar to the solitary large apes of the chimpanzee, gorilla and orang-utan type [*61*], but rather from some social species resembling the modern gibbon or siamang [*62*]. The recent solitary, 'a-social' great apes armed with long powerful canine teeth for the fierce and passionate combats indulged in by the males in pursuit of the females—for instance among the present-day Hamadryas baboons [63]—seem to have evolved in a kind of blind-alley direction by a process of sexual selection which allowed only the strongest, tallest and most formidable males to transmit their individual characteristics to their offspring. This has led on the one hand to a constant increase in size of the species (gigantism), and on the other to a complete and permanent break-up of the social organism, such as can be observed temporarily during the mating period among otherwise gregarious species [64].

The social life of the monkey- and ape-herd that persists among the human species can, therefore, have been maintained and developed only among those Primates which refrained from the murderous sex fights [65] leading to the evolution of the strong and protruding canines [66] of the great apes and of Piltdown man [67] as well as to the gigantism of *Meganthropus palaeo-javanicus* and *Giganthropus sinensis* of Java and south-eastern Asia [68]—the biblical 'giants' that 'were on earth' [69].

A species of this non-jealous, non-fighting kind is the Central American howler-monkey *Alouatta pallida aequatorialis* [70]. The oestrous females of these wholly peaceful herds of leaf- and fruit-eaters, who are almost entirely free from sexual envy and jealousy, accept all the males as they come and retire after having assuaged their appetites. The wooing is done now by the male, now by the female. Quarrels between the males, patiently looking on and waiting for their opportunity, are very rare, presumably because the number of adult females is far superior to that of adult males (a proportion of 42 per cent to 16 per cent was counted in the herds observed by Carpenter). This behaviour-pattern allows all the males, not only the tallest and strongest, to transmit their characteristics to the offspring. It does not produce either dental or ungular armature or gigantism, but a completely integrated herd in which every female is conditioned to mating association with all males.

It is obvious that the peaceful, food-collecting pygmies, ignorant of war [33], who inhabit the jungles and virgin forests, must be descended from the non-fighting, howler-monkey type Primates whose sexual behaviour pattern survives 'archetypally' and atavistically in the average client of the public brothel, in the so-called *voyeur* [71] and in the *mari complaisant* whose tolerance is despised by the average Frenchman [72] and indeed by the possessive *homme moyen* of every nation.

This attitude has, however, been courageously defended by the great English poets Blake [73] and Shelley [74] and the equally great British philosopher Bertrand Russell against the prevailing public opinion which supports the possessive attitude of the jealous, sexually combatant male [75] who considers himself entitled to kill both his rival and his faithless mistress or wife [76].

The peaceful, non-jealous attitude of the *Alouatta* has survived in a number of primitive tribes [77], such as the North Siberian Chukchi, where up to ten pairs may live together in a mating community and where a particular degree of kinship, 'new-tungit', 'men having their wives in common,' is recognized [78]. The Polynesian inhabitants of the Pelew Islands have free-love clubs [79]. What else were the witches' covens, *esbats* or sabbats, described with such picturesque detail in the reports of the witch-trials [80] held all over Europe and in New England down to the eighteenth century? 'The Yakuts see nothing immoral in free love, provided only that nobody suffers material loss by it' [81]. The exchange of wives between brothers, cousins, friends, hosts and guests is often recorded as customary by ethnologists in many parts of the world [82]. Only sociologists unfamiliar with the ways of our modern world would be willing to assert that group relations of this kind are entirely unknown among our contemporaries, although reliable evidence from written, let alone printed, documents is difficult to come by [83].

All through the history of mankind isolated attempts have been made to consolidate and safeguard the cohesion of the herd by eliminating the socially disruptive effects of sexual jealousy and possessiveness: the constitution of Sparta, attributed to Lycurgus [84], Plato's Utopian 'Republic' [85], probably influenced by 'Lycurgus', intended to restore the primitive sexual communism said to have prevailed in pre-Hellenic Athens [86], the *Niyoga* doctrine of the Indian Arya Samaj [87], mating every man with eleven women, every woman with eleven men, the Oneida community of the Christian mystic John H. Noyes (b. 1811) [*88*] are the best-known examples.

The atavist or, to use Jung's term, 'archetypal' [*89*] character of these ideas is particularly clear where the principle of Free Love is encountered in connection with a strict 'paradisic', ethical vegetarianism and the absolute prohibition of killing any living creature, as for instance, in the case of the 'Angel Dancers' of Hackensack in New Jersey [*90*].

We do not here attempt to decide the question whether the vegetarianism observed by several hundred millions of Hindus [*91*] is a survival of a primeval, originally subhuman diet or rather an atavistic revival like the Orphic and Pythagorean abstention from all animal food [*92*] among the ancient Greeks and Romans, among Oriental Christians [*93*] and Manichaeans [*94*], as well as among some Occidental Christian sects, Humanitarians and Ethical Societies [*95*]. What interests us in this context is rather the mysterious origin of the carnivorous or, more exactly, omnivorous diet of the vast majority of recent hunting, slaughtering and belligerent mankind.

The decisive step towards the solution of this fundamental problem was made by Wilfred Trotter (1872–1939) [*96*] the famous surgeon in ordinary to King George V. He it is who added to the Aristotelian zoological foundation of sociology [*57, 58*] a momentous complement by pointing out the essential difference between a herd of mouflon or bison armed only with horns and hooves, but with their leading rams and bulls and properly posted sentries, all ready at a signal to take up a defensive formation against an attacker, and a pack of wolves, wild dogs, jackals, hyaenas, stoats, etc. organized for hunting in common [*97*]. The pack itself contrasts with the feline stalking its prey alone, each animal for himself, with even the sexes keeping no permanent functional family company [*98*].

Because the Primates, including 'ape-man' and the earliest forms of man, must have been in the main harmless frugivorous animals [*48*], the gregarious structure of the Primate population can be described only as a number of herds [*99*], not of aggressive hunting packs. 'Good at shouting', like Homeric heroes [*100*], they frightened away threatening aggressors by a concert of raucous cries, their nearest attempts to offensive defence consisting presumably in a sustained pelting of their approaching carnivorous enemies or vegetarian competitors with stones and sticks [*101*].

> *Arma antiqua manus, ungues dentesque fuerunt*
> *Et lapides et item silvarum fragmina rami* [*102*]

['The weapons of old time were the hands, the nails and teeth, stones, and broken-off branches of trees.']

At the end of the pluvial period, however, man—described by Schiller [*103*] and by Thomas Jefferson [*104*] as the 'imitative animal'—driven by hunger to aggression, learned by 'aping' the habits of the gregarious beasts of prey that pursued these early Hominidae to hunt in common, biting and devouring alive the surrounded and run-down booty.

This horrible procedure survives today in the atavistic religious rites still performed annually by the Moroccan brotherhood of the 'Isâwîyya [*105*]. In the course of it men disguised as cats, lions, wolves, hyaenas—formerly by the appropriate pelt, now by means of garments painted to resemble animal skins [*106*]—work themselves up by ritual dancing into a frenzy that enables them to tear to pieces with their bare hands living kids and lambs and to lacerate the victims with their teeth. I was able to show in 1929 the identity of this Berber rite with the Bacchic orgies of the Maenads or 'raving women' dressed in lynxes', [*107*], leopards' or foxes' pelts and called, in a lost tragedy of Aeschylus [*108*], 'the vixens' (βασσαραί), tearing to pieces and 'devouring raw' fawns, kids, lambs, snakes, fish and even children; as well as with the tearing to pieces of the 'scapegoat' in the ancient Hebrew ritual of the Day of Atonement [*109*], originally part of the vintage-feast, when the people dwelt in primitive booths of foliage, the 'tabernacles' of the Bible. In the cult of Bacchus, too, this frightful orgy [*110*] is closely connected with the ritual of the grape-harvest and the drinking of the heady new wine—forbidden to the Moslem 'Isâwîyya—which would combine with the ecstatic dancing to produce the required delirious intoxication.

The great number of ancient Indo-European tribal names, such as Luvians, Lycians, Lucanians, Dacians, Hyrcanians, etc., meaning 'wolf-men' or 'she-wolf-people' found in Italy, Greece, the Balkan peninsula, Asia Minor and North-west Persia [*111*], and the numerous Germanic, Italic and Greek personal names meaning 'wolf' and 'she-wolf' [*112*], clearly prove that the transition from the fruit-gathering herd of 'finders' [*113*] to the lupine pack of carnivorous hunters [*114*] was a conscious process accompanied by a deep emotional upheaval still remembered by man's subconscious, superindividual, ancestral memory (Jung) [*89*], and reflected in the 'superstitions'—*i.e.* the surviving atavistic beliefs—about 'lycanthropy' [*115*]. This is the Greek term, formed from λύκος = 'wolf' and ἀνθρωπία = 'humanity', for the dread folk-lore of men converted into 'wer-wolves' (Germanic *wer*, the Latin *vir*, means 'man', 'male') [*116*].

The name 'lycanthropy' is used also by alienists [*117*] to denote a particular form of raving madness manifesting itself in the patient's belief that he is a wolf [*118*], with lupine teeth [*119*], refusing to eat anything but raw, bloody meat, emitting bestial howls and indulging in unrestrained sexual attacks on any victim he can overpower. Such cases, described by Drs. Hack Tuke [*120*] and Bianchi [*121*], are now easy to understand as throwbacks to the atavistic behaviour pattern ritually preserved in the cathartic orgies of the Moroccan 'Isâwîyya and the Thracian worshippers of Dionysos Bakkhos. Ancient medicine would naturally confuse this form of psychosis with contagious canine rabies [*122*], communicable to dogs by the bite of wolves and to man by the bite of a dog, which causes man and dog to snap at and bite everything within reach and thus to spread the dread disease [*123*].

According to Germanic legends [*124*], the magic change is brought about by donning a wolf's pelt [*125*]—just as the 'Isâwîyya and the Bacchic maenads wrap themselves in animals' skins—by taking to the woods and living a nocturnal hunter's and killer's wild and blood-stained vampire [*126*] life.

The uncanny word was resuscitated in Germany in the secret terrorist and para-military 'Organization Werwolf' after the first World War, and again in Himmler's rabid speech on the new *Volkssturm* of 1945 destined to harass 'like were-wolves' the allied lines of communication in occupied Germany [*127*]. It was of were-wolves that Hitler was thinking when he said in his programme for the education of the *Hitler Jugend* [*128*] 'Youth must be indifferent to pain' [*129*]. There must be no weakness or tenderness in it. He wanted 'to see once more in the eyes of a pitiless youth the gleam of pride and independence of the beast of prey' [*130*] and to 'eradicate the thousands of years of human domestication'.

A gang of terrorists who call themselves 'the Werwolf Organization' obviously intend to 'organize' themselves and to be dreaded as a pack of wolves hunting down their victims in the dark of the night; and that is exactly what these counter-revolutionary conspirators did in 1920 and the years following.

Outbreaks of endemic lycanthropism have occurred before, notably in France at the end of the sixteenth and the beginning of the seventeenth century, when rural poachers' gangsterism seems to have hidden behind the werewolf's mask, just as a recent native terrorist crime-wave in the French and Belgian Congo, Kenya, and other African regions operated behind the sinister masquerade of a secret brotherhood of 'leopard-men' disguised in leopard-skins [*131*], like the Dionysian maenads wearing panthers' or leopards' pelts [*132*], using appropriately carved sticks as stilts in order to leave leopards' spoor on the ground and iron leopards' claws to lacerate the victims of their nocturnal prowling.

The Chinese and, since the eleventh century, the Japanese had their 'wer-foxes' corresponding to the 'vixens' of the 'Great Hunter' god Dionysos *Zagreus* [*133*]. The Norsemen had their war-mad *berserker*, *i.e.* 'bear-skin coated' fighters, battalions of whom were employed as body-guards by the Byzantine emperors [*134*]. The ancient Arcadians of the Peloponnese were no idyllic shepherds, but rough northern invaders addicted to lycanthropic practices in the service of a wolf-suckled cannibal god Ζεύς Λυκαῖος [*135*], considering themselves as 'bears' (ἀρκτοί).

The Teutonic counterpart to this Arcadian wolfish god is the Germanic Wodan with his wolves, the 'Wild Hunter' [*136*] chasing through the stormy nights at the head of his 'wild hunt'.

Since we gather from Greek sources—notably two vivid passages in Plutarch [*137*]—that the fox-pelt-clad maenads or 'raving' women who worship the Thracian 'Great Hunter' god Zagreus [*138*] did actually chase and beat the woods by night,

35

armed with torches, staves and wooden spears, it is safe to conclude that the hounds of the northern 'Wild Hunt' [*139*] heard
'coursing and barking' in the dark by frightened peasants
awakened from their sleep, were neither imaginary spooks nor
mythical personifications of storms and clouds, but secret gangs
of poachers keeping up the old bloodthirsty pagan custom of the
nightly were-wolves' hunt a long time after Europe had adopted
the milder rites of Christianity. So, also, the witches' rides to a
meeting-place, where orgiastic dances and matings with goat-
shaped 'devils' were performed, are the exact counterpart to the
wild and primitive *Bacchanalia*—orgies idealized by the con-
summate art of the Greek sculptors, vase painters and tragic
poets, whose accounts we cannot understand unless we retrans-
late them into the language of the original barbaric folklore to
which they belong. The Moroccan compatriots of the above-
mentioned 'Isâwîyya believe in men who walk about by night
in the shape of hyaenas and who cannot be shot [*140*].

'Lycanthropy', the transformation of the frugivorous human
herd into a carnivorous pack through the hunters' lupine
travesty, must be at least as old as the remains of that primitive
Chinese cave-dweller known as *Sinanthropus* [*141*] whose cannibalistic habits were betrayed by the discovery of skulls the base
whereof had been removed to give free access to the brain [*142*],
and of others that bore external marks of violence. Similar
evidence is afforded by the fossil remains of the ancient men of
Java [*143*] and of *homo Neanderthalensis* whose stone tools
(Mousterian), obviously those of non-vegetarians, were found
associated with animal long bones charred and split for
marrow [*144*].

While the jaw of Neanderthal 'man' shows the bovine type
of molars adapted to the eating of hard seeds and tough roots by
a species formerly feeding on the tender shoots and soft fruit
available in plenty in a former warmer habitat, the dog-like
type of teeth in the Piltdown mandible and the jaw of recent
man has been very plausibly explained by Marett [*145*] as
caused by a change of diet reducing the intake of vitamin C,
that is by the transition to essentially carnivorous habits.

It seems legitimate to conclude that the bones of *Sinanthropus*
and the flake-tool-making Neanderthalers (so closely associated

with glacial Europe), represent the earliest human werwolf-packs, while the African and South Asiatic core-tools—the so-called 'hand-axes', eminently suitable for root-grubbing and crushing—are the remains of the original innocuous vegetarian herds of early Man, whose mothers accidentally discovered gardening and agriculture [146] when like squirrels they buried grain and other seeds or roots in the ground to store them up for the hungry winter season and found them sprouting and multiplying in the womb of the earth.

While these vegetarian herds are the ancestors of the recent wholly peaceful food-gathering tribes and of the primitive grain- and fruit-growing populations, the lupine packs of carnivorous predatory 'wer-wolves', running down and tearing their game to pieces, as the canine predatory beasts do, became the ancestors of the 'hunting'—i.e. 'hound'-ing—tribes who attacked not only what we would now call 'subhuman' animals, but also preyed on the more conservative fruit-gathering human herds reluctant to adopt the bloodthirsty new mode of life, killing the males, raping and enslaving the females, falling upon them while they were gathering and treading the ripe grapes of the wild vines in the wood [147] and enjoying the new must.

While the food-gatherers had left in peace 'every beast of the field and every fowl of the air' [148] amidst the 'trees pleasant to the sight and good for food' [149], using 'for meat' 'every herb-bearing seed' and 'the fruit of every tree' [150], the new hunting type 'filled the earth with violence', putting the 'fear and dread of them into every beast of the earth, into every fowl of the air, into all that moveth upon the earth and into the fishes of the sea' [151], 'delivered into' their 'hand even as the green herb' [152].

Man, who cannot eat grass, could move from the forest and jungle, where food-gathering pygmies live to this day, into the park-like glades, prairies and steppes of the post-glacial age and could survive and multiply during a phase of drought and forest recession by preying upon all the animals that feed on grass and leaves, assuming a more erect position with a wider outlook and developing the legs of a runner instead of the long arms of a Tarzan-like tree-dweller, climbing, dangling and swinging from limb to limb, from branch to branch.

But another, even more important, step forward in the conquest of the earth is involved in the process.

No subhuman animal makes or wears clothes, although not a few build 'houses'. But the characteristic transformation of 'man into wolf' is effected through man 'aping' the beast of prey by donning—like the cunning Dolon in Homer's *Iliad* [*153*]— the pelt of a wolf found dead or trapped in a pit covered with sods of turf and leaves, then killed and skinned with stone-knives and scrapers. The palaeolithic hunters of mammoth, reindeer, wild cattle and horses on the plains of south Russia and central Europe must have made themselves 'clothes of skin', since the stone scrapers for preparing these, and beautifully finished bone needles for sewing them together, are found in close proximity to each other [*154*].

The 'aprons' they 'made themselves' by 'sewing fig leaves together' [*155*], are the garments of the so-called 'leaf-wearing races' [*156*], such as the Kolarians of the Indian Deccan or the ancestors of the Sumerians, represented by their sculptors as wearing woollen kilts shaped so as to resemble aprons of palm or sacred fig-tree leaves [*157*]. They are but another protective camouflage worn by the hunter [*158*] chasing and stalking the animals of the jungle. The 'Green Wolf' of Jumièges [*159*] gets his name from the wolf's mask, the *wolfhede* of the outcast in the Anglo-Saxon laws [*160*], worn over the face, and from the costume made of grass and leaves covering the body.

Versi-pellis, 'the turn-pelt' [*161*], as the werwolf is called in Latin, manages to 'change his fur'. But he cannot at once divest himself of his own simian hair-coat, the *lanugo* surviving to this day in the embryonic state of man and in some individuals who preserve it throughout their adult life [*162*]. A remarkable Greek tradition actually says that Adam and Eve were as shaggy as bears [*163*]. Equally hairy was the Sumerian hero Engidu, who lived in peace with the wild animals at their drinking-place in the Babylonian Gilgamesh epic [*164*].

The Wambuttu dwarfs in the north-west of the Congo forest-region, first seen by Stanley, fully described by Stuhlmann [*165*], still have their bodies completely covered with a down of this woolly hair (*lanugo*), between three and five millimetres long. On top of this they have long dark hair on their breasts and legs, especially the lower parts [*166*]. The prehistoric bone-sculpture known as the Venus of Brassempouy, and even more the well-known '*Femme au renne*' of Mas d'Azil and another male figure, are covered with lines which are clearly meant to indicate long hair covering the whole body [*167*].

But among people who chase game at top speed under the cover of a double fur, those can run best whose own hair-coat is thinnest. Because of this advantage, the members of the were-wolves' hunting pack grew hairless [*168*], through natural selection [*169*] among the 'cunning hunters', underneath the mimetic fur-coat still worn by the nomadic gazelle-hunters of the Syrian steppe and Arab desert [*170*], the main feature in the story of the shepherd Jacob impersonating the 'hairy' Esau. Having shed their own hair and adopted hunters' clothes of vegetable and animal matter which can be cast off in the heat and put on in the cold, these hunting were-wolves were enabled to spread northwards and southwards beyond the temperate zone and to survive the successive glacial periods [*171*].

The proverb 'Clothes make the man' [*172*] is true in the most fundamental sense. As the naked 'hairy hermit' of the St. Onuphrius type [*173*] represents the ascetic return to the atavistic animal 'state of nature' and the 'in-nocence' of the 'naked savage' of a Paradisic age, the adoption of clothing to cover a nude, hairless body [*174*] is generally believed to constitute the essential advance from sub-human bestiality to civilized humanity.

We can now see that it was the 'clothes of skin' and the 'aprons of fig-leaves', that produced the nakedness of man, and not the other way round, the urge to cover man's nudity that led to the invention of clothing. It is obvious that neither man nor woman could be 'ashamed' (Gen. ii. 25) or 'afraid because they were naked' (Gen. iii. 10 f.) before they had donned their animal's pelt or hunters' 'apron of leaves', and got so accustomed to wearing it that the uncovering of their defenceless bodies gave them a feeling of cold, fear and the humiliating impression of being again reduced to the primitive fruit-gatherer's state of a helpless 'unarmed animal' [*48*] exposed to the assault of the better-equipped enemy. For nudity to be felt as contrary to 'modesty', *i.e.* the *modus vivendi*, and to 'decorum', the covering or decoration of the hunter's body with skins or leaves must have been firmly established as the habitual *modus* of living; the uncovered body could not have been considered 'indecorous' or 'im-moral' before the *mores* of clothing the hairless body, the custom of the costume, the habit of the habit had been acquired.

The very feeling of sin, the consciousness of having done something 'im-moral', contrary to the *mores*, customs or habits of the herd, could not be experienced before a part of the herd had wrenched itself free from the inherited behaviour-pattern and radically changed its way of life from that of a frugivorous to that of a carnivorous or omnivorous animal. The urge of the inherited 'mimetic' instinct—the automatic repetition of movements seen in others, which is the basis of all conformity within the herd—becomes a cause of change and non-conformism as soon as the mechanism of imitation extends its function beyond the bounds of the species, and *Pithecanthropus*, whose superior intelligence is but an extended range of imitation [175], begins to ape the beasts of prey.

William James's [44] 'most formidable of all beasts of prey', 'the one that preys systematically on its own species', lives henceforth in permanent fear of punishment and retribution for what the poet-philosopher Empedocles of Akragas [176] called 'the miserable deeds of devouring'.

Knowing that their ancestors were not carnivorous [177], men try to placate their resentment of the new ways by inviting the ancestral spirits of the tribe to take their share in the meat of the slaughtered victim, which becomes a 'sacrifice', or they return the red blood which 'is life' [178] to the earth [179], before they allow themselves to eat the meat of the killed animal.

Unable to draw a dividing line between animals and plants [180], the primitive savage now feels guilty of having tortured 'John Barley-corn' when he mows down the cereal plants and mills or malts them [181], or of having torn the vine- and grape-god Dionysos limb from limb in the process of the vintage rites [182]. He invents the most artful methods of placating the outraged spirits of fauna and flora and of atoning for the fatal necessity of living by taking life [183]—which not even the

Manichaean 'perfect ones' can avoid by living on 'fruit fallen by its own motion', brought to them by their 'not yet perfect' disciples [184].

The idea that it is 'sinful' to shed the blood that is 'life'—retained in the course of the transition from the vegetarian to the carnivore—and the belief that expiatory rites are required to avert the dangers connected with a practice that it was never really intended to abandon, since its results had proved so advantageous to the lupine pack, caused a consciousness of 'sin' and of a need for apotropaic ceremonies to attach itself even to the effusion of blood resulting from sexual intercourse with virgins [185]. These the aggressive pack would, whenever occasion offered, kidnap and carry away from among the females of the weaker fruit-gathering tribes [186] so as by this new practice of 'exogamy' [187] to avoid the otherwise inevitable, risky fight with the leader of the wolf-pack claiming for himself the females of the lupine clan. Judges xix. 22–28; xxi. 19–22, shows how violently the children of *Ben Jamîn*—the 'Yemenite' or 'southerner'—roaming on the fringe of the desert of Judah, 'ravening as a wolf, in the morning devouring the prey and at night dividing the spoil' (Gen. xlix. 27), wooed the females [188] of the more peaceful bovine and ovine, quietly grazing herds who called themselves the 'Sons of the Wild Cow' (*benê Le'ah*) [189] and the 'Sons of the Ewe' (*benê Rachel*) [190]. It is easy to understand that blood-lustful rape of this kind could not fail to appear, even to the lupine hunters, as a sinful perversion of the gentle folkways customary among the peaceful food-gatherers, which survive to this day among the Trobriand Islanders studied by Malinowski [191] and the Tahitians painted by Gauguin [192].

There is no other possibility of explaining the widespread, evidently archetypal feeling of guilt attached to sexual cohabitation, in itself a perfectly 'in-nocent' harmless biological function which must have been, in the original peaceful state of herd-life, as unrestricted by inhibitions as the equally 'in-nocent', 'natural' and biologically necessary act of feeding without killing.

On the basis of all these observations it seems legitimate to describe recent man—*Homo neanthropus*—as a crossbred species.

We are all descended from males of the carnivorous lycan-thropic variety, a mutation evolved under the pressure of hunger caused by the climatic change at the end of the pluvial period, which induced indiscriminate, even cannibalistic pre-datory aggression [*193*], culminating in the rape and sometimes even in the devouring of the females of the original peaceful fruit-eating *bon sauvage* remaining in the primeval virgin forests.

The characteristics of the fruit-collecting, seed- and root-planting agricultural mothers, worshippers of the ancestral goddesses Dêmêtêr and Korê, as well as those of the lupine, omnivorous fathers, sons of the *Lupa Romana*, raping the 'Sabine' women of the vineyards [*194*], worshipping a skygod Ζεύς Λυκαῖος, 'he of the she-wolf', [*195*], an apple-god Apollo [*196*] Λυκηγενής, 'born of the she-wolf', and a 'virgin' bear- and wolf-goddess Artemis Λυκείη [*197*], the representative ancestress of the sterile women in the bear-skin or wolves' pelt who hunted with the men, while the child-bearing mothers kept at home in cave or hut, are handed down in various proportions and combinations according to Mendelian laws. The two sets of characteristic functions combine and develop under the con-ditions created by the mating and breeding laws or customs of the various hunting, pastoral and herding man-wolf packs, who rule so sternly their subject-herds of peaceful bovine and ovine slaves and serfs: as Horace [*198*] says

Nos numerus sumus et fruges consumere nati,

'We are the masses born to eat the fruits' of the earth [*199*] and to leave the meat to our masters [*200*].

All of them have, therefore, common 'archetypal' race-memories of an original peaceful life among the fruit-bearing trees of some terrestrial paradise [*201*]. This is the reason for the quiet bliss felt by so many of us when walking through or resting in woods and forests (for Tacitus [*Germania* 5, 1] and the other sons of the *Lupa Romana* the wooded regions of northern Europe were, on the contrary, *silvis horridae*); why we love nothing so much as picking nuts and berries and the ripe fruits of the trees; why we can still feel tempted by a dessert of fruit at the end of a lengthy dinner when nothing could induce us to start on another dish of meat or fish.

To make it a true 'paradise', it must, of course, be a *pairi-daësa*, an 'enclosure' of trees protected from the dangers 'outside', a park (Anglo-Saxon *pearroc, parrak*), a *garth, hortus* or 'garden', such as Macaulay described nostalgically in his diary in June 1834: 'We passed through a garden which was attached to the residence of the Nabob of the Carnatic, who anciently held his court at Arcot. The garden has been suffered to run to waste, and is only the more beautiful for having been neglected. Garden, indeed, is hardly a proper word. In England it would rank as one of our noblest parks, from which it differs principally in this, that most of the fine trees are fruit trees.' Who can read these lines without wishing to live in this park for ever after? This is why, at all times and everywhere, men who have had the wealth, power and time to do so have crowned their worldly achievements by laying out parks modelled on the archetypal idea of 'paradise' and 'the garden' out of which man has been driven. Macaulay was well aware of this: 'After going down for about an hour we emerged from the clouds and moisture, and the plain of Mysore lay before us—a vast ocean of foliage on which the sun was shining gloriously. I am very little given to cant about the beauties of nature, but I was moved almost to tears. I jumped off the palanquin, and walked in front of it down the immense declivity. In two hours we descended about three thousand feet. Every turning in the road showed the boundless forest below in some new point of view. I was greatly struck with the resemblance which this prodigious jungle, as old as the world and planted by nature, bears to the fine works of the great English landscape gardeners. It was exactly a Wentworth Park as large as Devonshire.'

This longing for the lost paradise is the reason why children love nothing so much as a seat high in the fork of a tree up to which they can climb, retire from this world of worries and day-dream. The Plessis-Robinson near Paris—now built over with modern blocks of flats in the 'functional' style of architecture—used in my young days to be such a paradise, a group of big old planes with primitive tables and seats in the tree-tops where students and other *bohémiens* could have lunch with their girls, undisturbed by the Philistines [*200*]. There lived at that time, in this country, a very eminent Peer of the Realm who had to be called by a liveried flunkey from his retreat in the top of an immense tree in his park, whenever visitors arrived whom he had agreed to see.

As Jung saw so clearly [202], the tradition of a 'Fall from the Garden of Eden' is an archetype. The vast sales of the naïve Tarzan novels and the immense success of the acrobatic cinema star Johnny Weissmüller swinging by the strength of his arms from one tree-branch to another in the films derived from these stories can be understood only if we know that it is the archetypal background of the human mind that is stirred by these infantile day-dreams. Recurrent dreams of flying, not by flapping one's arms, but by swinging oneself through the air as a circus athlete flings himself from one trapeze to another, rise from the same layer of the subconscious.

Prof. Jung, whose undying merit it is to have shown that archetypes may be rooted not only in the ancestral, but even in the subhuman animal strata of the 'collective unconscious' [203], has published a series of dreams recorded, without any interference on his part, by one of his pupils, Dr. Erna Rosenbaum, now in London; at a time, moreover, when he was not yet acquainted with my own studies of lycanthropy and was therefore entirely unaware of the striking confirmation which his most illuminating theory has received from certain features of these dreams. After what we have been discussing so far, they will now appear completely transparent to the reader.

In the sixteenth dream of the second series [204], the patient, obviously familiar with Darwin's *Descent of Man* or at least with some popular book on the subject, sees 'many people. All walk in the direction from right to left around a square.' (The square is a familiar symbol of the *quattuor cardines mundi*, the τέσσαρα κέντρα κόσμου, the 'four corners of the world', East, South, West, North. Walking in this square 'widdershins', that is counter-clockwise, means running counter to the movement of the sun, that is, in the wrong direction.) Somehow they all have taken 'the wrong turn'. At least it seems so, although we should know that our world, the earth, does turn round in this way and carries us, willy-nilly, along with it. 'It is said' in the reported dream: 'it is intended to restore the gibbon'. On this striking statement Jung remarks [205]: 'This apparently means nothing

44

else but that it is proposed to restore the anthropoid, the archaic state of man.' The operative word is, however, 'the gibbon', the particular Primate species which is still a social being living in a herd [62], and not the solitary suspicious a-social great ape of the gorilla, chimpanzee or orang-utan type [49].

In the first dream [206] of the first series, the dreamer 'found himself in a society'—obviously the herd—'from which he takes leave', that is to say, he prepares to withdraw from the social organism. About to go, he 'puts on a strange hat' [207]. This is, of course, the disguising head-gear of the *haunskull* or wolfs-head, the *κυνέη* or *λυκείη* or *ἰκτιδέη*, as the Greeks called the original protective helmet [153] of the were-wolf about to take to the woods and to become an outlaw. In the third dream [208], 'just before falling asleep', he sees himself 'at the sea coast'. 'The sea breaks the dykes and invades the land, flooding everything.' This is, of course, the Deluge, called in the German language of the dreamer '*die Sintflut*', a word popularly understood as 'the flood avenging the sins' of men after the Fall. Then he finds himself 'sitting on a desert island' (like Noah on the top of mount Ararat or Robinson Crusoe on his island). For man isolated, as Jung [209] interprets the vision, by the breaking in or welling up of the flood of the unconscious, the task is to 'reconstruct the gibbon', *i.e.* the gregarious life of the original hominid from which he has broken away through the process of individualization. In the fourth dream [210], he is 'surrounded by many indistinct women's figures', evidently the undifferentiated females of the herd. That the dreamer is perfectly aware of the distinction between the social and the solitary Primates becomes manifest [211] in dream No. 22 of the first series: 'He is in the virgin forest, an elephant is rather threatening'—the dreamer is apprehensive of larger animals and formidable tusks—'then a large anthropoid ape or bear'—the '*berserk*,' man masquerading as a bear [114]—'or a cave-man with a club, threatening to assault the dreamer'.

In the 32nd dream [212] of the second series there are 'many apes' (*Affen*) 'in the primeval forest. Then a view opens upon extensive glaciers.' This is clearly an archetypal reminiscence of the 'racial memory' of the creatures in the virgin forests seeing

45

with anxiety for thousands or myriads of years the northern glaciers engulfing more and more of the vegetation of the temperate zone at the beginning of the glacial age. The reader may say it is simply the educated dreamer remembering speculations of his own on what the monkeys and apes in the virgin forest must have felt while their 'way of life' was more and more threatened by the slow climatic change [*213*]. That may be so. But he certainly showed no sign of being able to understand his dream, otherwise Jung would have given the above explanation of the glaciers instead of what he says on their connection with a previous dream-vision of the Milky Way.

The vision of the apes in the virgin forest bordering upon glaciers is preceded by a drawing contained in 'a letter from the unknown woman who writes that she feels pains in her womb'. The drawing shows unmistakably a winding serpentine path with a directional arrow showing the way from the 'Primeval Forest'—threatened by the approaching ice-flood—back into the warm womb of Mother Earth. She is the 'unknown woman' who receives her children back into her womb with a feeling of pain as a mother gives birth to her children.

In the preceding 'visual impression [*214*] No. 21 he is surrounded by Nymphs'—mythological figures whose name means nothing but 'brides', with a connotation of alluring sylvan beings. A voice says 'We were always there, only you have not noticed us'. The dreamer realizes that he has all the time been surrounded by fascinating females, only he was not aware of it. Dream No. 11 [*215*] explains why this was so: A voice says 'But you are still only a child,' meaning that he has still to grow up. In the ninth dream [*216*] he sees 'a green country where many sheep are browsing. It is the Sheep Country.' In the tenth dream—a visual impression—'the Unknown Woman is seen standing in the Sheep Country, showing the Way'.

Nothing could be clearer. The green and pleasant land where sheep are browsing is the promised land where the original frugivorous herd is living in peace. The 'Unknown Woman' is the *Anima* or archetypal representation of the dreamer's own soul pointing the right way of life.

The best illustration of this dream is an early Christian catacomb painting [*217*] from the Coemeterium Ostianum, illustrating the *Vision of Perpetua*. It shows the departed soul in the
shape of an *orans* or praying woman standing among a herd of
sheep. These symbolize the true Israel, the *benê Rachel* or 'sons
of the Ewe' feeding on God's pastures. In the sixth dream [*218*]
he had seen 'a veiled female figure sitting on steps'—a vision
that corresponds closely to Botticelli's famous *Derelitta*. The
picture shows Tamar having been raped by her brother Amnon
and thrown out from the royal palace in her shame [*219*]. In
the seventh dream [*220*] 'the shrouded woman unveils her face'
—a vision that can be wonderfully illustrated by a relief from
the archaic Greek temple [*221*] of Selinus in Sicily showing the
'Αναϰαλυπτῆρια Κοϱῆς, the unveiling of the sky-god's divine
bride. 'Her face shines like the sun.'

Clearly the dreamer has achieved the radiant illumination of
his own subconscious soul. The previously veiled *anima* now
reveals her hitherto shrouded face.

I do not think that there could be a more striking revelation
of the archetypes we have just discussed than in this series of
wish-dreams concerning the 'restoration of the gibbon'.

I myself remember vividly how, having gone up to the top
of the Eiffel Tower in Paris some twenty years ago on a windy
day, I felt with dismay the steel structure swaying like a reed in
the storm. The most astonishing features of the adventure were
two strange experiences: first of all, my soles, enclosed in socks
and shoes, contracted in a curious sort of cramp, as if my feet
were still prehensile limbs, clinging to the branch of a tree [*222*].
Secondly, while I was looking down on the city from behind a
seven-foot-high steel and wire lattice-railing, surrounding the
platform, I felt an overwhelming urge to throw myself down,
head forward, into the abyss—the very temptation of the devil,
sensed by Jesus [*223*] on the top of the mountain, and according
to Josephus [*224*] by every visitor to ancient Jerusalem who
looked down from the ramparts of the Temple into the valley
below.

This urge, fatal to a human being of our time seized
by vertigo on a projecting height, was eminently beneficial for
the Primate climbing by means of his prehensile arms and feet,

who would be killed by falling vertically to the ground from a swaying or breaking branch high up on a tree, but could save himself easily by jumping off in good time head forward and getting hold of another branch with his hands. Every parachutist knows how much easier it is to 'bale out' by jumping forward than by allowing oneself to fall passively out of the trapdoor. All this is archetypal.

So is, of course, the erotic fascination exerted upon the contemporary, masochist by the naked 'Venus in the fur', [225] representing 'la femme fauve', the nude blood-stained maenad or 'raving woman' in her bear-, lynx- or fox-pelt, coursing with her furiously excited male partners in the pack of the Wild Hunter through the primeval forests, vying with them in bloodlust when they came 'in at the death' and finally assuaging in a wild embrace [226] their common, mad excitement after the omophagic orgy, feasting on the live, raw and bloody meat of the quarry.

The tender young poetess [16], so 'fond of grief' as a source of artistic inspiration, who describes 'thoughts as assailing the poet, whose lust cries out from inside', 'like wolves' that have to be 'tamed', has unwittingly and with the deepest intuition revealed the atavistic, archetypal Dionysian, Orphic and Apollonian background of her 'love of pain'. It was not unusual in Austria or Germany before 1926, as it is now in the English-speaking countries, to call any 'Don Juan' and successful 'big dame hunter' a 'wolf' [227]. The expression, which is certainly archetypal, became current only during World War II. Being archetypal it can, nevertheless, be used to explain the striking metaphor of the poetess assailed by 'thoughts as by wolves',— by imaginary 'wolves', that is, by rough suitors [228] or rapers who have to be 'tamed'. At the same time she identifies herself with the (non-existent) 'Princess upon the Swords'. What she means is the 'Madonna of the swords', the suffering great Virgin Mother of the Logos, the poet's inspiration, whose birth she was to celebrate in later years in a magnificent mystical poem [228] equal to the greatest creations of Blake.

As archetypal as the male masochist's ideal of the nude 'Lady in the Pelt' and the feminine wish-dream of being assaulted by wolves [188], 'lust crying out from the inside', followed by the pains of motherhood in consequence of such rape suffered by the maiden 'lover of pain', is the male Actaeon's conversion into a stag torn to pieces [229] by the hounds of merciless wolfish Artemis Lykeia because he has seen her naked, that is, without her pelt, bathing in a woodland lake.

Archetypally, these hounds are rather 'bitches', as we know that the English-speaking peoples call the loose-living primordially promiscuous woman a 'bitch' [230], just as the Romans and the Greeks called her a 'she-wolf' (*lupa* and *λυκή*) [192].

Archetypal also are the sadist murderer's practices of beating his quarry with the hunting rider's horse-whip, of binding the victim like a captured animal, dragging the naked body over the ground and through the undergrowth [19]. So are the cannibalistic and at the same time infantile bitings into the breasts, the disembowelling and sometimes tearing or cutting to pieces of the body.

Wild archetypal dreams of this sort may break through into the consciousness of persons otherwise apparently quite harmless. An Oxford psycho-analyst was consulted in 1946 by a young don, just back from the war, who wanted to be cured of homosexual habits acquired under the circumstances described by T. E. Lawrence in his *Seven Pillars of Wisdom* [230], so as to be able to marry and 'settle down again'. It so happened that he met at that time a charming girl who fell for this very good-looking man and began to make advances to him in the way best described by Bernard Shaw. The psycho-analyst encouraged his patient to respond and to take the young lady out now and then, to see how this experience would react upon the feelings he wanted to get rid of. The result was that the patient remorsefully reported a few days later a frightful dream he had had of cutting the girl in pieces—like the victim of the Benjaminite ravening 'wolves' in the Book of Judges [186]. No-one can say, of course, whether or not the lycanthropic impulse manifested by such a dream will or will not break out into an actual blood-curdling crime [231].

As a matter of fact, murderous sadistic assaults are sometimes committed by well-educated, highly intelligent persons with no previous convictions [232] or with a record showing no more, at the worst, than minor sexual irregularities, especially so-called exhibitionist practices, now easily understandable as throwbacks to the habits of the hairy Primate who had not yet donned the hunter's 'coat of skin' or 'apron of leaves' and grown naked under it. Such self-exhibitions, which can be and are made respectable and socially acceptable by the organization of nudist societies [233] keeping apart from the rest of the community, are like 'ethical vegetarianism', radical pacificism, 'simple living', etc., symptomatic defence reactions against the pressure of the archetypal lupine urge that is subconsciously experienced by individuals unable to give free expression to their passions through the so-called 'blood-sports' of riding to hounds, big-game shooting, soldiering and similar 'cathartic' [234] 'ab-reactions.' Individuals, impelled to cast off their clothes and to yield to Rousseau's nostalgic *cri de cœur* 'retournons à la nature', but who nevertheless do not join one of the many terrestrial 'paradises' of organized nudism, reveal by this reluctance to follow the path of least resistance an invincible a-social 'lone wolf' character which under certain conditions may easily become very dangerous.

It is very important to state quite frankly that in many cases sadistic murders are unpremeditated reactions to the provocative behaviour of their female victims, yielding up to a point to the suitor's quite normal, though rather rough and pressing, wooing, and then infuriating him by a final, frightened or coy withdrawal [235]. Nothing could be more apt to rouse the lupine beast in a man, however slightly affected by a predisposition to lycanthropy.

Teachers assuming the delicate, but absolutely necessary, task of sexual instruction and education of the young should not fail to warn their charges against embarking on a dangerous path of erotic adventure where sudden, timorous or capricious retreat may be fraught with extreme risk. There will always be women as well as men who have decided to 'live dangerously', but I can see no reason why, young or old, they should go on living as ignorantly as they now do.

The main purpose of this paper [236] is not, however, either to enlighten them or to tell judges and juries that a sadistic murderer is no more 'responsible' for the werewolf behaviourpattern re-emerging from the abyss of the collective unconscious in this particular individual than another person is 'responsible' for being an atavist throwback to the 'hairy ape' type and having a body as shaggy as a bear [237]. There is no point in such an argument, since the vindictive attitude of judges and juries, rationalizing their behaviour as due to their anxiety to protect the potential victims of other such 'criminal perverts', is no less 'determined' by their ancestral and personal, archetypal and recent conditioning than that of the criminal. As he must kill, they must condemn him to be killed, until the peaceful, non-aggressive, 'bovine' or 'tauric' herd of 'John Bulls' succeeds in preventing, by a majority vote, the lupine pack from killing by legal process. We must not forget that the establishment of rule by majority-vote with the concomitant respect for minority opinion—misleadingly called 'democracy'—itself represents such a victory over the violent and revengeful of the meek who shall inherit the earth.

Thus we arrive at the final conclusion of an inquiry originally started, not for a psychological, but for a sociological purpose. What has been so far written is really meant to be the starting-point for a new approach to the greatest and most topical problem, not of this age of supreme anxiety only, but of all history: must wars, 'human nature being what it is', go on [238] until the human race has killed itself off for good and all by mutual annihilation, or is there a hope of peace on earth left for the non-violent who do not want to kill?

The plain answer is that if it were true [65] that all our ancestors have been carnivorous, or even omnivorous, predatory beasts, I would resignedly admit that, 'human nature being what it is', wars [239] must inevitably go on to that bitter end which may be as near as many of us fear. If there was never a Fall, there can never have been and there can never be a redemption in the future. If, however, there was a most definite Fall, if 'human nature' was originally not lupine but that of a peaceful, frugivorous, non-fighting and not even jealous animal [70], which developed its present predatory, murderous and jealous habits only under extreme environmental pressure by extra-specific imitation of the blood-lustful enemies of its own species, then there is hope of changing our social organization and our environment, gradually or suddenly, in such a way that we can throw off the fatal wolf's mask, tame the 'archetypal' beast in ourselves [*234*], and restore mankind to its pristine state of *ahimsa* or in-nocence [*240*], so achieving peace on earth for men of good will.

NOTES

NOTES TO AUTHOR'S FOREWORD

*Letter to Macvey Napier, Calcutta, 26 Nov. 1836 (ed. Sir G. O. Trevelyan, *Life and Letters of Lord Macaulay*, popular ed., London (Longmans), 1901, p. 327).

†According to Schlichtegroll, *op. cit.* below, note 2, p. 66, the earliest mention of what is now known as *algolagnia* is said to be found in Caelius Aurelianus (*A.M.*, I, 5): *ex amore melancholicos aut insanientes, si alia nihil possint, non pauci sunt qui vapulare iubent* ['There are not a few people who, when they are melancholic because of unhappy love, if they cannot do anything else, order themselves to be whipped']. Caelius Aurelianus is a late 5th-cent. A.D. physician (Wellmann in Pauly-Wissowa, *Realenzyklop.*, III, col. 1256, 63, No. 18), but what he says is a more or less literal translation from the Greek of Soranos who practised and wrote under the emperors Trajan and Hadrian (Kind in Pauly-Wissowa, *op. cit.*, III A, col. 1114, 2).

The quotation would therefore be very important—*if* it were genuine. I have, however, been unable to verify it. Dr. Gerhard Bendz of Lund, the specialist about to prepare a new edition of Caelius Aurelianus, confirms in a letter of 20 July 1949 that there is no such passage. There is no such book by Caelius as *Antiquae Lectiones lib.* 6 quoted by Brunfels (below, p. 54), since Caelius wrote only three books *Celerum Passionum* and five books *Tardarum Passionum*. Brunfels would seem to be referring to some Renaissance book of quotations from ancient physicians. This so far unidentified collection may have misunderstood Caelius Aurelianus, who says in Bk. I, ch. 5 of *Tardae Passiones*, §175 of the Amsterdam edition: 'Alii flagellis aiunt coercendos ut quasi iudicio mentis pulso resipiant' 'Other [physicians] say that [the

53

insane] are to be held in check with floggings, as if to recover their senses through the driving away of their mental state.' It is not the insane who ask to be beaten, but some ancient psychiatrists who think their patients might be cured by a good hiding. It is well known that up to the 18th-century reformers of the Salpetrière, Pinel and Esquirol, the violent insane were indeed beaten up by male nurses. The following §176 says: 'alii vero amorem furentibus aiunt procurandum' ['but others say that love is to be displayed towards the insane'], and condemns this method as patently absurd. Someone seems to have mixed up the two paragraphs and produced the above-quoted misunderstanding of §175.

The first detailed description of a case of 'algolagnia' is due to the famous humanist scholar Count Pico della Mirandola (1463–1494) who says in his treatise *Contra Astrologos*, XXVII: 'homo mihi notus prodigiosae libidinis et inauditae: nam ad venerem nunquam accenditur, nisi vapulet et tamen scelus id ita cogito: saevientes ita plagas desiderat ut increpet verberantem, si cum eo lentius egerit haud compos plene voti nisi eruperit sanguis et innocentes ortus hominis nocentissimi violentia scutica desaevierit. Efflagitat miser hanc operam summis precibus ab ea semper femina quam adit, praebetque flagellam, pridie sibi ad id officii aceti infusione duratum et supplex a meretrice verberari postulat: a qua quanto caeditur durius ita ferventius incalescit et pari passu ad voluptatem doloremque contendit' ['I know of a man of extreme and unheard-of lechery: for he is never enkindled to venery unless he is flogged; he desires the cruel blows to such a degree that he chides the person who is flogging him if she is too lenient with him, and is not fully satisfied of his desire unless the blood flows and the whip violently tears the wicked man's innocent buttocks. The wretch always begs ardently for this task to be performed by any woman he approaches, and offers her a whip which he has hardened for that office by pickling it in vinegar the day before, and eagerly begs the harlot to beat him; and the harder she whips him the more fervently aroused he is, and strives equally after pleasure and pain'].

The next mention of the abnormality in question, with the full name of the patient, is found in Otto Brunfels, *Onomasticum*

Medicinae, Argentorati [Strasbourg], MDXXXIII, *s.v.* 'coïtus':
. . . 'ad coïtum quidam sunt impotentes nisi plagiis et virgarum
conuberationibus immodice caedantur, de quo vide memora-
bile exemplum apud Caelium "antiquarum lectionum"' lib. 6,
c. 37 [above, p. 53]. 'Quin et hodie apud Monacum Bavariae
quendam superstitem adhuc agere, Wolfgang Steiermeister
Francofordianus bene aestimatus civis qui cum uxore sua rem
habere non potest, nisi acriter ante caesus. Tantam esse natium
densitatem ut vix multis verberibus illi queat sanguis elicere'
['Even today at Munich in Bavaria Wolfgang Steiermeister of
Frankfurt, a highly esteemed citizen, cannot have congress with
his wife unless he is first of all soundly beaten. His buttocks are
so thick that even after many stripes it is difficult to draw
blood'].

All these testimonies are quoted in what seems to be the first
monograph on the subject: Meibomius, *De Flagellatione usu in re
Veneria et Lumborum*, Lugduni Batavorum [Leiden] 1643.

For a recent Freudian treatment of the subject and an
analysis of a number of case-histories see Wilhelm Stekel, *Sadism
and Masochism, The Psychology of Hatred and Cruelty*, Engl. trans. by
Louise Brink, London (John Lane), 1935.

The best short summary of the knowledge available twenty
years ago, still worth reading, can be found in Bertrand Russell's
Marriage and Morals, London (Allen & Unwin), 1929, p. 216:
'Both sadism and masochism, although in their milder forms
they are normal, are connected, in their pernicious manifestations, with the sense of sexual guilt. A masochist is a man
acutely conscious of his own guilt in connection with sex. A
sadist is a man more conscious of the guilt of the woman as
temptress. These effects, in later life, show how profound has
been the early impression produced by unduly severe moral
teaching in childhood. On this matter, persons connected with
the teaching of children, and especially with the care of the very
young, are becoming more enlightened. But unfortunately
enlightenment has not yet reached the law-courts.'

See also the posthumous edition of Magnus Hirschfeld, *Sexual
Anomalies and Perversions*, compiled by his pupils, London (Torch
Publ. Co.), s.a. [1936], book IV, ch. XV, on 'Sadomasochism',
and chs. XXI ff., pp. 451 ff. on 'Sex murder'.

I cannot find in the British Museum Library and have never seen Oswald Zimmermann, *Die Wonne des Leides*, 2nd ed., Leipzig, 1885, quoted in J. M. Baldwin's *Dict. of Philos. and Psychol.*, New York (Macmillan), vol. III, p. 1056, nor H. Rau, 'Schmerz und Wollust', *Bibliothek der Seelenkunde und des Sexuallebens*, I, No. 10. Oswald Zimmermann is mentioned in C. F. von Schlichtegroll's book on Masochism (below, note 2), p. 15, as a critic and violent enemy of Leopold von Sacher-Masoch.

§ *The Messiah Jesus and John the Baptist according to Flavius Josephus' recently rediscovered 'Capture of Jerusalem' and the other Jewish and Christian Sources*. Engl. trans. by Alex. Krappe, London (Methuen), 1931.

NOTES TO THE TEXT

1. MARQUIS DE SADE

Janin, *Le Marquis de Sade*, German trans., Leipzig, 1835; Marciat, 'Le Marquis de Sade et le Sadisme' in A. Lacassagne, *Vacher l'Éventreur et les crimes sadiques*, Lyon et Paris, 1899; Eugène Dühren (pseudonym of Dr. Iwan Bloch), *Der Marquis de Sade und seine Zeit*, Harsdorf, 1901; Henri d'Almeras, *Le Marquis de Sade*, Paris (Albin Michel), 1906; *Neue Forschungen über den Marquis de Sade*, Harsdorf, 1904. A bibliography of de Sade's works has been compiled by the poet Guillaume Apollinaire, *L'Œuvre du Marquis de Sade*, Paris (Bibliothèque des Curieux), 1909. Montague Summers, *The Marquis de Sade, A Study in Algolagnia*, London, 1920 (Publ. No. 6 of the British Society for the Study of Sex Psychology); Paul Bourdon, *La Correspondance inédite du Marquis de Sade*, Paris, 1929; C. R. Dawes, *The Marquis de Sade, His Life and Work*, London (Holden), 1927 (bibliography on pp. 229 ff.); Salvatore Sarfatti, *Essai médico-psychologique sur le Marquis de Sade*, Lyon (Boze), 1930, with bibliography; Otto Flake, *The Marquis de Sade*, trans. by Edward Crankshaw, London (Peter Davies), 1931; Geoffrey Gorer, *The Revolutionary Ideas of the Marquis de Sade*, with foreword by Prof. J. B. S. Haldane, London (Wishart), 1934; Jean Desbordes, *Le vrai visage du Marquis de Sade, précédé d'une étude graphologique* par J. Crépieux-Jamin et

André Lecerf, Paris (Nouv. Revue Critique), 1939. There is no need to read Beresford Egan and Brian de Shaw, *De Sade, being a series of wounds inflicted with brush and pen upon sadistic Wolves garbed in Masochistic Wool*, London (Fortune Press), 1929. This book contains a reproduction of the apocryphal portrait of 1929, a self-portrait of Beresford Egan and the essay, 'In Defence of sadism': . . . 'man's *differentia*, his patent of nobility in the realm of created things' . . . 'For all nature kills the weak and ailing; man alone devises torture and death for his strongest and most gifted sons.' 'The barbarism of prehistoric times, the savagery of savages are axioms', . . . 'with sadism the gods too were endowed' . . . etc. These quotations will be sufficient to characterize this eccentric publication.

There is a biography of the Marquise de Sade by Rachilde (Comtesse de Mérimée), *La Marquise de Sade*, Paris, which I have not seen.

The Marquis Donatien Alphonse François de Sade, son of the Comte de Sade, was born at Paris on 2 June 1740. Nothing is known of his early childhood and family background, but some conclusions may be drawn from the fact that one of the heroes of his novels[1]—not, of course, to be rashly identified with the author—puts forward an elaborate defence of matricide. He was educated by an uncle who wrote a three-volume biography of Petrarch's adored Laura de Sade.

The decisive factor in de Sade's mental evolution—not sufficiently stressed by any of the authors mentioned above—was this uncle's decision to send the boy into the army at the age of fourteen (Desbordes, *op. cit.*, p. 23). He joined the aristocratic cavalry regiment of the *Chevaux Légers*, accompanied by a somewhat older valet recruited to serve as his batman from among the peasant serfs of his family, implicated later in the trial of his master when he was accused of having poisoned a number of

---

[1] *Infortunes de la Vertu*, pp. 55 ff.: 'L'homme ne peut détruire. Qu'importe à la nature que la masse de chair conformant aujourd'hui une femme se renouvelle incessamment sous d'autres figures et se reproduise sous la forme de milles insectes différents? Quand on m'aura prouvé la sublimité de notre espèce, quand on m'aura démontré quelle est tellement importante à la nature que nécessairement ses lois s'irritent de sa déstruction, je pourrai croire que cette destruction est un crime.'

filles publiques by mixing cantharides in their drinks, a rascal whom the Marquis used to whip and by whom he allowed himself to be whipped. The *Chevaux Légers* were just then campaigning with the contingent of the French army engaged in the Seven Years War. At the age when an English boy of the same class would find himself at a public school, subject to its particular discipline (see below, end of note 232), this fair-haired, blue-eyed aristocratic cadet found himself in the company of equally noble elder comrades and superior officers who would find his youthful charms more to their taste than those of the average plebeian drummer-boy.

As a French nobleman he was not subjected to corporal punishment, but would constantly see common soldiers receive the *bastonnade* or even run the gauntlet for minor or major offences against strict military discipline. Whenever a village or town was occupied in enemy country he would see young and old women raped, and, with their men-folk, tortured to make them reveal the hiding-places of any hidden treasure. It is these war-time experiences which must have filled the impressionable imagination of the young cadet, soon promoted to ensign, lieutenant, and—at eighteen—captain, with the lurid subject-matter of his later fantastic literary productions. Should the reader ask why not more than one *Chevaux Légers* cadet among the many who saw service in the Seven Years War, or before or after, wrote such books as did de Sade, the reply is that literary gifts such as his are rare, and that the algolagnic day-dreams which, no doubt, excited many of his comrades throughout their lives have vanished without trace because the dreamers could not, and, what is even more to the point, dared not, write them down.

It is, as Anatole France has pointed out (Introduction to De Sade's *Dorci ou la Bizarrerie de la Mort*, Paris, 1881), absurd to compare the Marquis de Sade with Gilles de Rais, the 'Bluebeard' Marshal of France, alleged mass-murderer of hundreds of children. De Sade's own sexual crimes were insignificant erotic experiments so awkwardly improvised as to get him into troubles which many contemporary sinners managed without difficulty to avoid. While they and their successors, until the 20th-century abolition of *maisons tolérées*, could always arrange in Paris for a consideration to flagellate and otherwise torture or see tortured with impunity helpless victims of human cruelty,[1] he got himself into trouble, not by the crime itself, but by neglecting the required prearrangements.

On being accosted in the street by a woman named Keller—who did not afterwards deny this fact in court but only protested that she was not a common prostitute—the Marquis took her into a pavilion in his garden, locked it on the inside, undressed her and himself and proceeded to give her a severe spanking. He was also accused of having pricked her with a knife and dressed the wounds with an ointment to alleviate the pains and cure the lesions—both of which allegations he denied. The doctor, to whom she went as soon as she could escape from the pavilion, found stripes but no wounds. She consented to withdraw her complaint on receipt of a hundred louis-d'or. 'C'est assez cher pour une fessée, dit à ce propos le docteur Béliard' (Sarfatti, *op. cit.*, p. 33). The social ostracism he incurred in consequence of the sordid lawsuit was a heavier penalty than the monetary loss. Henceforth, and even more after the second lawsuit in which he was charged with having at a banquet mixed cantharides in the drinks offered to a company of prostitutes, none of whom was any the worse for it after a few days, though they all claimed to have been 'poisoned', he was treated as an outcast by his peers. For them, the judges, and the Church, he conceived a passionate hatred, reinforced by the resistance which the family of his fiancée—belonging to the high *noblesse de la robe*—opposed to their projected and finally completed marriage. Falling in love with his wife's younger sister, he eloped with her, but was forced to return to France and was interned in the fortress of Vincennes on the strength of a royal *lettre de cachet* obtained at the instigation of his influential in-laws. For nothing worse than these more or less venial

[1] Touts accosting tourists with the words 'Voulez-vous voir, monsieur, une jeune fille crucifiée?' were by no means rare between 1926 and 1931 when the present writer lived and lectured in Paris. A guide-book entitled *How to See Paris by Night*, surreptitiously distributed in the streets to foreign-looking persons, advertised a notorious establishment in the rue Colbert, quite near the Bibliothèque Nationale, where an underground vault with a wooden cross used as a whipping-post and shackles for both sadist and masochist clients of both sexes was available and, it was currently supposed, well patronized by people who could afford to pay for their strange pleasures.

offences—easily seen in their real character of headstrong escapades since the official protocols of the trials in which he figured have been rediscovered by the untiring efforts of Maurice Heine,[1] de Sade passed the seven years 1777–1784 in the prisons of the Château de Vincennes, and five more years up to 6 July 1789 in the Bastille. Freed by the destruction of that notorious prison, he was re-interned under Napoleon I in Sainte-Pélagie from 1801 to 1803 and at Charenton from 1803 until his death in December 1814. According to the expert opinion of Dr. Royer-Collard, confirmed by the graphological analysis of his last manuscripts, he was, although eccentric, in no way insane. In his will he expressed the wish to be buried in the densest forest-thicket on his estate, the mound of earth to be sown with acorns—a very characteristic desire of the unfortunate man to return to the virgin forest[2] (see below, note 201, p. 222).

It is the merit of that excellent anthropologist Geoffrey Gorer to have pointed out that de Sade was persecuted mainly for political reasons. He was one of the *déclassé* aristocrats who had come passionately to hate and despise their own class, the Church, the high-ranking judges and crown officials as well as the financiers of his age. So far from identifying himself with the main figures in his novels, he describes these wicked dukes, bishops, presidents, etc., as veritable monsters of ugliness—fat, deformed 'hairy satyrs', his obvious intention being to make all these multiple sexual perverts appear both detestable and contemptible.

His contemporaries who kept him imprisoned for most of his life were well aware of the white-hot hatred and searing con-

---

[1] See the French medical review *Hippocrate*, No. 1, March, 1933, where the whole material is printed and commented upon.

[2] 'What need has man to live in society? Return him to the wild forests where he was born. Savage man knows only two needs, copulation and food. Both are natural, and nothing which he can do to obtain either can be criminal.' 'All that produces in him other passions is the work of civilization and society'. . . 'How tempted I am to go and live among bears' (see below, note 116 on going *berserk*) 'when I consider the multitude of dangerous abuses', etc. (de Sade, *Aline et Valcourt*, IV, 115, quoted by Gorer, *op. cit.*, pp. 170 f.). This, as the reader will soon understand (notes 38–56), is the clue to de Sade's subconscious regressive personality.

tempt for the governing classes of the *ancien régime* which inspired all his writings, while his modern readers—oblivious of his political motives, and turning to his novels mainly for the vicarious gratification of their own erotic desires—condemn him, hypocritically, as if he intended to glorify his rogues' gallery of perverts, pitilessly described without the slightest gleam of sympathy. 'On n'est point criminel' he says in the *Epigrammes de Juliette* (quoted by Gorer, *op. cit.*, p. 127) 'pour faire la peinture des bizarres penchants qu'inspire la nature.' Obviously nobody could have written these books who did not to a large extent project his own strange feelings and desires and attribute them to the objects of his hatred. But his hatred is genuine, and it is not the author but the objects of his characterizations and the puppet-creatures of his imagination which are a-moral and/or antimoral.

He was a powerful writer and an original though not always strictly logical thinker,[1] and it is not wholly absurd of Maurice

[1] While he rightly states (Gorer, *op. cit.*, p. 186) 'no act of possession can ever be exercised on a free person', he also speaks of the 'blind submission to man's caprices which Nature prescribed' (see below, note 4, on his curious concept of 'Nature' as the supreme all-powerful, hypostatized Great Mother). The apparent contradictions are, however, easily resolved by remembering that the conflicting statements are put into the mouths of different persons. An example of this method is his curious political scheme for a European Federation—criticizing the plan of the Abbé de Saint-Pierre, who wanted to preserve intact all the small European states—which is developed in a dialogue (Gorer, p. 162) between a brigand, a kind of Robin Hood, and a nobleman who considers 'aristocratic government' as 'the worst of all.' The outlaw proposes to divide Europe into four republics, of the North, South, West, and East, after driving the Turk out of Europe and uniting European Turkey with Russia. The Southern Republic is to consist of Germany, Hungary, and Italy, including Sicily, Corsica, Sardinia (the Pope, whom the brigand calls 'a Sodomite priest with an income of twelve million', is to be expelled from Rome), the Northern Republic is to consist of Scandinavia with Greenland, the British Isles and their dependencies, Belgium, Holland, Westphalia and Pomerania, and to have 'a single religion without the insolent vermin that has constituted itself mediator between Heaven and human weakness.' The West is to consist of France, Spain, Portugal and their overseas dependencies. All laws are to be abolished. 'Without laws I shall be oppressed. What does it matter, if I have the right to do likewise?' It would be absurd to forget that it is a brigand who is made to advocate this anarchic constitution of club and sword law, and this arbitrary redistribution of political sovereignty.

Heine, Guillaume Apollinaire, and the French surréalistes 'de placer l'œuvre de de Sade parmi les monuments de la pensée humaine'.

On the basis of his own bitter experience he anticipates modern penological ideas where he writes (*op. cit.*): 'If the Law were wise it would never inflict any punishment except one which tends to correct the guilty and preserve them to the State.'

In the present context the most important of his works— correctly described as an anticipation of the modern textbooks on *Psychopathia sexualis*, surpassing them all in the wealth of material collected—is the unfinished *Les cent-vingt journées de Sodome ou l'École du libertinage*, first mentioned by Restif de la Bretonne. It was written in prison on loose sheets, afterwards glued together into a scroll 40 feet long, covered on both sides with his small handwriting, which he left behind in the Bastille in 1789. It was acquired, probably, from a turnkey, and came into the possession of the Villeneuve-Trans family, being discovered by 'Eugen Dühren', that is, Dr. Iwan Bloch, and published in 1904 in a private edition for the *Club des Bibliophiles*. The *Catalogue générale des livres imprimés de la Bibliothèque nationale*, tome CLIX, Paris (Imprimerie Nationale), 1940, p. 1071, col. b, lists only a later edition (Paris, aux dépenses des bibliophiles souscripteurs, 1931–1935, in 3 volumes 4° pl. (shelfmark *Enfer* 975–977). The British Museum possesses only (among its 'Private Case Books', which are by no means as inaccessible as Geoffrey Gorer states, *op. cit.*, p. 255; he must have been or looked very young when he asked to see them!) the German translation by Karl von Haverland of Brussels, privately printed in 1,650 numbered copies, illustrated by K. M. Diez of Rosenburg, Leipzig, 1909, copy No. 510, press-mark P.C. 31.k.3.

Of the '120 days' which he intended to describe and to contain descriptions of 600 'perversions', only 30 were completed. The last of them are mere sketches. The *dramatis personae* of the scheme are four; the duke, his brother the bishop, the president (of some high court of justice) and finally a *fermier-général* (one of the hated tax-farmers of the French *ancien régime*), all of them described as revolting characters without any redeeming feature. The duke, the president and the tax-farmer have wives, the duke has two grown-up daughters with whom he has incestuous relations. One of the daughters is also the bishop's mistress. The president and the tax-farmer likewise have each an adolescent daughter. The duke has poisoned his mother and a sister whom he had previously seduced. He 'has discovered that unfortunate aberration which makes men seek their own pleasure in the sufferings of their fellow-beings'—now known under a name derived from that of the author of the story. The duke is described as a man of gigantic size, tiger-like savage cruelty, with an immense *membrum virile*, fabulous potency, a glutton and a drunkard, yet a coward, addicted from his boyhood to passive sodomy, who has dishonoured himself in war, lived with three accomplices the life of a highway robber, holding up post-chaises, plundering and raping travellers.

The cowardice and military dishonour attributed to the duke show clearly that this figure is not a projection of the author's own personality (de Sade had a brilliant military career and was promoted for valour in battle). He stands for the marquis's superiors in the ranks of the nobility who had cut him after he had disgraced his noble name by his sordid adventures.

The president—representing the *noblesse de la robe*, the class of de Sade's persecuting 'in-laws',—is described as a mere skeleton, hairy like a satyr, so dirty in his habits that he stank—a characteristic by no means incredible or unusual in this polite, brilliant and perfumed, but unwashed society surrounding a king the ritual of whose ceremonial morning *lever* included no other ablution than the perfunctory dabbing of his face with cotton-wool moistened with a drop of *esprit de vin*, and whose disagreeable smell is mentioned in contemporary memoirs. Again there is no way of overlooking the spiteful intention of the characterization. The four men make an arrangement to hold their wives—and daughters—as common property (incidentally none of these ladies is consulted about the matter). They subscribe a million livres for the purpose of procuring a bevy of the most entrancing girls and boys and a retinue of the best cooks and servant-maids, all of whom, including their wives and daughters, they lock up in a remote and inaccessible castle amidst forests and mountains belonging to the duke in order to explore in a hundred and twenty nights all the six hundred erotic possibilities and combinations which a libertine's unrestrained and extravagant fancy could imagine, including the voluptuous enjoyment of torture and murder. De Sade aimed at (vol. I, p. 80 of the German version) and certainly succeeded in producing 'the most lascivious story invented since the world exists, a book whose like is not found either in ancient or in modern literature'. 'One can hardly imagine (*ibid.*, p. 137) in what diverse ways man can develop his debauches when his imagination is inflamed; however great is variety in all other passions, it is even greater here. He who could set down in detail all the aberrations in this kind would perhaps be able to write one of the most beautiful (!) and interesting investigations of human manners and customs.' He does not realize the difference between describing real phenomena from observation and the pure invention and imagination of merely conceivable variations, the very thing which distinguishes this exuberant fantasy from the sober scientific catalogues of the modern psychiatric text-books. What makes the book, in spite of a certain weird and satanic grandeur, more repulsive than any of his other productions is the amount of space given to coprophily and coprophagy. De Sade has never been accused by his worst enemies of any inclination towards these complete perversions (below, note 185); on the contrary, he is known to have been rather fastidious in all his tastes. The persistent affection shown for him in all his adversities by both his wife and her sister would be incomprehensible if he had been tainted with repulsive habits of this kind. It must have been his boundless resentment and hatred of his enemies in the nobility above the rank of count and marquis—there are no simple *chevaliers* or barons among the villains of his novels—of priests from poor friars upwards to cardinals and for the moneyed financiers, which made him describe them as addicts of the vilest and most debased practices. On the other hand, it is equally true that de Sade was no more a murderer than he was a coprophile or coprophage. It would probably be true to say that he preserved his sanity and succeeded in resisting his murderous impulses by 'abreacting' them through projection upon the imaginary villains of his novels.

His own passive algolagnia—attested by the fact that he

allowed or rather ordered himself to be whipped by his valet—
was mainly satisfied by the imaginary sufferings of the virtuous
heroes and heroines of his novels at the hands of the pitiless
scoundrels he invented.

The reader will remember that the most serene, urbane and
benevolent of all poets in history, Goethe, Prime Minister of
Saxony-Weimar, said with magnificent frankness that there was
'no crime of which he did not feel himself capable.' 'Nihil
humani a me alienum puto.' De Sade must have felt the same.
He had, no doubt, inherited a double dose of original sin, but
he yielded to the worst temptations of his tormented soul by
spilling, not the blood of human victims, but harmless pots of
ink on unfeeling notepaper. It is not *his* notorious books that
have been found in the hands of really murderous maniacs (see
below, Appendix IV and V, on the Book that inspired the mass-
murderers Haigh and Unruh).

What, finally, is the damage, if any, done by these notorious
books, clandestinely circulated mostly among neuropaths dominated by the same dark atavist urges as their author and equally
anxious to get imaginary relief for their passions rather than a
terrible real satisfaction in the sufferings of their fellow-creatures,
in comparison with, say, the Rev. Dr. Sprenger's *Malleus Male-
ficarum*, directly responsible for the torturing and burning as
'witches' of hundreds of innocent women and not a few men,
not to speak of more respectable and deservedly praised books
such as the *Summa* of St. Thomas Aquinas, which advocates
(II–II, qu. XI, art. 3) the death penalty for heretics, and
cannot therefore be absolved from responsibility for all
the judicial murders perpetrated, albeit indirectly, by the
Inquisition, or rather by the most saintly and well-meaning
inquisitors?

2. LEOPOLD VON SACHER-MASOCH

There is no literature in English on this curious personality.
In German there is a monograph by Carl Felix von Schlichtegroll, *Sacher-Masoch und der Masochismus*, Dresden (Dohrn), 1901,
with a portrait of Sacher-Masoch as frontispiece, and an article
on him by Richard M. Meyer in the *Allgemeine Deutsche Bio-
graphie*, suppl., vol. 53, 1907, p. 682. In French there are:

Leopold Stern, *Sacher-Masoch ou l'Amour de la souffrance*, Paris (Bernard Grasset), 1933; Marc Amiaux, *Un grand anormal, Le Chevalier Sacher-Masoch*, Paris (Éditions de France), 1938. His first wife Aurelia Sacher-Masoch, née Rümelin, published *Die Damen im Pelz*, Leipzig (Morgenstern), 1881, with a frontispiece photograph showing the author in her fur coat; *Confessions de ma vie avec deux portraits*, 4th ed., Paris (Mercure de France), 1907, as a reply to von Schlichtegroll's book, *Wanda ohne Pelz*, Leipzig, 1906.

Leopold von Sacher-Masoch was born on 27 January 1836 at Lwow (Lemberg) in Galicia. He was the son of the police-president Johann Nepomuk von Sacher, who had been knighted by the Emperor Francis I and had married Charlotte, a daughter of Prof. Franz von Masoch, Rector (equivalent to English Vice-Chancellor) of Lemberg University. The name Sacher is derived from the Hebrew *saḥar* 'hawk about', whence *soḥer* 'a hawker' or 'huckster', and there is no doubt that the family, although not mentioned in any Jewish reference work, was of Jewish origin. The father's Christian name, Johann Nepomuk, and his rise to high office in Austria show that he was a convert to Roman Catholicism. Masoch is a Polish place-name, such as were often used by Jews as family names, and Prof. von Masoch may likewise have been of Jewish origin, although Sacher-Masoch used to claim that his mother belonged to the Polish gentry (*schlachta*). This is possible but by no means certainly true. He also claimed an ancestor Matthias Sacher, who came, he alleged, with the Emperor Charles V to Germany, acquired a castle at Mühlberg and married a Marchesa Clementi. For this romantic story or family tradition there is no support whatever, but it may be true that he had Sephardi ancestors. If they came from Spain to Germany with Charles V —long after the expulsion of the Jews in 1492—they must have been *maraños* (*conversos*), which is quite possible. Police-president Ritter von Sacher was transferred with the same rank to Prague, where his son Leopold went to the humanist gymnasium (the Austrian equivalent of an English grammar-school with a classical curriculum) and passed the 'maturity' examination (='matriculation') at the age of sixteen (the normal age was eighteen). His father having by then been transferred as police-president to Graz in Styria, he studied law at the University of Graz and became a *Doctor Juris*, *i.e.* an LL.D., at twenty. He continued to study history at the University of Vienna and became an *Archiv-Praktikant*, or clerk in the State Archives. He is also said to have studied history under Prof. Schwind at the German University of Prague. In his twentieth year he published a historical monograph on the Flemish rising against Charles V (*Der Aufstand in Ghent unter Karl V*, Graz, 1856); and soon afterwards an essay on *The Downfall of Hungary and Maria of Austria*, Graz, 1857.

At the age of thirty he is said to have earned as a cavalry-officer of the reserve the Austrian medal for valour on the battlefield of Solferino (1866). Soon after the end of the war he started on his famous novel *Don Juan von Kolomea*, containing a sequence of colourful accounts of life inside and around the Jewish villages and towns of Galicia. Having hawked the manuscript from one publisher to another, he at last got it printed in Westermann's *Monatsheften*, where it had an immediate, spectacular and not undeserved success. It criticized with audacity the institution of monogamous marriage, which, it alleged, forced husband and wife by inexorable necessity to deceive one another, children separating rather than uniting their parents. Henceforth he was able to concentrate on a literary career and produced one successful novel after another: *Eine Mondnacht; Die Kapitulanten;* and then his best-known and most typical work, the *Venus im Pelz* ('Venus in the Fur'), the *Love of Plato*, and so forth. Most significant is his attempt to present a kind of philosophy of history or sociology in a book *The Legacy of Cain* (*Das Vermächtnis Kain's*, Stuttgart, 1870) with chapters on Love, Property, the State, War, Labour, Death, preceded by a prologue *The Wanderer* and followed by an epilogue *Peace on Earth*; also a book *Die Aesthetik des Hässlichen*, Leipzig, 1880, on the aesthetics of ugliness. The success of these books, none of which is in the British Museum Library, was spectacular enough to provoke a real crusade against their influence on the public, organized by two now-forgotten critics, Karl von Thaler and Otto Glagau. Twenty-four of his novels appeared in French in the respectable *Revue des Deux Mondes*. On his forty-seventh birthday in 1883 he received the *Légion d'Honneur* and the congratulations of the Grand Rabbi of France on the sympathetic treatment in his novels of Jewish characters and the Jewish problem in general.

Schlichtegroll says (p. 11) that, as a child, his greatest delight was to look at the pictures representing executions in the illustrated papers of the time; but it seems doubtful whether any illustrated papers existed at Lemberg about 1840, and if they did, whether the Austrian censorship would have allowed them to publish such illustrations. That the legends of the martyrs interested him more than any other literature (*ibid.*) sounds more credible. He remembered dreaming, at the age of puberty, of being in the power of a cruel woman, a Sultana before whom he was kneeling in fetters—a dream which holds no mystery for the modern psychoanalyst. He used to tell a story of how as a little boy he stayed in the house of an aunt Zenobia—according to him a Countess X.—whom he loved passionately. Having hidden himself in a wardrobe in the lady's bedroom to be near her, he saw her come in, followed by a gentleman, with whom she went to bed, only to be disturbed by the irruption of the enraged husband, the frightened lover departing through the window, the jealous husband being set upon and his ears boxed by his charming wife. Having betrayed his presence by an involuntary movement, the boy Leopold was dragged from his hiding-place and soundly thrashed by the adored Zenobia, wearing for the occasion the *kazabaika*, the fur-lined dressing-gown, henceforth associated inseparably with all his erotic imaginations.

In Graz the young Dr. von Sacher-Masoch is said to have had his first love-affair with a married lady, Anna von Hottowitz. But his great love was another married woman, Fanny von Pistor-Bogdanoff, at whose feet he is seen in a would-be romantic, but rather absurd photograph, showing her, of course, in the significant fur-lined *kazabaika*. By this lady he arranged to be constantly maltreated and humiliated. He went with her on long journeys by rail and road, paying all expenses, but dressed and acting as her liveried footman, until the lady got bored by this performance. While he lived in Graz he got acquainted with Wanda Rümelin, born 1845, who became his first wife. Her father, Wilhelm Rümelin, was then a trusted servant of the military governor of Graz, General Prince Alexander of Württemberg, but ended his life as station-master at Kranichfeld, quite a humble person and not at all a 'Herr von Rümelin', as she pretended in later life. His marriage was unhappy. Wanda relates (p. 14 of her *Confessions*) how she once surprised her father in making love to some trollop. As a child, she says, she had an ecstatic vision and went regularly to confession. She and her mother and sister earned some pin-money by making gloves. The photograph which displays her 'in the fur' does not show her exactly as a Venus, but she was probably once quite a good-looking girl, greatly flattered by the attentions of an infatuated young man who was not only a *Herr von* and a *Herr Doktor*, but also the author of two books to be seen in the windows of the local bookseller who had published them for the author. She tells, rather pathetically (*op. cit.* p. 55), how she was prevailed upon by the young bridegroom, immediately after the wedding, to put on the fur-lined dressing-gown which seemed so indispensable to his happiness and to treat him with the proper severity. She was more than perplexed to find that she was expected to consider her husband as her slave, to inflict upon him not only corporal punishment for any shortcomings of his as a lover, but also the tortures of jealousy by taking a paramour and committing adultery, not in secret, but brazenly flaunting in her husband's face her claims to complete matriarchal freedom and independence. (It is not likely that he himself understood the unconscious archetypal motives (below, App. I) of his behaviour.)

The reader can easily imagine the bewilderment that a bride of petty-bourgeois origins, with no more than an elementary education received in a Roman Catholic convent school, must have felt (her *Confessions*, p. 312) on being told: 'Quand tes fils seront grands, tu seras une mère encore très jolie et tu leur apprendra ce que c'est que l'amour!'

The most characteristic information about her husband's unconscious mental background is found on p. 275 of her *Confessions*, where she speaks of the time the young couple spent on the Hungarian estate of Ecśed near Hatvan, belonging to their friends, a Jewish family named Ries. There he used to organize nightly games of hide-and-seek in the park, at which all the young ladies, guests as well as members of the host's family, were dressed in their fur wraps to hunt for him, throw themselves upon him and scratch and bite him like wild beasts as soon as they had found him. Whether his classical education had acquainted him with the fate of king Pentheus, the 'sufferer', at the hands of the Maenads clad in panther-skins (below, note 108) in the *Bacchae* of Euripides—quite unknown beyond doubt to poor Wanda—or whether he acted under the impulse of unconscious archetypal motives the strange nocturnal panto-mime in which he played the helpless victim of the primeval fur-clad huntresses, the facts reveal the mental background of his passive algolagnia as clearly as De Sade's desire to live with bears (above, p. 60, note 2) the atavist motives of the latter's active cruelty. The most remarkable fact about Wanda—who assumed, apparently at his suggestion, the Polish noble family-name Dunayew—is that this half-educated young woman learnt so quickly—possibly by engrossing clean copies of her husband's manuscripts and reading his proofs—to produce successfully 'masochist' novels in competition with him (*Die Frauen im Pelz*, Geschichten von Wanda von Dunayew, Leipzig (Morgenstern), 1881, is the best known). It is not likely that he enjoyed this emulation; anyhow, the marriage became more and more com-plicated and ended in a divorce. He espoused a second wife, one Helene Meister, whose stolid common sense seems to have had a calming effect upon him, in spite of the interminable lawsuit with his first wife and others in which he became involved. He acquired an estate with a castle, tower and dungeon near Lind-heim in Hesse, where he lived the quiet life of a country squire and author until his death on 5 March 1895. In the previous year he went to Vienna on some legal business which brought him into contact with an uncle of the present writer, a pro-minent lawyer, who pointed out this strange client of his, sitting in the stalls just below us, to my parents in the Vienna Imperial Opera House. I was with them and still remember quite clearly the man's face and general appearance. So does Mr. Paul W. Emden, now living in Wimbledon, Surrey, whose father, a well-known banker of Frankfurt am Main, happened to be the executor of Sacher-Masoch's complicated will and had to cope with the lawsuits between his descendants by his two marriages, some of whom were still alive when my fellow-exile had to leave Germany.

The copyright of Sacher-Masoch's works has lapsed, and it would be well worth someone's while to produce an English version of the best of them. His bitterest enemy, Oswald Zimmermann (quoted by Schlichtegroll, *op. cit.*, p. 15) says of one of his novels, *Die geschiedene Frau* (*La Divorcée*), that 'its influence on contemporary German literature can be compared only with that of Goethe's *Werther*.' This is indeed a mouthful, and I cannot say whether it is true. His books were certainly reprinted again and again, until the real horrors of the First World War threw a shadow of oblivion on his sufferings and the imaginary ones of his tortured heroes.

Mr. Geoffrey Gorer censures the impropriety of the psychiatrists who have immortalized his and de Sade's names by attaching them to the strange mental types represented by these two writers. There is, however, no doubt that both de Sade and von Sacher-Masoch would have preferred this kind of notoriety to the obscurity to which so many, even better writers, have been condemned by an ungrateful posterity.

3. The exception is Havelock Ellis, *The Sexual Impulse*, p. 74, who says: 'In men it is possible to trace a tendency to inflict pain, or the simulacrum of pain, on the woman they love; it is still easier to trace in woman a delight in experiencing physical pain when inflicted by a lover, and an eagerness to accept subjection to his will. Such a tendency is certainly normal.' The acceptance of the undeniable fact as 'certainly normal' reveals the writer's own feelings. But it explains nothing, any more than does the criticism of the phenomenon as 'abnormal'.

4. THE LAWS OF NATURE

See on this concept, its history and meaning, Hans Kelsen, *Society and Nature, A Sociological Inquiry*, London (Kegan Paul), 1946, pp. 249 ff.; p. 382, note 40. Neither Dr. Edgar Zilsel, *Die Naturwissenschaften*, XIX, 1931, p. 275, nor Prof. Kelsen quoting him (*l.c.*, p. 382, note 5), seems to be aware of the fact that— like so many concepts still in use—the term 'laws of nature' is derived from Plato (νόμοι φύσεως), *Timaeus*, 83 E; *Gorgias*, 483 E;

cf. Aetii, *Plac.*, I, 28, 2; Diels, *Doxogr.*, p. 323, on Plato explaining fate (εἱμαρμένη) as 'the eternal law of the nature of the universe' (νόμον αἴδιον τῆς τοῦ παντός φυσέως). See *ibid.*, I, 28, 3, the Stoic Chrysippus on fate being κόσμου . . . νόμος . . . καθ' ὃν τὰ μὲν γεγονότα γέγονε, τα δὲ γινόμενα γίνεται, τα δε γενησόμενα γενήσεται ['The law of the universe according to which that which has been became, that which is becomes, and that which will be will become']. Latin *natura* is the literal translation of τα γενησόμενα at the end of this Stoic definition ['that which is going to be generated'].

The distinction between the fallible, conventional law (νόμος), set up by men for men, ignorant of the things about which they legislate, and the infallibly right order of nature as arranged by the gods, is first found in the Heraclitean treatise *De victu* (Περὶ διαίτας, VI, 478, ed. Littré; Diels, *op. cit.*, p. 83, ll. 27–34) attributed to the great Hippocrates, but possibly composed by Herodicus of Selymbria (Gomperz, *Griech. Denker*, 2nd ed., vol. I, p. 230). Through Marsilio Ficino's Latin translation of Plato's *Dialogues* humanist scholars came to know the *leges naturae*. The first to speak of 'natural law' in a vernacular language seems to have been Leonardo da Vinci (*Notebooks*, ed. McCurdy, p. 5): 'Nature never breaks her own law which lives and works within her' (Leonardo Olschki, *Machiavelli the Scientist*, Berkeley, Calif. (Gillick Press), 1945, p. 29, note 31; *id.*, 'Galileo's Philosophy of Science', *Philos. Review*, 1943, pp. 349–365). Nausiphanes, the disciple of Democritus (fr. 2; Diels, *Fragm. d. Vorsokr.*, 2nd ed., p. 465, ll. 3 ff.), speaks of 'the will of nature' and says that only the physician knows it on the basis of his observation (τὸν φυσικὸν μόνον, τοῦτο τεθεοροκότα, τῷ γινώσκειν ὃ βούλεται ἡ φύσις . . . δυνήσεσθαι πείθειν). If Nature has a will, the physician can, of course, tell what is 'according to nature's will' or 'natural' and what is 'contrary to her will' or perverse (κατὰ φύσιν and παρὰ φύσιν, Protagoras, Diels, *op. cit.*, p. 531, l. 21).

Although the opposition of φύσις and θέσις, φύσις and νόμος played a most important part in the history of ancient philosophy, it is undeniable that 'Nature' (*natura*, 'that which is about to be born', Greek φύσις, 'becoming', 'growth', 'procreation', 'generation') personified as the 'mother of all living beings' (*10th Orphic hymn*, Abel, p. 63; Nonnus, *Dionys.*, 2, 650;

41, 52, 103; *Anthol. Pal.*, 7, 561; 9, 738, 739, etc.; *Anthol. Planud.*, 116, 302, 373; Philodem., *Peri euseb.*, p. 79, Gomperz; Theodoros Hyrtakios ap. Boissonade, *Anecd.*, 1, 265; Artemidorus, *Onirocr.*, 2, 39, p. 233 Reifferscheidt; cf. 2, 34, p. 21; Stoll's article 'Physis' in Roscher's *Mythol. Lex.*, II, 2, col. 2488; *Natura* personified in the same way in Latin poets; passages collected in Forcellini-de Witt's *Thes. Ling. Lat.* and *Onomasticum*, *s.v.* 'Natura'; Rob. Eisler, *Weltenmantel und Himmelszelt*, Munich, 1910, I, p. 102, note 1 f.; pp. 221 f.; II, pp. 6506–6519, on the goddess *Physis*, Latin *Dea Natura* in Claudianus, *Dame Nature*, in Alanus de Insulis, the medieval *Échecs Amoureux*, the *Roman de la Rose*, etc.) is a purely mythical concept, completely useless for scientific distinctions. If the term 'natural' is used in contradistinction to 'artificial', 'that which is due to human intervention', a dam built by beavers will have to be classified as a natural phenomenon and lumped together with an obstruction across a river caused by a landslide due to a rain-storm. If everything due to the action of a living being is to be called 'artificial', then coral islands built up by *zoantheria* will have to be described as artificial structures comparable to stone-built jetties and iron piers. A cave will be praised as a 'natural', a house criticized as an 'unnatural' dwelling. The futility of such a distinction was already evident to the disciples of Empedocles quoted by Plato (*Laws*, X, 889 b), who taught that the universe and all in it came into being 'by nature and accident, not by a mind or some god or some artifice' (οὐ διὰ νοῦν, φασίν, οὐδὲ διά τινα θεὸν οὐδέ τινα τέχνην ἀλλὰ ... φύσει καὶ τύχῃ). If the reverse is true and the whole universe and all that is in it is taken to be the creation of a mind, the work of a god or of the one and unique God, then, of course, everything is the product of this divine artisan's work and all is 'artificial'. The distinction between what is God's work and what is due to the resistance of 'matter' or rebellious Nature, set forth in a series of myths beginning with the Babylonian Creation Epic and ending with the Manichaean cosmology, is the dualist mythological explanation of the universe. Nothing is gained by thus opposing 'natural' to 'supernatural' phenomena, because the latter cannot be defined in any other way than by the statement that 'supernatural' phenomena are those which cannot be explained by the alleged 'laws of nature'. This would force us to describe every unexplained occurrence as a 'supernatural event' and completely arrest the progress of so-called 'natural' science.

It is hardly necessary to say that anyone who speaks of 'Nature' as kind and generous, or as 'merciless' and 'red in tooth and claw', speaks as a poet and mythologist, not as a scientist or philosopher. To state this in so many words would seem otiose. But it is instructive to realize that while the unthinking and uncritical practitioner may think himself justified in calling sadistic acts 'un-natural' or 'contrary to nature', the Marquis de Sade could and did with equal naïveté protest that these practices conform with the intentions of cruel and merciless Nature to which he opposes 'education'.

The argument of fruit-trees in the natural and the highly cultivated state is likewise found in Ernest Renan, *Souvenirs d'enfance et de jeunesse*, Paris (Calmann Lévy), 1883, p. 341: '*Que tout cela, direz-vous, est . . . peu naturel. Sans doute, mais on n'est fort qu'en contrariant la nature. L'arbre produit de beaux fruits dès qu'il est en espalier, c'est à dire, dès qu'il n'est plus un arbre'* [*naturel*]). 'Cruelty is in Nature, we are all born with a portion of cruelty that only education modifies, but education is not natural. It contravenes nature as much as cultivation does in trees' (*Philosophie dans le boudoir*, I, pp. 175–176, Engl. vers. by Geoffrey Gorer, *op. cit.*, p. 238). 'Do not be astonished or blame me because I am following the movement that Nature has placed in me. One wants to give one's nerves a violent commotion . . . One realizes that that of pain will be far stronger than that of pleasure. One uses it and is satisfied' (*Juliette*, II, 94–102; *La Nouvelle Justine*, II, 213–220; Gorer, *op. cit.*, p. 240). In his *Cent-vingt journées de Sodome* (p. 74) Sade proposes to enumerate 'six hundred perversions' excluding 'the pleasure allowed or forbidden by that brute of which you talk ceaselessly without knowing it and which you call Nature'. In an epigram, intended to justify the publication of his book *Juliette ou les malheurs de la Vertu* (Gorer, *op. cit.*, p. 120), Sade calls what is known to the public opinion of his and our own times as 'unnatural vices' 'the strange urges inspired by Nature':

> *On n'est point criminel pour faire la peinture*
> *Des bizarres penchants qu'inspire la nature.*

'Once man was launched on to the earth he received direct laws from which he cannot depart; these laws are those of self-preservation and propagation, laws which affect him and depend on him, but which are in no way necessary to Nature, for he is no longer a part of Nature, he is separated from her. He is entirely distinct, so much so that he is no longer useful to her progress or necessary to her combinations, so that he could quadruple his species or completely annihilate it without in the least altering the universe. If he multiplies he does right in his own eyes, if he decreases, he does wrong, equally in his own eyes. But in the eyes of Nature, it is quite different. If he multiplies he deprives Nature of the honour of a new phenomenon. If those that had been launched did not multiply, she would launch new beings and would enjoy a faculty she has no longer. Proofs of how much multiplication annoys her are epidemics, and such criminals as Alexander, Tamburlaine, Genghis Khan and all the other heroes who devastate the earth.' There is hardly any need to remind the reader that man is by no means inexorably compelled to conform to the alleged natural laws of self-preservation and race-propagation. He can commit suicide or sacrifice himself to save others, and he can avoid propagation of his kind by the methods condemned in Gen. xxxviii. 9 f. So the alleged 'laws of Nature' are by no means compulsory for man. They cannot, anyhow, be appealed to for the purpose of justifying the practices in question. Whether they are 'natural' or 'unnatural', it is certainly natural for the potential victims to condemn them as dangerous and antisocial. De Sade's argument is no more valid or invalid than Comtesse de Sarotta's apology for her Lesbian practices: '*Dieu m'avait mis cet amour dans le cœur; s'il m'a créé telle et non pas autrement, est-ce ma faute ou celle des voies insondables de la Providence?*' (Prof. Étienne Martin, 'L'homosexualité', *Lyon Médical*, 1 Dec. 1907). Theologians will recognize in this argument the heresy known as 'Traducianism', and produce from their arsenal the appropriate counter-arguments which we have no desire to repeat.

5. ALGOBULIA

'Der Wille zum Schmerz, Ein psychologisches Paradox', *Vortrag gehalten am 29. Jänner 1904. Wissenschaftl. Beilage z. 17.*

Jahresbericht (*1904*) *der Philosophischen Gesellschaft an der Universität zu Wien*, Leipzig (Barth), 1904, pp. 77 f., repeated Feb. 1912 before the Munich Psychological Society. See *Zeitschr. für Psychotherapie und mediz. Psychologie*, ed. Alb. Moll, IV, No. 3, Stuttgart (Enke), 1912, pp. 188 f. The motto of the paper was taken from Shakespeare's *King John*: 'Then have I reason to be fond of grief.'

I might as well have used for the delight in pain the neutral term 'algophily'. I did not then know that the recognized Italian technical term is *algofilia*. See Prof. Emilio Seradio's articles 'algofilia' and 'sessuologia' in the *Enciclopedia Italiana* (1934). Neither the word 'algolagnia', nor any of its equivalents is found in either the 11th or the 14th edition of the *Encyclopedia Britannica* or in Baldwin's *Dictionary of Philosophy and Psychology*, New York, 1912, or in the *Oxford English Dictionary*. The phenomenon itself was, of course, not quite unknown. Alexander Bain (*The Emotions and the Will*, p. 177) says that in a state of anger gratification may be obtained from the suffering inflicted on other sentient beings; he speaks (p. 178) of the 'fascination of the sight of bodily pain inflicted or suffered', of (p. 195) 'the pleasure of power over others in its gross and brutal form.' Of all this James Sully, 'Gratification from the Infliction of Pain', *Mind*, I, 1876, pp. 285–287, tried to give an explanation from the evolutionary point of view, deriving it from the predatory animal's pleasure in the exploring of the prey, the cat's playing with the captured mouse, etc.; totally overlooking the fact that there is no predatory animal among man's ancestors. He mentions, in a brief sentence, the 'triumph over rivals', thinking obviously of animal sex-fights (below, notes 63 and 65). See also F. M. Bradley, 'Pleasure, Pain, Desire and Volition', *Mind*, XIII, 1888, p. 36; Tarozzi, 'La Filosofia del Dolore', *Rivista di Filosofia, Pedagogia, Scienze affine*, II, 1900, No. 2.

6. ALGOLAGNIA

According to C. G. von Schlichtegroll, *op. cit.* (note 2 above), p. 21, note **, the terms *Algolagnie* for masochism, *aktive Algolagnie* for sadism were coined by Dr. Albrecht van Schrenck-Notzing (18 May 1862–12 Feb. 1929) of Munich. In the Munich report on my lecture of 1 Feb. 1912 (above, note 5) its introduc-

tion is attributed to 'Offner and Schrenck-Notzing'. From his
books available in the British Museum I cannot find out when
and where he first used it. In his books *Die Suggestionstherapie bei
Krankheitserscheinungen des Geschlechtslebens,* Stuttgart (Enke), 1892,
p. 233c (a case reported by Moll) and p. 297e; *Kriminalpsycho-
logische und Psychologische Studien,* Leipzig (Barth), 1902, p. 69, he
uses the term as of something already well understood and
needing no explanation. So does von Krafft-Ebing in the 14th
ed. of his *Psychopathia Sexualis,* ed. Alfr. Fuchs, Stuttgart, 1912
(Engl. trans. of the 10th ed. by F. J. Rebman, London, 1901; a
trans. of the 7th ed. by Dr. C. G. Chaddock, Philadelphia and
London (Davis), 1892, quoting (p. 69, note 1) Eulenburg's
Klinisches Handbuch der Harn- und Sexualorgane, which is not in
the British Museum). The term *Algolagnie* is not found, any
more than the term *Masochism,* in the earliest editions of Krafft-
Ebing's *Psychopathia Sexualis,* of which the first (1886) and
second (1887) are in the British Museum. There is nothing relevant to be found in Schrenck-Notzing's *Gesammelte Aufsätze zur
Parapsychologie* (Stuttgart (Union Verlagsgesellschaft), 1929). I
strongly suspect that von Schlichtegroll's statement is erroneous
and that the term *Algolagnie* is one generation earlier than
Schrenck-Notzing. I trust the matter will be finally elucidated
by the German reviewers of this book.

7. Shakespeare, *Antony and Cleopatra*: 'the lover's pinch which
hurts and is desired', quoted by Krafft-Ebing, *Psychopathia
Sexualis.* An elaborate theory of erotic pinches and scratches can
be found in the *Kama-Sutra,* the Hindu *Ars amandi* of Vatsyayana,
Engl. trans. by Dr. B. N. Basu, Calcutta (Medical Book Co.),
1944, ch. xiv, pp. 117–124, and ch. xv, pp. 124–126.

8. First criticized, I believe, by H. Sidgwick, *Contemporary
Review,* 1872, p. 671. This is earlier than Nietzsche's 'Do I strive
for happiness? I strive for my work!' ('Strebe ich denn nach
Glück? Ich strebe nach meinem Werke').

9. *Confessions,* Book III, ch. 2. The first to see the problem and
to try to explain it by assuming a mixed feeling of pain and
pleasure is Plato, *Philebus,* 48 a (106): 'Socrates: Καὶ μῆν καὶ τὰς

γε τραγικὰς θεωρέσεις ὅταν ἅμα χαίροντες κλαῶσιν, μέμνησαι;
Protarchos: Τὶ δ'οὔ; 'And don't you remember the tragic
spectacles when they cry, enjoying themselves at the same time?
—Why should not I?' Socrates' question is preceded by the
query 'Must we be reminded of the fact that in the lamentations
(ἐν τοις θρήνοις) and longings (και πάθοις) there are pleasures
(ἡδονὰς) mixed up with the sufferings (ἐν λύπαις οὖσας
ἀναμιγμένας)?

10. The late Dr. W. A. Brend, *Sacred to Attis*, London (Heinemann), 1936, p. 169, described 'the enjoyment of tragedy' as 'a
relic of sadism'. This would not be denied by those who have
seen the horror plays regularly performed at the Paris *Théâtre du
Grand Guignol* and have observed both the actors and the audience. The serial killings in the 'Punch and Judy' plays for
children are so enjoyable because the puppets are of wood and
the beaten skulls sound so wooden and insensitive. Nevertheless
this enjoyment is certainly the harmless 'abreaction' of the cruel
urges of infancy.

11. R. Eisler, *Studien zur Werttheorie*, Leipzig (Duncker &
Humblot), 1902, pp. 64 f.

12. *Die Willenshandlung*, 1888.

13. 'What Is an Emotion?' *Mind*, IX, 1894.

14. The biological necessity of pain's functioning as a signal is
rarely taken into due consideration by the pessimist gnostic asking 'Unde malum?' as he inquires into the allegedly mysterious
origin of evil, instead of asking more intelligently why we are
not adapted more perfectly and 'fully automatically' to our constantly varying environment—a question which need only be
formulated in order to receive its self-evident answer. For a new
and original approach to the problem see Gerald Heard, *Pain,
Sex and Time, a New Hypothesis of Evolution*, London (Cassell)
1939, pp. 42 ff.

15. 'Leave well alone!'

16. Paula Schlier, *Petra's Aufzeichnungen*, Innsbruck (Brenner Verlag), 1926, p. 45.

17. By a curious and significant mistake not noticed either in the typescript or the printed proofs, she quotes this tale as 'The Princess on the Swords', obviously thinking of paintings of 'the Madonna of the Swords' and identifying herself with the suffering divine Mother.

18. See T. B. Macaulay's *Diary*, 1 Jan. 1839 (G. O. Trevelyan, *Life and Letters of Lord Macaulay*, popular ed., new impr., London (Longmans), 1901, p. 368): 'On my journey through the Pontine Marshes I finished Bulwer's *Alice*. It affected me much, and in a way in which I have not been affected by novels these many years. Indeed, I generally avoid all novels which are said to have much pathos. The suffering which they produce is to me a very real suffering, and of that I have quite enough without them.'

On ascetics inflicting pain upon themselves—allegedly in order to reap a recompense of happiness in a future life after death—see the articles by T. G. Hall, C. A. F. Rhys Davids, E. Anwyl, W. Capelle, A. S. Geden, M. Revon, A. E. Suffrin, R. A. Nicholson, W. Söderblom, J. S. Reid, G. A. Barton on Buddhist, Celtic, Christian, Egyptian, Greek, Hindu, Japanese, Jewish, Muslim, Persian, Roman, Semitic and Egyptian asceticism in the *Encyclop. of Rel. and Eth.*, II, Edinburgh (Clark), 1909, pp. 63–111, especially T. C. Hall, p. 63, col. a, §1: 'Pathological elements in Asceticism'; *ibid.*, VI, pp. 49, Prof. Rufus M. Jones's article 'Flagellants'.

19. HEATH AND OTHER CASES OF SADISM

Gerald Byrne, *Borstal Boy, the Uncensored Story of Neville Heath*, London (John Hill), *s.a.* [1947], with several autograph letters and documents in facsimile, but no portrait. The best photographs of the handsome killer were reproduced in the *Daily Mail* 25 and 27 Sept. 1946. Psychiatric evidence given by Dr. William Henry Duval Hubert—who was engaged on a book about the case at the time of his death—for the defendant (pp. 125 ff.), and for the prosecution by Dr. Hugh A. Grierson and Dr. Hubert Turner Young (pp. 128 ff.). The newspaper reports were in many details cruelly untrue; the book is a hurried compilation, superficial and lacks any deep psychological understanding. Neville Heath was by no means the monster he was made out to be. The last letter he wrote before his execution was addressed to the head master of the approved school to which Heath had been committed as a boy. The recipient, an outstanding, altogether admirable educationalist, will not allow me to quote from the text, which I had the privilege of hearing read at a private meeting of the Oxford magistrates' club. So the reader must take my word for it when I say that these few, simple and obviously sincere lines are a deeply moving *document humain,* quite incompatible with the composite image projected on to the screen from whose cold glare public opinion is wont to derive its blurred and inaccurate information. It would be quite misleading to compare this case with those discussed by Lombroso in his book *Verzeni e Agnoletti,* Roma, 1874, the horrors of the case of the German Fritz Haarmann (executed in 1924; William Bolitho, *Murder for Profit,* London, 1926, pp. 263–320), the cases of Cream (Teignmouth Shore, *The Trial of Thomas Neill Cream,* 1892, Notable British Trials Series, London and Edinburgh, 1923), of Vacher (A. Lacassagne, *Vacher l'Éventreur et les crimes sadiques,* Lyon et Paris, 1899), of the clerk Alton who entered in his diary: 'Killed to-day a young girl. It was fine and hot' (Krafft-Ebing, *op. cit.,* case 18). The perpetrator of the frightful crimes attributed to 'Jack the Ripper' (Iwan Bloch, *Sex-Life in England, Past and Present,* London (Aldor), 1938, p. 145; William Stewart, *Jack the Ripper, A New Theory,* London (Quality Press), 1939) has never been discovered. The 'new theory' is that the criminal may have been a midwife gone mad. It is, of course, often thought by the uninformed that the crime of sadistic murder is committed only by men. The truth is that women have rarely had the physical strength required for such outrageous crimes. But there was quite recently the case of a Mrs. Nora Patricia Tierney, aged 29, of St. John's Wood, London, who took her own daughter and a neighbour's three-year-old daughter into a house, hit the child on the head with a hammer and killed her. 'She did not know how often she hit her', could give no reason for the crime, but tried to blame it on her husband (*News of the World*, 11 Sept. 1949, p. 3). There was also a female counterpart of the terrible 'Bluebeard', the Maréchal de France Gilles de Rais (Abbé Eugène Bossard, *Gilles de Rais*, Paris (Champion), 1886; Vincent and Binns, *Gilles de Rais*, London, 1926) convicted of having killed some three to four hundred children, namely the Hungarian Countess Ersze (= Elisabeth) Bathory, a 17th-century feudal lady in her own right, said by K. von Elsberg (in a paper extensively quoted by C. G. von Schlichtegroll, *op. cit.* in note 2 above, pp. 176 ff.) to have killed 650 girls, most of them forcibly brought into her bed by her menials, to be literally bitten to death.

20. Schizophrenes and 'feral children' (below, p. 138, note 111) are said to be characterized by a total lack of power to show empathy (P. G. Hoskins, *Biology of Schizophrenia*, London (Chapman & Hall), 1946, p. 60. This is relevant because of the gazelle-fostered boy (note 111) and the possibility of such individuals having taken the lead in the process outlined on p. 33.

21. 'The pain must not be too intense and must not be too serious.' . . . 'If the pain becomes too intense, the displeasure outweighs the erogenous stimulation and pleasure ceases.' See the chapter on 'Masochism' in Dr. Otto Fenichel's *The Psychoanalytical Theory of Neurosis*, London (Kegan Paul), 1945, pp. 359 f. Quite recently the American periodical *Time* of 7 Feb. 1949 carried the following news item: 'In Quito, Ecuador, Bersabe Cachago refused to press charges against her husband, explained that she does not really mind his beating her if he doesn't beat too hard.'

22. PLEASING PAIN
Shakespeare, *Antony and Cleopatra*. Cf. Montaigne, *Essays*, Book III, ch. 12: 'rien ne chatouille qui ne pince' ('nothing tickles that doeth not pinch'). See also Spenser's *Faerie Queene*, III, 10, str. 60, 'and painful pleasure turns to pleasing pain' and Swinburne's *Laus Veneris*:

> . . . *with nerve and bone she multiplies*
> *Exceeding pleasure out of extreme pain.*

See Havelock Ellis, *Sexual Impulse*, pp. 66 f.; Westermarck, *Evolution of Moral Ideas*, I, p. 657: 'Among the Slavs of the lower classes the wives feel hurt if they are not beaten by their husbands; the peasant women in some parts of Hungary do not think they are loved by their husbands until they have received the first box on the ear; among the Italian *camorristi* a wife who is not beaten by her husband regards him as a fool.' The relation between the sexes among the French Apaches constantly represented on the variety stage in the so-called Apache dances, and between gangsters and gunmen's 'molls', are too well-known and too often shown on the cinema screen to need further documentation. To my own tutor, in later life an Austrian Supreme Court judge, a woman—not a Slav—of Lower Austria applied for a divorce. Asked for her reasons she said: 'He does not love me, he never beats or kicks me.'

23. In Kleist's tragedy *Penthesilea* the Amazon queen not only has Achilles whom she loves torn to pieces by her own pack of dogs, but joins them in biting into the living flesh of her victim. Cf. below, note 229, on Artemis and Actaeon rent by the dogs. *Penthesi-leia* means 'smoothed by sufferings.' Krafft-Ebing, *op. cit.*, p. 70, quotes Alfred de Musset's *Andalousienne*:

> *Qu'elle est superbe en son désordre*
> *Quand elle tombe, les seins nus*
> *Qu'on la voit béante se tordre*
> *Dans un baiser de rage et mordre*
> *En hurlant des mots inconnus.*

C. G. v. Schlichtegroll, *op. cit.*, p. 126, quotes from Baudelaire's *Fleurs du Mal*:

> *Quelque fois pour apaiser*
> *ta rage mystérieuse*
> *Tu prodigues sérieuse*
> *ta morsure et le baiser.*

24. INTOXICATION IN MATING AND BY BLOOD

Blumröder, *Über Irresein*, 1836, p. 51 (quoted by Krafft-Ebing, Engl. trans. by Chaddock, *op. cit.*, note 6 above, p. 57), treated a man for severe bites in the pectoral muscles made by a woman in great sexual excitement during copulation. Cf. the Marquis de Sade's *Les infortunes de la Vertu*, texte établi sur le manuscrit original autographe et publié pour la première fois par Maurice Heine, Paris (Editions Fourçade), 1930, p. 103: 'J'étais bien loin de croire que l'homme, à l'exemple des bêtes féroces, ne peut jouir qu'en faisant frémir ces compagnons. Je l'éprouvais maintenant et dans un tel degré de violence que les douleurs naturelles du déchirement de ma virginité furent les moindres que j'eusse à supporter dans cette dangereuse attaque; mais ce fut au moment de sa crise qu'Antoine termina par des cris si furieux, par des excursions si meurtrières sur toutes les parties de mon corps, par des morsures enfin si semblables aux sanglantes caresses des tigres qu'un moment je me crus la proie de quelque animal qui ne s'appaiserait qu'en me dévorant.' It is hardly necessary to add that the tiger's mating caresses, observed in more than one zoological garden, are in reality no more sanguinary, although somewhat more raucous, than those of a domesticated tom-cat. The 'cruenta voluptas', the actual intoxication by the mere sight of flowing blood, is impressively described by St. Augustine, *Confessions*, VI, ch. viii (Migne, *P.L.*, t. 32, col. 726), speaking of the effect of gladiatorial combats in the circus on the spectator: 'Alypius ut enim vidit illum sanguinem, immanitatem simul ebibit, hauriebat furias, cruenta voluptate inebriabatur.' ['For as soon as Alypius beheld that blood he drank it down with a kind of savageness; and drinking up the cup of fury, he became drunk with a delight in blood.'] Blood was actually drunk by the Iranian Sarmatae (Pliny, *H.N.*, XVIII, 10). The ecstatic effect of the practice is mentioned by Pausanias, II, 24, 1. Madness caused by blood-drinking, Aeschylus, *Eumenid.* 859 ff.; blood-drinking orgies of North American Indians, Kurt Breysig, *Geschichte d. Menschheit*, I, Berlin, 1907, p. 123; Kircher, *Sacrale Bedeutung d. Weines*, Giessen, 1910, pp. 82, 88 f.; Eisler, *Orphisch.-Dionys. Myster.*, Leipzig, 1925, p. 247, note 5.

25. The well-known adage of St. Thomas 'amare est velle alicui bonum' occurs in the *Summa Theol.* I–II, art. IV, Migne, *P.L.*, Suppl., vol. 2*, cols. 217s.: 'Respondeo dicendum, sicut Philosophus dicit in secundo "Rhetorices" capitulo quarto in

principio "amare est velle alicui bonum". Sic ergo motus amoris in duo tendit, scilicet in bonum quod quis vult alicui vel sibi vel alii et in illud cui vult bonum. Ad illud ergo bonum quod quis vult alteri habetur amor concupiscentiae, ad illud autem cui aliquis vult bonum, habetur amor amicitiae'. ['I reply that it is to be held, as the Philosopher [Aristotle] says in *Rhet.*, II. 4, that "to love anyone is to wish him good". And so the emotion of love is directed towards two things, namely, towards that good which one wishes to an object, be it either oneself or some other, and towards that object to which one wishes good. Towards that good which one wishes to another is experienced the love of concupiscence, but to the object to which one wishes good, is experienced the love of friendship.'] See M. C. d'Arcy, S.J., *The Mind and Heart of Love*, London (Faber), p. 69.

26. The portrait—now in the Vienna Museum—was, of course, never meant to be sold. Rubens left the picture, which he called 'het pelsken', to his wife by his will. But it was subsequently acquired by the Archduke Leopold Wilhelm of Habsburg and thus passed into the collections of the Austrian Imperial House. See Rudolf Oldenbourg, *Rubens, Klassiker der Kunst*, volume V, 4th ed., Stuttgart, 1927, p. 424; Glück, *Jahrbuch der Kunsthist. Sammlungen*, Vienna, XXXV, 1920/21, pp. 580 f., pl. x.

27. TITIAN'S PORTRAIT OF BELLA

Thausing, 'La Bella del Tiziano', *Zeitschrift f. Bild. Kunst*, XIII, 1878, pp. 62–64, thought it to represent the young Duchess Eleonora Gonzaga, but this is extremely unlikely. Phot. reprod. in Hans Tietze's *Tizian*, Vienna (Phaidon Press), 1936, II, p. 317; Oscar Fischel, *Klassiker d. Kunst*, vol. III, Stuttgart, 1906, top of p. 64. The same model was used for Titian's *Bella* in the Palazzo Pitti and the reclining Venus of the Uffizi. Sacher-Masoch knew these three pictures. They suggested the title, *Die Venus im Pelz*, of his most famous novel. An ideal portrait of 'Petrarca's Laura' (thus described in Christian Mechel's catalogue of the Vienna Gallery, 1738; so also by Dr. Johannes Wilde, 'Ein unbekanntes Werk Giorgione's', *Jahrb. d.*

Preuss. Kunstsamml., Berlin, 1931, p. 97), painted and signed by Giorgione in 1506, symbolizes the lady's Christian name by branches of laurel sprouting, as it were, from her head and shoulders and shows her baring the 'white', 'angelic bosom' ('suo candido seno'. . . 'l'angelico seno' praised by her poet-lover, *Rime di Petrarca*, comm. da Giosué Carducci e Severino Ferrari, Firenze, 1905, p. 247, No. cl; *ibid.*, p. 184, No. cxxvi). The model—the same which the painter used for the almost nude figure of the young shepherdess in the so-called *Tempesta*, formerly in the Palazzo Giovanelli, now in the Accademia di S. Luca in Venice—was painted 'by order of Messer Giacomo (d)e Stra(da)' (possibly the father of the homonymous art collector and dealer Jacobus de Strada, portrayed by Titian in 1556), dressed in a blood-coloured mantle lined with marten's fur. It is a most curious coincidence that this earliest of the naked 'ladies in the pelt' or *femmes fauves* should be meant to represent Petrarca's chaste and unrelenting love Laura de Sade, the direct ancestress of the notorious Marquis de Sade, whom her descendant remembered with pride (he quotes Petrarch 'the sweet singer of Vaucluse' in *Juliette*, II, pp. 79–82; see Geoffrey Gorer, *op. cit.*, note 1 above, p. 217). There is also a portrait by El Greco of a 'lady in the fur' now in Sir John Maxwell's collection, recently exhibited at the National Gallery, London. In Baluchistan it is believed that 'the black bear takes the form of a beautiful woman at night and hugs men to death if they are not wary' (M. L. Dames, *Folklore*, XIII, 1902, p. 265, and the literature quoted below, note 92).

28. Chateaubriand, *Hercule préféré à Adonis*, quoted by Krafft-Ebing, *op. cit.*, p. 22, note 1.

29. LOVE AND DESTRUCTION

E. A. Crawley, article 'Love (Primitive)' *Encyclop. of Rel. and Eth.*, VIII, p. 156, col. b: 'The intimate psychology of love reveals not only an impulse for union, but an association in the male psychosis with an impulse for destruction and even for devouring. Love often uses the language of eating.' Unfortunately this is not a matter of mere language. See, for instance, Jean Français, *L'Église et la Sorcellerie*, Paris (Nourry), 1910,

p. 259, the confession of a French Sergeant Bertrand of the revolutionary year 1848: 'Je coupais une femme en morceaux avec un extrême plaisir.' *Ibid.*—'George Leyer tua une jeune fille dans les environs de Versailles, la viola et lui mangea une partie des seins, du ventre et des parties sexuelles'. A similar case concerning one Andreas Bichel who killed and dissected like a butcher the bodies of girls he had raped, opening the breasts with a knife and cutting out the fleshy parts of the body, is recorded in Feuerbach's *Aktenmässige Darstellung merkwürdiger Verbrechen*, I, Giessen, 1828, pp. 97 ff.; C. Goldhammer's *Archiv*, xxx; quoted by Krafft-Ebing, *op. cit.*, p. 62.

30. On the phenomena known as atavisms, reversions or re-crudescences see J. Arthur Thomson's article 'Atavism' in the *Encyclop. of Rel. and Eth.*, II, p. 167.

31. Krafft-Ebing, *op. cit.*, p. 69.

32. *The Criminal*, 1875; *L'uomo delinquente*, Turin, 1896–1897.

33. See W. A. Perry, 'The Peaceable Habits of Primitive Communities,' *Hibbert Journal*, 1917, pp. 28 ff.; *id.*, *The Growth of Civilisation*, London (Methuen), 1924, p. 6, and pp. 191 ff.; Sir Grafton Elliot Smith, *Human Nature* (Conway Memorial Lecture), London (Watts), 1927; M. R. Davis, *The Evolution of Man in Early Society*, Yale Univ. Press, 1929, ch. IV, pp. 46 f.: 'Where war exists and where not'.

34. *Morals in Evolution*, 3rd ed., London, 1915, p. 234.

35. *Essays on Human Evolution*, London (Watts), 1946, p. 178.

36. *Op. cit.*, p. 176, against W. C. Allee, *Social Life of Animals*, who rightly regards war as an 'acquired habit'.

37. *The Twilight of Man*, Harvard, 1939, p. 273.

38. We have now a Sumerian parallel found in Nippur (c. 2000 B.C.), published by N. Kramer, *Journ. Amer. Orient.*

Soc., LXIII, 1934, p. 191, to the Hebrew account of the primeval peace between fruit-eating man (Gen. i. 9; ii. 16) and the animals in the oasis or 'garden of the desert' (that is what *gan 'eden* means, *edin* being Sumerian for 'steppe', 'desert'). On the Sumerian story of the eviction of man from the garden of the gods (A. Chiera, *Amer. Journ. of Sem. Lang. and Lit.*, XXXIX, 1922, pp. 40 ff.) see R. Eisler, 'Food and the Fall', *Modern Churchman*, XXXVI, Nos. 1–3, June, 1946, p. 96. For the parallel Persian tradition see Windischmann, *Zoroastr. Studien*, p. 212. The Greek and Latin tradition, Empedocles and Posidonius ap. Porphyry *De Abstin.*, II, 21 ff.; Plato, *Laws*, VI, 782 E; Seneca, *Epist.* CVIII (Sôtiôn); Clem. Alex., *Strom.* VII, 32, etc., see E. Graf, 'Ad Aureae Aetatis Fabulam Symbola', *Leipzig. Studien z. Klass. Philol.*, VIII, 1885, pp. 20 ff. Kirby Flower Smith, *Encyclop. of Rel. and Eth.*, I, p. 195, note ‡.

39. Ovid, *Metam.*, XV, 96 ff.

40. On occasionally meat-eating apes see T. K. Penniman, *A Hundred Years of Anthropology*, Oxford, 1935, p. 305, quoting S. P. Tolstoy, *Sovietskaya Etnografia*, 1931, pp. 69–103. On apes eating insects, chrysalids and grubs, ant-eggs, butterflies, caterpillars, flies and spiders, see Moriz Hörnes, *Natur- und Urgeschichte d. Menschen*, Vienna (Hartleben), 1909, I, p. 485, who insists on classifying the apes as 'omnivorous', although 'preponderantly frugivorous', 'the anthropoid apes being less eager for meat than other apes although they could easily procure it with their great strength and formidable teeth'. Much relevant material has been collected by Steinmetz, 'Endokannibalismus,' *Mitt. d. Anthropolog. Gesellschaft in Wien*, 1896, XXVI, p. 35; see also J. A. MacCulloch's article 'Cannibalism among animals', *Encyclop. of Rel. and Eth.*, III, 194 No. 2.

41. *Cambridge Natural History*, X, p. 576.

42. Letter dated London, 16 Jan. 1945. The misleading abuse of serving, to the amusement of an ignorant public, fried chicken as Sunday dinner to one of the gorillas, still remembered by older visitors, has long been abandoned by the present, more

enlightened administration. Free gorillas have been seen to catch little birds, lizards, etc., but never to eat them. Presumably they throw them away as the captured chimpanzee was seen to do.

43. It was the veteran editor of the *Hibbert Journal*, Dr. L. P. Jacks, who proposed to supplant the Linnæan term *Homo sapiens* by this more realistic denomination for the fools now preparing to blast each other and all their works to extinction.

44. *Memories and Studies*, p. 301. Cf. also Oswald Spengler, *Der Mensch und die Technik*, Engl. trans. ['Man and Technics'] by C. F. Atkinson, London, 1932, p. 43: 'Man is a predatory animal. He knows the feeling of intoxication when the knife enters into the flesh of the enemy and brings to the triumphant senses groans and the smell of blood.' These words are true enough, and also characteristic of the mentality gloating upon such horrors, let loose upon the world in 1933. But when he goes on to say: 'All the paragons of virtue and thinkers on social ethics are merely beasts of prey with their teeth drawn' he goes off the rails. For the truth of the matter see the dream cited on our p. 213, note 205, about 'restoring the gibbon'.

45. ABSENCE OF CANNIBALISM IN ANIMALS
The accent in this sentence is on 'systematically'. Juvenal (*Satire* XV) may be right when he says:

> *What lion takes advantage of his strength*
> *To kill his kind? What bear will e'er succumb*
> *To boar with larger tusks?*

It is, generally speaking, true that 'dog.does not eat dog'. Polar expeditions have, however, often had to slaughter some of their Eskimo dogs to cut them up and feed the others who do not object to eating dogs' meat. It is also a fact that wolves some- times attack, kill and devour old and sickly members of the pack (Brend, *Sacred to Attis, op. cit.*, p. 24). See further MacCulloch, *op. cit.*, note 29. A lady member of the recent International Congress of Mental Health in London who keeps lions 'had observed that they ate rabbits or anything like their normal prey without digestive anxiety'. But when she fed them Great

NOTESn. 49

Danes, one of which they had 'known socially', 'they showed signs of severe guilt' (*News Chronicle*, 9 Sept. 1948). The name of the speaker is not on record, so no more details could be ascertained about the guilt-feeling of the lion or of the speaker who may have 'projected' these sentiments on to her somewhat idealized pets.

46. *Laws*, VI, 765 ff.; *Sophist*, 222b: man 'no wild animal' (ἄγριον ζῷον), but a tame (ἥμερον), indeed the tamest (ἡμερότατον) of all animals.

47. Cf. Aristotle, *Polit.*, 1253, a, 21. Repeated by Philo, *De praemiis*, p. 423 Mangey; Epictetus, *Diss.*, IV, 1, 120; IV, 5, 10; Pseudo-Philo, 'On the imperishability of the world', ed. Jacob Bernays, *Abh. Berl. Akad. d. Wiss.*, 1876, p. 217 (quot. Critolaus of Phaselis); Ocellus (1st century A.D.), *On the Nature of the World*, ed. Mullach, IV, 4. See Max Mühl, *Philol. Wochenschr.*, 1924, col. 405. Cf. on this problem Sir Arthur Keith's essay, 'Is Man a Domesticated Animal?', *op. cit.* above (note 35), pp. 37 ff.

48. ἄνθρωπος ἄοπλος, *animal inerme* [an unarmed animal] in Protagoras's story of man's creation by Prometheus (Plato, *Protagoras*, 321c), who gave him, instead of the natural weapons of the other animals, fire and the knowledge of handicrafts (ἔντεχνος σοφία). See Zeller, *Arch. f. Gesch. d. Philos.*, 5, 176 f.; Gomperz, *Griech. Denker*, I, 313, on Protagoras's authorship of the story).

49. Cf. Sir Arthur Eddington, *Science and the Unseen World*, Cambridge, 1929, p. 15: 'a being of no great size, almost defenceless, defective in at least one of the most important sense organs, one gift saved him from threatened extinction, a certain stirring, a restlessness in the organ called the brain'. This 'stirring' of the brain is more technically described as 'progressive cerebration' by the late Prof. Constantine Economo, *The Cytoarchitectonics of the Human Cerebral Cortex*, Engl. trans. by Dr. S. Parker, Oxford Medical Publications, Oxford Univ. Press, 1920, p. 177. Also Dr. Richard J. A. Berry, 'Some Recent Advances in the Study of the Brain as the Implement of the

Mind', *Proc. R. Soc. Edinburgh*, Ser. 3, LXII, paper No. 11, p. 89, on the supergranular cortex as the most recent evolutionary addition.

50. On the reasons why the successive races of mankind are connected with the various metals see my lecture on 'Plato, the Philosopher' in *Quarterly Journal of the Philosophical Society of England*, Sept. 1948, pp. 7 f. (illustrated and amplified in the book *Plato, his Personality and His Politics*, London, Tower Bridge Publications Ltd., 1951); and my paper 'Metallurgical Anthropology in Plato and Hesiod', *Isis*, vol. 40, No. 120, 1949, pp. 108–112.

51. FRUGIVOROUS DIET OF EARLY MAN

Ovid, *Metam.*, XV, 96 f.; Schmekel, *De Ovidii Pythagoreorum Adumbratione*, Diss., Greifswald, 1885. The primitive Arcadians in the mountains feeding on the acorns of the *phêgoi* are mentioned by Apollonius Rhodius, *Argon.*, IV, 265; Lycophron, 482; Scholia to Lycophr., *l.c.*; the younger Philostratus, *Imagg.*, V, 1; cf. IV, 1; Pausanias, VIII, 5. Pelasgos, ancestor of the Arcadians, teaches them to eat the fruits of all δρύες, *i.e.* trees, not only of the φήγοι. They had previously lived on leaves and roots (Pausanias, VIII, 1, 5). The physician Galen (VI, 778) says that acorns (βαλανοί), although now a pigs' food, were still eaten by men in times of famine. But in another passage (VI, 620) he speaks of his own home country, Mysia, where *Quercus vallonea* Ky. with eatable acorns is found, and says that the peasants eat them after submitting them to a process of fermentation in clamps covered with earth. He then continues: 'It is said that once all men lived on acorns (βαλανοί), but the Arcadians kept to this diet long after the other Greeks had turned to the gifts of Demeter.' According to Suidas (s.v. ἀληλεσμένον) and Eustathios on *Odyss.* XIX, 163, p. 1859, 48, the ancients contrasted the 'acorn diet' (βαλανιτής βίος) with the more civilized 'milled flour diet' (ἀληλεσμένος βίος). The comic poet Nicochares (*Athen.*, I, 34c) speaks of a cooked beverage made of acorns, probably what is now called acorn coffee, a decoction of roasted acorns made in Central Europe before and during the First World War, probably now drunk again instead of malted corn-coffee. In the pile-dwellings excavated in the plain of the river Po acorns have been found in great quantities, often stored in big clay vessels. W. Helbig, *Die Italiker der Po-Ebene*, 1879, pp. 16 f., thinks they were used for human consumption rather than as pig-food. In the pile-dwellings of the Swiss lakes also acorns have been found in quantities (Schrader, *Reallexikon*, p. 528). Appian (*Bell. Civ.*, I, 50) reports that a defeated group of the Roman army tried to live on acorns during the hard winter march from Etruria to the Ionian Sea, but that half of the men died of starvation. This does not mean that such a diet is in itself inadequate to sustain life, but that even of acorns there were not enough for all. The acorn diet of primitive man is mentioned by Lucretius, V, 692; 1414; Horace, *Sat.*, I, 3, 100; Tibull., II, 3, 69; Juvenal, 6, 10, 13, 57; Vergil, *Georg.*, I, 148; Ovid, *Fast.*, IV, 508; Pliny, VII, 191; Apuleius, *Metam.*, XI, 2: Ausonius, *Idyll.*, 12; *De cibis*, 3; Claudian, *R. Pros.*, III, 43 ff.; Vesp., *Iud. coci et Pist.*, 22; Bährens, *Poetae Lat. min.*, IV, 327; Cicero, *Orat.*, 31; Pliny, *H.N.*, XVI, 15, on Iberian tribes in Spain eating bread baked from crushed acorns and acorns baked in ashes (of *Quercus ballota* Derf.). Cf. Aelian (*Var. Hist.*, III, 39): 'The Arcadians fed in old times on acorns, the Argives on pears, the Athenians on figs, the Tirynthians on wild pears, the Indians on cane, the Carmanians on palm-fruit, the Maeotians and Sarmatians on millet, the Persians on pistachio-nuts and cress' (also Dioscur., V, 32; Pliny, *H.N.*, XIV, 103; Pallas III, 25, 11, on the diet of pears of Argos and Tiryns). See Ed. Dupont, 'Le régime frugivore est le régime naturel de l'homme', *Bulletin de la Soc. d'Anthropologie de Bruxelles*, XII, 1893/4. The psychologist Wilhelm Wundt, the geographer Peschel and the ethnologist Karl Schurtz, *Speiseverbote*, 1893, have all attributed a frugivorous diet to earliest man. The objections of Moriz Hörnes, *Natur- und Urgeschichte d. Menschen, op. supra cit.* (note 40), I, p. 489, are based on the alleged 'demonstration by the physiologist' that 'the digestive system of man requires a mixed diet' —a prejudice refuted not only by the vigorous longevity of Bernard Shaw, but by millions of equally active and healthy vegetarians. (The present writer has to confess to omnivorous habits and is quite unprejudiced in this controversy.)

52. See Eisler, 'Das Quainszeichen und die Qeniter', *Le Monde Oriental*, Upsala and London (Williams & Norgate), 1929, pp. 67 ff.

53. Tablet I, ll. 35–41; IV, 6–12; col. IV, 1–5, col. 1, Engl. trans. by R. Campbell Thompson, Oxford, 1928.

54. W. Mannhardt, *Antike Wald- und Feldkulte*, Berlin (Bonträger), 1877, ch. III, §3, pp. 126 ff. Sir James Frazer, *Spirits of the Corn and of the Wild*, London (Macmillan), 1912.

55. Title of Emile Zola's famous novel. The original model for the hero was the fourfold murderer Eusebius Pieydagnelle (1871) (Magnus Hirschfeld, *Sexual Anomalies*, p. 458b). See also Georg Brandes, 'Das Tier im Menschen', *Essays*, Frankfurt a.M., 1894, pp. 376 ff.

56. *animal sociale*, Seneca, *De beneficiis*, 7, 17; *De clementia*, 1, 3, 2. Macrobius, *Somnium Scipionis*, I, 8, 6; Lactantius, *Instit.*, 6, 10, 10. St. Bernard of Clairvaux, *Sermones de diversis*, XVI, 3, *Opera*, I, 2350 D.

57. *Hist. anim.*, I, p. 488a, 7 ed. Imm. Bekker.

58. *ibid.*, p. 351a.

59. Curiously enough, he omits the dam-building beavers, although he knows the animal by the name of κάστωρ.

60. This is the title of an interesting book by Dr. Rudolf Jordan with the subtitle *Principles of the Philosophy of Responsibility*, published by the Central News Agency of South Africa Ltd., 1944.

61. S. Zuckerman, *The Social Life of Monkeys and Apes*, London (Kegan Paul) 1932; E. Westermarck, *History of Human Marriage*, 5th ed., London, 1921, vol. I, p. 37; on the Orangutan—keeping the young ones for two years with the old pair —see Moszkowski, *Auf neuen Wegen durch Sumatra*, p. 246; de

Crespigny, 'On North Borneo', *Proc. R. Geograph. Soc.*, XVI, p. 177; Rajah Brooke, *Narrative of Events in Celebes, Borneo, etc., from the Journals of James Brooke*, I, pp. 227 and 221; on the gorilla living in bands with one male only fighting against any other male approaching with horrible cries, see Savage, *Description of Troglodytes Gorilla*, p. 9 f; Schweinfurth, *Heart of Africa*, I, p. 522; Jenks, 'Zulu Knowledge of the Gorilla and Chimpanzee', *Americ. Anthropolog. Review*, New Ser., XIII, pp. 56 and 57; Westermarck, *l.c.*, p. 37: 'None of these apes can be called gregarious animals', the reason being that because of their great size a herd would need too much food if it kept together. As to the chimpanzee and gorilla, the bands which have sometimes been observed in the Cameroons under conditions of relative abundance of food in the neighbourhood of the modern plantations are a composite group of polygynous families. Ample material can be found in E. Westermarck, *History of Human Marriage*, 5th (re-written) ed., London (Macmillan), 1921, p. 32.

62. On these gregarious apes see Robert Yerkes, *The Great Apes*, New Haven (Yale Univ. Press), 1929, p. 558, and Zuckerman, *op. cit.*, ch. xiii, pp. 208 ff.

63. See Zuckerman, *op. cit.*, pp. 251 and 256. The London Zoological Society has in a few years lost thirty-six Hamadryas females literally torn to pieces by the males. Since there was always a sufficiency of females and complete freedom of movement for both sexes, there is no reason to think that the baboons behave otherwise when not in captivity. The constant loss of females in the course of these jealousy-fights must diminish their numbers and thus exacerbate the fighting. The process is therefore necessarily self-accelerating.

64. See F. B. Kirkman, *Bird Behaviour, A Contribution based on the observation of the black-headed gull*, Edinburgh, 1937; Schelderup Ebbe, 'Social Behaviour of Birds', *Handbook of Social Psychology*, ed. Carl Murchison, Worcester, 1935; David Katz, *Animals and Men, Studies in Comparative Psychology*, London, 1937, p. 212.

65. Charles Darwin, *Descent of Man*, 1871, I, part II, ch. 8, 'Sexual Selection', §8, says: 'It is certain that among all animals a fight of the males for the possession of the females takes place, a fact which is so universally known, that it is superfluous to produce examples.' This is still so widely believed and so often used for the purpose of explaining an allegedly universal 'instinct of pugnacity'—derived from jealousy—that the falsity of the statement and the exception discussed in note 70 below cannot be overemphasized.

66. See J. R. de la H. Marett, *Race, Sex and Environment*, London (Hutchinson), 1936; R. A. Fisher, *The Generical Theory of Natural Selection*, Oxford, Univ. Press, 1930, p. 483, note 12.

67. LARGE CANINE TEETH IN EARLY MAN

A canine tooth very similar to that of a chimpanzee was found in close connection with the skull of the so-called *Eoanthropus* in the gravel-pit of Piltdown in Sussex. Many authorities consider it as having once belonged to this skull (Gordon Childe, *What Happened in History*, Harmondsworth (Penguin Books), 1942, pp. 8 and 24). See also Reche's article 'Piltdown' in Ebert's *Reallex. d. Vorgeschichte*, X, 1927/8, pp. 157 f., and the photographic reproduction in L. S. B. Leakey, *Adam's Ancestors*, London (Methuen), 1934, pl. xii; fig. 23 to p. 64 of Henry Fairfield Osborn, 'Man Rises to Parnassus', *Critical Epochs in the Pre-History of Man*, Princeton and Oxford Univ. Press, 1927. Birkner and Schwalbe's contrary opinion ('Die Abstammung des Menschen,' *Anthropologie*, 1923, p. 24), assuming that the tooth belonged to a chimpanzee co-existent with *Eoanthropus*, is improbable, although Dr. L. S. B. Leakey (*The Times*, 23 August 1947, p. 5) has now discovered in Rusinga (Kenya), within fifteen feet of one another, a jaw of the anthropoid *Proconsul* and, a few minutes later, a jaw of *Xenopithecus*, 'quite as great a coincidence as the association of a fossil human skull and an ape jaw in the Piltdown gravels'. I still think that the efforts to separate the canine from the skull are merely based on a prejudice concerning the limited variability of the prehistoric genus *Homo simius*. See also M. Boule, *Les hommes fossiles*, 1923, pp. 158 ff.; Hans Weinert, *Menschen der Vorzeit*, Stuttgart, 1930, p. 32, fig. on p. 31. Dr. Gordon Childe, *What Happened in History*, *op. cit.*, p. 8 (cf. p. 26), admits the connexion between the Piltdown skull and the jaw and tooth, concluding that 'some very early men . . . had projecting canine teeth set in very massive jaws that would be quite dangerous weapons, but these have disappeared in modern man whose dentures will not inflict mortal wounds'. I am inclined to think that these simian large canine teeth survived because of the manifest advantage they offered for a predatory omophagous life and disappeared only when the hunters had perfected their extraneous weapons and began to roast and cook their game by fire.

This book had already been typed when Dr. K. P. Oakley of the Geological Dept. of the British Museum of Natural History, South Kensington, announced in his address to the Anthropology and Archaeology Section of the British Association for the Advancement of Science at Newcastle-on-Tyne on 5 Sept. 1949 that he had established, by estimating the fluorine absorption of the Piltdown skull and jawbone, the age of both these fossils—formerly estimated as 500,000 years old—as more nearly 50,000 years. They are contemporary and appear to have belonged to a race 'part man, part ape'. Dr. Robert Broome, Keeper of the Anthropology Dept. of the Transvaal Museum, supported Dr. Oakley's theory. He said that during a recent visit to this country, he had examined the Piltdown remains and now had scarcely any doubt that the jawbone and the skull belonged to the same individual—a big-brained type of man who evolved concurrently with *Homo sapiens*.

68. LARGE JAWS OF EARLY MAN

See Franz Weidenreich, *Science*, vol. 99, 16 June 1944, Lancaster, Pa., No. 2581, pp. 479 f.; phot. illustr. in XV, 1945, of the *Anthropological Papers of the American Natural History Museum*, New York. Dr. R. von Königswald found a skull-cap fragment, more complete than Dubois' 'ape-man' skull, morphologically not the skull of a giant gibbon, but of a true hominid, much like *Pithecanthropus pekinensis* of the Chu-ku-tien cave. In 1939 the site where the skull-cap was found yielded an upper jaw larger than any known fossil or recent human jaw, with a canine tooth not tusk-like but with all the peculiarities of the truly human canines of *Sinanthropus*. In the same place the calvaria and a fragment of a lower jaw still larger than the 1937 find were recovered. The year 1941 yielded a fragment of the lower jaw, the most primitive human skeletal part ever found, which exceeds in size every known fossil or recent jaw, including that of *Homo heidelbergensis*. The teeth participate in this astonishing gigantism of the species now called *Meganthropus palaeo-javanicus*, while the 1937 find has been labelled *Pithecanthropus robustus*. In South China, between 1939 and 1944, three right-side lower molars of gigantic size were acquired, not belonging to some giant fossil ape, but to a true hominid now called *Giganthropus sinensis*. They are six times larger than the teeth of modern man and twice the size of gorilla molars. These teeth come from the caves in the yellow deposit south of the Yang-tse and belong to the Lower and Middle Pleistocene, where tapir, stegodon and orang-utan remains are encountered. Cf. Robert Eisler, 'Food and the Fall', *Modern Churchman*, XXXVI, No. 1–3, June, 1946, pp. 95 f. It should not, however, be overlooked that Prof. Le Gros Clark, reviewing Prof. Weidenreich's book in *Nature*, No. 4013, 28 Sept. 1946, p. 427, thinks it 'misleading to refer to the owner of the *Meganthropus* jaw as a giant, if this term is meant to indicate unusual stature. All jaws of *Pithecanthropus* are massive compared with those of the modern European, yet, so far as stature is concerned, it is the latter who would appear as a 'giant'. *Giganthropus*, which is described by Dr. von Königswald as a giant ape, is classified by Weidenreich as a giant hominid. Prof. Le Gros Clark finds himself quite unable to follow Prof. Weidenreich: 'The simian appearance and properties of the teeth far outweigh in significance any suggestion of hominid traits.' He notes the 'unexpected combination of the peculiarly primate skull and jaw of *Pithecanthropus* with the delicately modelled limb-bones of the modern human type recently discovered in East Africa and the association of a simian skull with teeth of human properties in the *Australopithecinae*, and concludes: 'Incidentally such odd associations greatly weaken the arguments of those who still refuse to accept the possibility that the Piltdown jaw and skull may belong to the same individual.' It is evident that a final verdict will have to be postponed until the publication of Prof. Le Gros Clark's eagerly awaited book on the new East African finds of the British Kenya Miocene Expedition. Speaking at the recent Brighton meeting of the British Association (*The Times*, 10 Sept. 1948), Prof. W. E. Le Gros Clark said that particular interest attached to the discovery of limb bones, for hitherto our knowledge of the extinct apes had been practically confined to jaws and teeth. The bones discovered consisted of the shaft of a humerus, fragments of clavicle, an almost complete femur, and portions of others, with some ankle bones. They evidently belonged to one of the large apes and were similar in general dimensions to those of a chimpanzee, but showed significant differences, particularly in the slender proportions of the shafts of the long bones. They appeared to indicate that those early Miocene apes—lightly built creatures which had not become specialized for a completely arboreal existence—were capable of running and leaping with considerable agility, in strong contrast with modern anthropoid apes. Those observations had an important bearing on the problem of human evolution.

69. Gen. vi, 4.

70. C. Roy Carpenter, 'A Field Study of the Behaviour and Social Relations of Howling Monkeys', *Comparative Psychology Monographs*, ed. Knight Dunlop, X, No. 12, Baltimore, 1934, written on the basis of eight months' observation on an island reserve where the animals lived wholly undisturbed. P. 140, pl. 5 A, gives the portrait of an adult male howler, pl. 11 C a photograph of primary sex-activity in dorso-ventricular position, pl. 11 D shows a male following an oestrous female. See also Prof. Ernest Albert Hooton, *Why Men behave like Apes and Vice Versa*, Princeton Univ. Press, 1940, p. 31.

71. VOYEURISM
Krafft-Ebing, *op. cit.*, p. 390, note 1, quoting A. Moll, who speaks of 'mixoscopia'; Ivankow, *Archive d'Anthropologie Criminelle*, XIII, p. 697, quoting Merzejewsky, *Gynécologie Médico-legale*. The most recent term is 'scoptophilite'. Provision made for voyeurs in bawdy houses of Vienna is mentioned by Stefan Zweig, *World of Yesterday*, London (Cassell), 1945, p. 75; the

same in Paris, Elliot Paul, *A Narrow Street*, London (Cresset Press), 1942, p. 122. It is, of course, absurd to treat the *voyeur* or 'Peeping Tom' of the Coventry legend as a psychopath. Dr. Walter Riese, 'The Psychology of the Voyeur', *Sexual Reform Congress, London 1929*, ed. by Norman Haire, London (Kegan Paul), 1930, pp. 641 f.: 'every healthy human being is to some extent a *voyeur*'; p. 642 on the *voyeur* in the theatre identifying himself with the hero or heroine acting as lover and beloved.

An observation, interesting for the self-analysing psycho-analyst, is found in Louis Bromfield, *Twenty-Four Hours*, London (Cassell), 1930, p. 11: 'There was much of the voyeur in Hector, and the trait found its expression in a morbid desire to pry into the lives of other people.' On the contrary, the furiously jealous possessive type cannot bear to look at even a pictorial representation of a mating couple without being irrationally enraged. The best example is the impotent Ruskin destroying in the basement of the National Gallery Turner's magnificent drawings of such subjects, left to the nation by the artist (W. M. Rossetti, *Rossetti Papers*, 1903, p. 383; Bernard Falk, *Turner the Painter*, London, 1938, pp. 233 ff.).

72. Even Romain Rolland, *Jean Christophe*, Engl. trans. *John Christopher* by Gilbert Cannan, IV, '*Journey's End*', London (Heinemann), 1913 (2nd ed., 1916), p. 314 says: 'Adultery with the consent of the husband is a filthy thing ... the doglike promiscuity in which some of the rich people in Europe lived appalled him.' The phenomenon is, of course, by no means peculiar to the rich. It is only that Jean Christophe, *i.e.* middle-class Romain Rolland, was not acquainted with the equally 'promiscuous' life of the poor.

73. See Denis Saurat, *Blake and Modern Thought*, London (Constable), 1929, p. 21: ... 'jealousy was to him an unbearable thing'. His poem 'Visions of the Daughters of Albion' is directed against the vice of jealousy. Saurat, *op. cit.*, p. 28: Crabb Robinson reports that Blake believed in 'having women in common'. See Crabb Robinson's *Diary*, ed. Symon, p. 269: 'He' (*viz.* Blake) says that, from the Bible, he has learned that *eine Gemeinschaft der Frauen stattfinden sollte*' (thus in the original).

Saurat, p. 27 and p. 162, on Blake's idea that exclusive love for
one woman is wrong, love for all women right. See Blake,
Poetical Works, ed. John Sampson, Oxford, 1905, p. 372:

> *For the sexes.*
> *The Gates of Paradise.*
> *Mutual forgiveness of each Vice*
> *Such are the Gates of Paradise.*

74. FREE LOVE AND JEALOUSY
  See especially his poem 'Epipsychidion', ll. 149–173, where
the Manuscript has:

> *Free love in this differs from gold and clay*
> *That to divide is not to take away.*

Of this poem Francis Thompson wrote in his famous essay on
Shelley (*Dublin Review*, 1908): 'It presents his theory of Free
Love in its most odious form.' In one of the letters recently published by Walter Sidney Scott in his book *Harriet and Mary, being
the Relations between Percy Bysshe Shelley, Harriet Shelley, Mary E.
and Thomas Jefferson Hogg*, London (Golden Cockerel Press),
1944, p. 15, letter II, Shelley writes to his friend Hogg: 'I hope
I am not prejudiced. I attempt to be otherwise. I hope,
generally speaking, I have appeared to you so. I attach little
value to the monopoly of exclusive cohabitation. You know that
frequently I have spoken slightingly of it . . . this I would not
value . . . Harriet (the last great complication) still cherishes,
still cherishes (it) as a prejudice interwoven with the fibre of
her being—this is the point.' P. 21, letter V: 'I am not jealous.
Jealousy has no place in my bosom. But Harriet does not think
so. She is prejudiced.' In order to appreciate the nobility of
Shelley's statement the reader should contrast it with the
explanation of jealousy in Spinoza's *Ethics*, pt. III, on 'Affects',
L. 35 E (Germ. trans. J. H. v. Kirchmann, 5th ed., Berlin
(Salinger), 1893, p. 137): 'Jealousy is called the hatred of the
beloved object combined with envy . . .' (the jealous man) 'is
forced to combine with the image of the beloved object the
image of the hated one. This situation occurs principally in the
case of love of woman; since whoever imagines that the woman

whom he loves has given herself to another, will be sad not merely because his own desire is thwarted, but because he will feel disgust and abhor the woman, because he is compelled to associate the image of the beloved object with that of the privy parts and excreta of the other', etc. The psycho-analyst of a jealous neurotic may easily be able to offer confirmation of this definition. But what a vile attitude towards the 'beloved object'(!) for an educated human being to assume! L. L. White, *The Next Development in Man*, London, 1944, p. 191, quotes Spinoza's definition and adds this remark: 'To the unitary consciousness organic facts are innocent, but dissociated man may by a shudder reveal that his divine comprehension is no more than an intellectual pretence.' If the said shudder occurs, it reveals nothing but the disgust felt by the unwashed—who included, at the time of Spinoza, all classes of European society—for their own bodies and especially for those parts that are more in need of frequent washing than the rest. On jealousy as the great vice poisoning human relations, see Bertrand Russell, *Marriage and Morals*, London (Allen & Unwin), 1929, pp. 17, 25–26, 36 f., 113 f., 153, 182, 186, 246 f., especially p. 17: 'Love and jealousy are both instinctive emotions, but religion has decreed that jealousy is a virtuous emotion to which the community ought to lend support, while love is at best excusable'; also p. 36, which is to be compared with the passage quoted from Spinoza: 'Wherever jealousy is aroused, even if it be only faintly, the sexual act appears to us disgusting, and the appetite which leads to it, loathsome'. 'The purely instinctive man, if he could have his way, would have all women love him and him only; any love which they may give to other men inspires in him emotions which may easily pass into moral condemnation. Especially is this the case when the woman is his wife' (all this does not apply to the *voyeur*-type who is as 'instinctive' as the jealous one). 'The good life cannot be lived without self-control, but it is better to control a restrictive and hostile emotion such as jealousy, rather than a generous and expansive emotion such as love. Conventional morality has erred not in demanding self-control but demanding it in the right place.' For a psychological study of this passion, see Dr. Boris Sokoloff, *Jealousy*, London (Carell & Nicholson), 1948.

75. '*La Tyrannie de l'homme a converti la possession d'une femme en une propriété*' (Diderot, *Supplément au Voyage de Bougainville*). It should not be forgotten, however, that the reverse is now equally true. We do not know whether it was so already in the matri-archal age. It is certainly contrary to the principle enunciated by M. C. d'Arcy, *op. cit.* (above, note 25): 'Love between per-sons means that each wants the other to be more himself.'

76. '*Tue-la!*' has always been a popular principle in Latin countries. Romain Rolland (*op. cit.* note 72 above, p. 149) makes John Christopher say: 'Puisqu'elle t'a trompé, elle ne peut pas avoir été ton amie. Elle est ton ennemie. Oublie-la ou tue-la.' Here in Britain, returned soldiers have killed not a few wives who sat less faithfully at their looms than Penelope, although the returning Ulysses himself has but too often yielded in the mean time to the charms of Circe, Calypso and Nausicaa. The House of Lords has had to remind juries that murder of this kind must not be classified as mere homicide and *crime passionnel*.

77. Spencer and Gillen, *op. cit.*, p. 99 f.; A. E. Crawley, *Encyclop. of Rel. and Eth.*, VIII, p. 154, col. 1, note 7: 'Among the Australian natives with whom we have come in contact, the feeling of sexual jealousy is not developed to anything like the extent to which it would appear to be in many other savage tribes.'

78. Thurnwald, article 'Promiscuität' in Ebert's *Reallexikon der Vorgeschichte*, X, p. 322, col. b.

79. *ibid.*, p. 323, col. b.

80. WITCHES' SABBATS
It is the merit of Margaret Alice Murray, *The Witch-cult in Western Europe*, Oxford Univ. Press, 1921, to have established a realistic approach to the study of these documents. See especially pp. 173–185; also Grillot de Giory, *Witchcraft, Magic and Alchemy*, London (Harrap), 1931. These associations are pre-agrarian, and the interpretation of the ecstatic dances and promiscuous matings, celebrated in the course of the esbats, as

'fertility rites' is in no way established. See below, note 226, on Dionysian analogies. There is ample evidence for connecting the accounts of the witches' Sabbats with the werewolf masquerade (below, note 92). In Brittany, at the end of the 18th century, sorcerers were believed to take the form of wolves or to clothe themselves with a wolf's skin when going to the Sabbat (La Tour d'Auvergne-Corret, *Origines Gauloises*, 2nd ed., Paris, 1794, p. 39; MacCulloch, *op. cit.* note 105, p. 209, note 5). Wizards are believed to go to the witches' Sabbat in animal-shaped spirit bodies. If one rubs the real bodies with pepper, they cannot re-enter them, but must die (R. H. Nassau, *Fetichism in West Africa*, London, 1904, p. 123). In 1521, Pierre Burgot and Michel Verdun were tried by the Prior of the Dominicans of Poligny in the diocese of Besançon. Burgot confessed that Verdun taught him at a Sabbat how to become a werewolf by rubbing himself with a certain ointment. Then he saw himself with four paws and his body covered with hair, while he was able to run like the wind. Verdun also transformed himself in the same way; the ointment had been obtained from his demon master. In the form of wolves they killed several children, sucked their blood, and ate part of their flesh, finding it excellent. Burgot also said that he had sexual relations with wolves. Both men were burnt alive at Besançon. (Bodin, *De Magorum Demonomania*, Francofurti, MDCIII, p. 225.)

81. Westermarck, *op. cit.*, II, p. 423; W. G. Sumner, *Journ. of the Anthropological Institute*, XXXI, 1901, p. 96.

82. Thurnwald (see note 78 above), p. 321, col. a.

83. A case was recently tried and reported in *The Times* of 11 June 1948, p. 3, Col. 3, of two husbands exchanging wives for their vacations, but only because the fact was mentioned many years later in a divorce suit started by one of the wives. At the beginning of the Soviet régime the European and American press was full of reports about the 'nationalization of women' in Russia. But it is well known that they were mainly products of Western imagination, and that Lenin—a *déclassé* nobleman named Ulianov, with the subconscious background of his fight-

ing, hunting and possessive ancestors—firmly opposed and repressed the theory that a man should be able to assuage his
sexual appetites with the same ease as he could deal with his
thirst by 'drinking a glass of water'. The present Russian society
is as firmly based on the patriarchal family as that of any
bourgeois-capitalist country. Divorce has recently been made
more difficult than before, adultery is frowned upon by the
Communist Party, etc.

84. See the testimonies quoted from Plutarch's *Lycurgus* in
Bertrand Russell's *History of Western Philosophy*, London (Allen
& Unwin), 1946, p. 122.

85. 459–460.

86. Clearchus of Soloi ap. Athen., *Deipnosoph.*, XIII, 2,
p. 555 D.

87. Engl. trans. by Sathiarth Prakas, ch. iv, p. 150, quoted
Encyclop. of Rel. and Eth., II, p. 60, col. b.

88. *ibid.*, III, p. 780; p. 785, col. b, and p. 787, col. a.

89. THE CONCEPT OF ARCHETYPES
The concept, without the term 'archetypes', occurs first in
Jung's *Wandlungen und Symbole der Libido*, 1912 (Engl. trans.
The Psychology of the Unconscious, 1921) where they are called,
by a name derived from Jacob Burckhardt, 'primeval images'
(*urtümliche Bilder*). The term 'archetypes' appears for the first
time in Jung's 'Instinct and the Unconscious', *Brit. Journ. of
Psychol.*, X, No. 1, 1919; repr. in *Contributions to Analytical Psychology*, London (Kegan Paul), 1928, where he says (p. 279) that
the term is derived from the *Diversae Quaestiones* of St. Augustine.
He admits now (letter of 17 July 1946) that this was a slip of his
memory. On p. 280 he explains: 'archetypes are typical forms
of apprehension'; on p. 279 archetypes are said to be 'natural
images engraved upon the mind'. This metaphor points to the
real source of the concept. It is derived from the famous passage
in Plato's *Theaetetus* (191 f.) where the soul is said to contain a

wax-tablet (κήρινον ἐκμάγειον), a gift of *Mnêmosynê*, mother of the Muses, upon which our thoughts and sensations imprint, as it were, the images, engraved upon signet-rings (δακτυλιῶν σημεῖα). As long as this seal-impression (σφραγίς) remains, we remember; when it is wiped out, we forget. This theory is repeated by Aristotle (*De Memoria*, ch. 1), Zeno the Stoic, Cleanthes, Epictetus and, in modern times, by Locke (the passages are collected by E. Stölzel, *Die Behandlung des Erkenntnisproblems bei Plato*, Halle (Niemeyer), 1908, p. 96, note). Varro speaks of 'seal-impressions left in the mind by Love's fingerring' (*sigilla impressa Amoris digitulo*; Valckenaer, *Scholia in Nov. Test.* II, p. 235). Richard Semon's 'engram' is the last reflex of it. Curiously enough, two clay disks have been found in Minoan Crete at Phaestus into which an inscription has been imprinted by means of engraved sealstones, each one carrying an elaborate pictogram in *intaglio* (reproduced by David Diringer, *The Alphabet*, London (Hutchinson), 1948, p. 78, figs. 40 a and b). It was the Stoic philosopher Arius Didymus, a friend of the Emperor Augustus, who represented Plato's theory of ideas (Diels, *Doxogr.*, p. 447, cf. 72) by comparing the eternal 'paradigmatic ideas' of the species 'man', 'horse', etc., to the image engraved on a seal and the individual empiric men, horses, etc., to the impressions imprinted into matter by this eternal, imperishable stamp from which innumerable prints could be taken. The 'ideas' thus become 'archetypes of the sensed bodies' (ἀρχήτυπα τῶν αἰσθέτων σωμάτων). This account seems to refer to such passages as Plato, *Timaeus*, 50C/D–51C: ἐκμαγεῖον γὰρ φύσει παντὶ κεῖται . . . τὰ δὲ εἰσιόντα καὶ ἐξιόντα τῶν ὄντων ἀεὶ μιμήματα, τυπωθέντα . . . τὸ μὲν δεχόμενον μητρί, τὸ δ' ὅθεν πατρί, τὴν δὲ μεταξὺ τούτων φύσιν ἐκγόνῳ, νοῆσαί τε ὡς οὐκ ἂν ἄλλως ἐκτυπώματος ἔσεσθαί . . . [For it is laid down by nature as a moulding-stuff for everything . . . And the figures that enter and depart are copies of those that are always existent . . . it is proper to liken the Recipient to the Mother, the Source to the Father, and what is engendered between these two to the Offspring; and also to perceive that, if the stamped copy is to assume diverse appearances of all sorts . . .] and parallels. The combination of the ἀρχήτυπος idea with the notion of the seal (σφραγίς) that creates the empiric individuals is found more than once in Philo (the passages have been collected by F. J. Doelger, *Sphragis*, Paderborn (Schoeningh), 1911, pp. 67 f.; more in Leisegang's *Index* to Philo under *sphragis, archetypos, idea*, etc.). Latin testimonies are collected in the *Thesaurus Linguae Latinae*, II, p. 460, s.v. *archetypus*.

The term 'archetype' is always used for the one original engraving upon a seal or stamp contrasted with the many impressions, the original in contradistinction to the copy, never in the sense in which Jung uses it for a primeval, archaic impression in the 'wax-tablet' overlaid by later memory engrams. This usage is wholly new and original. In his *Two Essays on Analytical Psychology*, London (Baillière, Tindall & Cox), 1928, pp. 103 ff., he writes: 'The contents of the collective unconscious are not only the archaic residuum of specific human modes of reaction, but also the residuum of the functions of the animal ancestral chain of humanity, the duration of which in time must have been infinitely longer than the relatively short period of specifically human existence . . .

'These residues, or, to speak in Semon's terms, these engrams, are extremely liable, when active, not only to arrest the progress of development, but to divert the libido into regressive channels until the store of energy that has activated the collective unconscious has been used up.' Cf. *Psychological Types*, London (Kegan Paul), 1923, ch. xi, 'Definitions', No. 8 '*image*': 'These archetypes, whose innermost nature is inaccessible to experience, represent the precipitate of psychological functioning of the whole ancestral line, *i.e.* the accumulated or pooled experiences of organic existence in general. In these archetypes all experiences are represented that have happened on this planet since primeval times.' In Jung's *Two Essays on Analytical Psychology*, London, (Baillière, Tindall & Cox), 1928, p. 67 f., we find what is perhaps the most useful presentation of the facts for our purpose: 'There are present in every individual besides his personal memories the great "primordial images", as Jacob Burckhardt once aptly called them, those potentialities of human representations of things as they have always been, inherited through the brain structure from one generation to the next. The fact of this inheritance explains also the really amazing phenomenon that certain legends and themes repeat themselves the whole world over in identical forms. It explains, further, why it is that our mentally diseased patients can reproduce exactly the same images and associations as those we are familiar with in old texts. I have given some examples of this in my book *The Psychology of the Unconscious* (*Wandlungen und Symbole der Libido*). . . . In this further stage of the transference, then, when these phantasies that no longer depend on personal memories are reproduced, we have to do with the manifestations of the deeper layers of the unconscious, where sleep the primordial images common to humanity. To these images I also apply the term archetypes (*Urbilder*). The personal unconscious, of which I also speak as the "subconscious", in contrast to the absolute or collective unconscious, contains forgotten memories, suppressed (purposely forgotten) painful ideas, apperceptions, sometimes described as below the threshold (subliminal), that is, sensory perceptions that were not strong enough to reach consciousness, and, finally, contents that are not yet ripe for consciousness. This discovery leads now to the fourth stage of the new conceptual scheme, that is, to the recognition of two levels in the unconscious. We have to differentiate between a personal unconscious and an impersonal or super-personal unconscious. We speak of the latter also as the collective unconscious, because it is apart from the personal and quite universal. For its contents can be found in all minds, and this is obviously not the case with personal contents.

'The primordial images are the deepest, the most ancient and the most universal thoughts of humanity. They are as much feelings as thoughts, and have indeed an individual, independent existence, somewhat like that of the "partial souls" which we can easily discern in all those philosophical or gnostic systems that base themselves upon the apperception of the unconscious as the source of knowledge.'

I should like, finally, to recommend to the reader that strange and impressive book of searching self-analysis by the late John Cowper Powys, *In Defence of Sensuality*, London (Gollancz), 1930, from which I cannot quote here more than the following sample (p. 93): 'Loneliness is at once the soul's supreme achievement and its strongest link with all the earlier stages of its evolution. In loneliness a human being feels himself backward,

down the long series of his avatars, into the earlier planetary
life of animals, birds and reptiles and even into the cosmogonic
life of rocks and stones.' The author may be influenced in the
interpretation of his day-dreams by Jung, whom he quotes in
his *Autobiography*, London (John Lane), 1934, p. 275, speaking
of 'this pathological theorizing that Freud has started—my own
sympathies are very much in favour of Jung.' He is, however,
far more detailed and vivid in the description of what he calls so
impressively his 'ichthyosaurus ego' than the theoretical passages in Jung quoted above. As a matter of fact, there never was
a true reptile in man's direct ancestry, but that does not very
much matter. Powys could just as well have spoken of the
archaeopteryx ego, only his readers would not have understood him
so well.

90. On these originally Methodist sectarians and their ecstatic
dances (see below, pp. 117–18) cf. F. D. Arsdale's article in
Encyclop. of Rel. and Eth., I, p. 474.

91. RELIGIOUS VEGETARIANISM

The Laws of Manu (V, 48, 49, 52) declare that 'meat can
never be obtained without injury to living creatures, and injury
to living beings is detrimental to the attainment of heavenly
bliss. There is no greater sinner than that man who though not
worshipping the gods or the ancestral *manes* seeks to increase the
bulk of his flesh by the flesh of other beings.' Meat-eating is thus
considered as bad as cannibalism (Percival, *Land of the Veda*,
London, 1854, p. 272). The protest against killing is an important tenet of Buddhism and Jainism. King Aśoka proclaimed
himself a vegetarian in the first of his edicts (T. W. Rhys Davids,
art. *'ahimsa'*, *Encyclop. of Rel. and Eth.*, I, p. 231, col. b), although
Kassapa the Buddhist laid it down that 'it is not meat-eating
that defiles but evil deeds'. The sin is, according to Buddhist
doctrine, on the slayer of the animal. Vegetarianism is enjoined
by Taoism. Temporary vegetarianism is observed by all Chinese
during the pilgrimage to the Sacred Mountain. The Ch'an
School of Buddhism known as *'Chai-kung'*, 'the Fasters', is bound
to strict vegetarianism (*Encyclop. of Rel. and Eth.*, XII, p. 648 a).
Westermarck, *Development of Moral Ideas*, II, p. 338, thinks that

the earliest Egyptians were vegetarians. The theory is, however, based only on Greek traditions of the Ptolemaean epoch, asserting that the god Osiris travelled about weaning men from cannibalism by teaching them how to grow corn. Cannibalism is, on the basis of the belief in metempsychosis, found in Egypt at the time of Herodotus (II, 123; Eisler, *Orph.-Dionys. Myst.*, p. 313, note 2), but certainly not before the Persian dominion over Egypt, when Mithraic and even Indian doctrines may have been introduced into the Nile valley, interpreted as including the eating of all animals, because a human soul may be dwelling in any animal to expiate its sins. Among Moslems the agnostic Abu'l 'Alā Aḥmed ibn 'Abdallah of Ma'arrah (d. 1057 A.D.) preached extreme vegetarianism, as did the earlier Zindiqs or Moslem gnostics (Margoliouth, *Encyclop. of Rel. and Eth.*, II, p. 189, art. 'Atheism'). Among the Jews the Therapeutae of Alexandria were vegetarians (Philo, *De vita contempl.*, 9) and ate only bread with salt and hyssop (E. Lyttelton, art. 'Vegetarianism', *Encyclop. of Rel. and Eth.*, XII, pp. 618b–623a).

92. Eisler, *Orphisch-Dionys. Mysteriengedanken* (Warburg Lectures, 1923), Leipzig, 1925, pp. 30 f. and 353.

93. Eisler, *Orpheus*, London (Watkins), 1921, p. 132 f.; Kieferndorf and Duke Max of Saxony, *Vegetarische Warte*, 1921, p. 188; 1922, p. 1 ff.; *id.*, *Iesoûs Basileus*, Heidelberg Univ. Press (Winter), 1931, II, pp. 27–31; p. 514, note 3.

94. A. A. Bevan, *Encyclop. of Rel. and Eth.*, VIII, p. 399, col. a.

95. See E. Lyttelton's article 'Vegetarianism', *Encyclop. of Rel. and Eth.*, XII, pp. 618–623. Historical data can be found by means of the Index volume, s.v. 'Vegetarianism'.

96. Cf. on this author and his admirable book *Instincts of the Herd in Peace and War*, London, 1916, 13th ed. 1948 (Benn), Dr. R. W. Chapman's bio-bibliographical notes and gleanings, *Sociological Review*, XXXV, Nos. 1 and 2, April 1943, pp. 44 ff.

97. Alverdes, *Social Life in the Animal World*, London, 1927,

p. 76, saw in 1915 near Eydtkuhnen in East Prussia in the regions devastated by the advance of the Russian army, how the dogs of the burnt villages and farms had formed themselves into hunting packs and were combing the woods for game, in chain-formation like wolves. There are also insects which hunt in packs. See Julian Huxley, *War a Biological Phenomenon*, 1942; repr. in *On Living in a Revolution*, London, 1944, p. 9, on the so-called harvester ants fighting in swarms: 'they are the wolves of the insect-world'.

98. SOLITARY ANIMALS CONVERTED TO GREGARIOUS LIFE
Such 'habits' (inherited 'conditioned reflexes') are not un-alterable, but can be re-conditioned either by changes in the surroundings or by 'spontaneous mutation'. H. G. Wells reports in his *Outline of History*, London (Cassell), 1937, p. 281— evidently on good authority—that 'nowadays the lions in East Africa are apparently becoming social animals . . . by the young keeping with the mother after they are fully grown and hunting in a group. Hitherto the lion has been much more of a solitary beast'. The reader will notice that it is the mother-animal who tolerates the formation of the hunting pack. There is no sugges-tion that the old male abandons his solitary hunt. It would seem that the fox, generally found as a lonely hunter, does occasion-ally chase in pack-formation. The following item was printed in the *Sunday Express* of 16 Dec. 1945: ' *"King" fox ambushed*. A magnificent "king" fox, leader of a "flying column" of marau-ders, was trapped and shot with eleven of his followers when a County Leitrim, Eire, farmer tied two cubs near poultry houses on Friday night. When the raiding foxes came, the cubs gave the alarm'.—An ἀρχιβασσάρα, 'chief vixen' or 'leading vixen', is mentioned in connexion with the βασσαραι or were-vixens of the god Dionysos in a Greek inscription (*Corp. Inscr. Graec.*, I, 2152; cf. Jensen's article 'Bassarides' in Pauly-Wissowa, *Realenzyklop.*, III, col. 104).

The leader of the canine pack need not be a male. To this day the inhabitants of the Swedish and Estonian coasts believe in the existence of female werewolves (*wargkelng*, Hoops, *Reallexik. d. Germ. Altert.*, art. 'Werwolf'.) The existence of hunting goddesses like the Greek and Asianic Artemis Lykeia or Arktemis (Hartung, *Religion d. Griechen*, III, p. 181), the Latin Diana with her following of female huntresses—sterile females described by our late poetic sources as maidens because they are not married in the sense of the later patriarchal society, although they have occasional lovers—shows that the pack may be led by a female 'dominating the beasts' (πότνια θῆρων). The pack may equally be led by a female beyond the age of child-bearing, a 'Great Mother' or 'grandmother of the cave' or layer (the Phrygian *matar Kubile*) of the tribe hunting through the densely wooded mountains with torches, clubs, spears and later bows and arrows.

99. The term 'human herds' (*greges humanae*) is used by Varro, *Ling. Lat.*, VI, 34, in his description of the *Lupercalia* (below, p. 254 ff.): 'lupercis nudis lustratur antiquom oppidum Palatinum gregibus humanis cinctum'. See on the Orphic origins of this Platonic idea (*Phaedo*, 62 E) Eisler, *Orph.-Dionys. Myst.*, p. 58, note 2.

100. βοὴν ἀγαθός, *Iliad*, II, 408, and elsewhere.

101. *Alouatta* monkeys were observed breaking sticks from the tree and throwing them at Captain Dampierre (Carpenter, *op. cit.* note 70 above, p. 12). See E. A. Hooton, *Why Men Behave Like Apes*, Princeton University Press, 1940, p. 30, on the South American howler-monkey of the genus *Alouatta*: 'The howler clans have their restricted territories... they move around in ordered processions led by one or more males. A conflict arises when another clan attempts to trespass. But the conflict is largely vocal.'

102. Lucretius, *Rer. Nat.*, V, 1282 s.

103. *Wallenstein's Tod*, III, iv, 9:

'*Der Mensch ist ein nachahmendes Geschöpf.*'

104. EDUCATION BY IMITATION
Thomas Jefferson (1743–1826), *Writings*, II, p. 225: 'Man is an imitative animal. This quality is the germ of all education in

him. From his cradle to his grave he is learning to do what he sees others do.' Man cannot swim 'by nature' any more than he can fly. But he acquired the first faculty by imitating frogs (not dogs or wolves crawling through water in a manner adopted by man only quite recently) and the second by trying to learn from birds and dragon-flies. 'Extraspecific imitation' was first noticed by Democritus (*fragm.* 154, Diels, *Fragm. d. Vorsokratiker*, 2nd ed., I, p. 412): 'We have become disciples of the animals in the most important things: of the spider in weaving and darning, of the swallow in house-building, and of songsters such as swan and nightingale in singing, through imitation (κατὰ μίμησιν).' This behaviour pattern is, of course, inherited from the proverbial imitative behaviour of the apes. See Wolfgang Köhler, trans. Ella Winter, *The Mentality of Apes*, London (Kegan Paul), 1927, repr. 1931, ch. VII, pp. 185 ff.: 'Chance and Imitation'; pp. 221–224 on apes imitating man. The sociological importance of imitation has been studied by Gabriel Tarde, *Les Lois de l'imitation*, Paris, 1890 (Engl. trans. entitled 'Social Laws'). See also Bosanquet, *Philosophical Theory of the State*, ch. II, 3. Further literature in J. M. Baldwin and G. F. Stout's articles 'Mimetism', 'Imitation', 'Crowd' and 'Contagion, social' and 'mental' in Baldwin's *Dict. of Philosophy and Psychology*, I, New York, 1901. See now N. E. Miller and John Dollard, *Social Learning and Imitation*, London (Kegan Paul), 1945. See also below, note 114 c. *finem* on birds of various species learning by imitation to open milk bottles on doorsteps.

105. THE ʿISÂWÎYYA

René Brunel, *Essai sur la confrérie religieuse des ʿAissâoûa au Maroc*, Paris (Geuthner), 1926; R. Eisler, *Archiv f. Relig. Wiss.*, 1929, vol. 27, pp. 173–183; W. Wittekind, *ibid.*, vol. 28, p. 386, note 3, where the analogous Bacchic and early Hebrew rites of tearing living animals to pieces are discussed.

The confraternity of the ʿIsâwîyya (French transcription ʿAissâoûa (*Encycl. of Islam*, II, 26, 1921, col. 527) was founded by the faqîr and mystic Shêikh Abû ʿAbd ʾAllah Sîdî Muhammed ben ʿIsa as-Sofiani al Mukhtârî, born in 1465/6 A.D. (A.H. 872), d. 1526/7, also known as the *Shêikh al Kâmil* ('The Perfect', Brunel, *op. cit.*, p. 15, note 2). ʿIsa is generally taken as an

ordinary personal name—the Arabic equivalent of Biblical
'*Esau*— and *ben 'Isa* as an ordinary Arab patronymic. It would,
however, be a strange coincidence if this were the true explanation. The still existing relics of this saint, called 'the son of the
Hairy One', consist of two panther-skins on which he slept and
prayed, one in Meknâs, one in the Ouzrâ near Palikao (Brunel,
p. 20, note 1). He had—although he is not described as a
'cunning hunter' like the Biblical 'Esau—the gift of catching
('*captiver*') the wild animals and of rendering poisonous snakes
harmless (Brunel, p. 213). In the *qaṣida* At-Tâîya which he composed, he defines his own power in these words: 'Men as well as
the jinns are all devoted to me, also the venomous reptiles and
the beasts of the desert.' It is a well-known fact that the Quran
and therefore all the Moslems call Jesus Christ '*Isa bin Maryam*,
that is to say they believe that His name was '*Isa* (A. Mingana,
art. 'Quran', *Encyclop. of Rel. and Eth.*, X, p. 540, col. b), that
is 'Esau and not *Jeshu'*, short for *Jehoshua'*. (Curiously enough
the present Earl [then Mr. Oliver] Baldwin, who wrote a *vie
romancée* of *Aïssa*, meaning Jesus, in 1935, apparently believed
this to be true). The Moslems expect 'Isa to return as the
Mahdi to judge the world (D. S. Margoliouth, art. 'Mahdi',
Encyclop. of Rel. and Eth., VIII, p. 337, col. a). Now, we have a
picture painted during the lifetime of Muhammed ben 'Isa by
Moretto da Brescia (Alessandro Bonvincino, 1498–1544) of
Jesus sitting among the animals of the desert, among them
snakes and the venomous basilisk (Eisler, 'Jesus among the
Animals by Moretto da Brescia', *Art in America*, vol. 23, no. 4,
Oct. 1935, pp. 137–140, fig. 1), just as Orpheus among the
animals is pictured in the early Christian catacombs (Eisler,
ibid., fig. 3; *Orph.-Dionys. Myst.*, p. 56, fig. 24) as illustrating
the Gospel of Mark (i. 3): 'Jesus was in the wilderness forty days
and forty nights, and was with the wild beasts, and the angels
ministered unto him'. The passage is an exact parallel to ben
'Isa's claim that 'the jinns . . . and the animals of the desert are
devoted to me'.

The idea is archetypal. Even as, according to Gen. i. 28, the
first Adam (I Cor. xv. 45) before the Fall in Paradise ruled over
all the animals 'over the fowl in the air and over every living
thing that moveth upon the earth', even so the Christ as 'the

second' or 'future Adam' (I Cor. xv. 45; v. 14)—having been
purified by the baptism of St. John and having victoriously
resisted the temptations of Satan—rules again over all the
creatures. Thus in the 18th and 19th chapter of Pseudo-
Matthew's Gospel of the Infancy (M. R. James, *Apocr. New
Test.*, Oxford, 1924, p. 73), dragons, lions, leopards and wolves
come meekly to adore the infant Jesus, and in ch. 35 Jesus plays
in the lion's cave with the lion's whelps, as it is foretold by the
prophet Isaiah (xi. 6–9) that 'the sucking child shall play on
the hole of the asp and the weaned child shall put his hand in
the cockatrice' den, the wolf also shall dwell with the lamb',
and so forth. There is a famous book by the Swiss poet Victor
Widman, *Der Heilige unter den Tieren* (*The Saint among the Animals*),
one of a long series of stories about various saints—Christian
hermits as well as Moslem *walis* and Brahman or Buddhist
ascetics—living in the solitude of the forest, desert or jungle,
amidst and in friendly intimacy with the wild beasts. There may
be a certain amount of truth in them, for General Howard Bury
seems to have found in the Rongchar valley of the high Hima-
laya hermits living in rock-caves surrounded by all kinds of wild
animals who were fed regularly by those ascetics (Eisler, *Orph.-
Dionys. Myst.*, p. 350, note 2). On the whole they are certainly
meant to illustrate the eschatological doctrine that the pure
and sinless in the Kingdom of God will again rule over the
animal world in peace and freedom, as man did in Paradise
before the Fall.

There was a *walî* said to have lived for twenty years among
the gazelles (Curtiss, *Ursemitische Religion im Volksleben des heutigen
Orients*, p. 64) which receives colour from the story and photographs of the captured boy who had lived among the gazelles
in our own days (below, p. 139, note 111). Muhammed ben 'Isa
is said to have tamed the wild beasts, especially the lions, with
astonishing ease. Al Ghâzâli reports that a fellâh of the region
of Miknâs complained to the shêikh that a lion had carried away
his cow. 'Ibn 'Isa, by an extraordinary miracle, restored the cow
to him and tamed the lion (Brunel, *op. cit.*, p. 21). When Al
Basrî asked him, at the request of the people of Miknâs, to
restrain the eccentricities of his followers, he replied: 'Calm their
worries, my followers are hyenas (*D'boûa*) at Miknâs and lions

(*Sboû'a*) in the field' (cf. next note). The curious analogy between 'Ibn 'Isa and the tamer of all beasts, Orpheus, is further
emphasized by the two lines in the above-quoted *Mendoûma
Attâïa* of 'Ibn 'Isa (Brunel, p. 88), where the author says 'I have
abandoned my friends, my family, my neighbours; I have made
my children orphans and have separated myself from those near
to me'. This sounds almost like an explanation of the name
Orpheus, from Greek *ὀρφενω*, Latin *orbare*, 'make orphans'
(Greek ὀρφανους); Armenian *orb*, see Eisler, *Orph.-Dionys. Myst.*,
p. 349.

In a *qaṣida* by Hajj Dris al Honch ('the Serpent'), sung in the
course of the nocturnal assemblies of the 'Isâwîyya, the shêikh
'Ibn 'Isa is implored to open the locks of the soul with the keys
(*mafâtih*) of assistance and of mystery' (Brunel, p. 104). The
mention of the 'keys' (*mafâtih*, also = 'arcana') is most interesting,
because we have fragments of an Orphic poem (O. Kern,
Orphic. Fragm., Berlin (Weidmann), 1922, p. 155, No. 82) which
mentions the 'key of the mind' (κλεῖδα νοῦ).

The bull or calf sacrificed in honour of 'Ibn 'Isa on the third
day of the celebration (Brunel, *op. cit.*, p. 120) is 'dressed up
specially for the ceremony with women's girdles around its
flanks and silk kerchiefs around its horns'. While it is led in procession (Brunel, p. 110) the animal is *recouvert de toiles aux couleurs
rutilantes, portant au cou un collier de cauris et aux cornes un cache de
soie jaune*. This is obviously intended to dress up the sacrificial
animal as a substitute for a human victim and corresponds
exactly to the Greek sacrifice to Dionysos 'Ανθρωπωραίστης,
'Smiter of men', described by Aelian, *De Nat. Anim.* XII, 34,
Engl. trans. by Prof. A. B. Cook, *Zeus*, Cambridge Univ. Press,
1914, I, p. 659: 'The Tenedians keep a pregnant cow for
Dionysos 'Ανθρωπωραίστης and, when it has brought forth, they
tend it like a woman in child-bed. But the new-born calf they
sacrifice after binding buskins upon its feet.'

The parallel is all the more important because the descendants of 'Ibn 'Isa divide and eat this animal, in spite of the
Quranic prohibition of eating the flesh of any beast immolated
in honour of any other than Allah.

Considering the low esteem in which the dog is held in
Islamic countries it is remarkable that the *murid* or initiate into

the 'Isâwîyya confraternity is told (Brunel, p. 63) to acquire the ten virtues of the dog, enumerated one after the other. The reader will be reminded of the well-known punning description of the Dominican Order as *Domini canes*, 'watchdogs of the Lord', illustrated in Orcagna's famous fresco celebrating the Canonization of St. Dominic. But the real source of this feature seems to be the role played by the shepherd's dog, among the animals surrounding the lyre-playing Orpheus—*e.g.* on the fresco in the catacomb of St. Priscilla (De Rossi, *Bull. archeol. crist.*, 4, 5 (1887), pp. 29 ff.; Wilpert, *Röm. Quartalschrift*, II, 1888, p. 91). In all probability this is an allusion to the Cynic school of philosophers and the itinerant Cyno-Stoic preachers who had constituted themselves a pack of watch-dogs over public morals throughout the Roman Empire (Eisler, *Orph.- Dionys. Myst.*, pp. 59 ff.) and survive in this strange figure of the Moroccan *murid*, trying to imitate the ten virtues of the perfect 'dog'. All these facts may be interpreted as mere coincidences, but considering that Orpheus is described as wearing fox-pelts (βασσαριδες) and that the word βασσάρα, 'fox', is a Libyan, *i.e.*, Berber word (Herodot. IV, 192) or a Cyrenaean one (Hesych., s.v. βασσαρή; cf. the word *bashar* 'fox', in Reinisch's *Lexikon der Afar- und Sahosprachen*; Comte de Charencey, *Muséon*, Nouv. Série, V, 1904, pp. 279 f.; Eisler, *op. cit.*, p. 110, note 2) and considering the close analogy of the Dionysian and the 'Isâwîyya rites, I should think a revival of Bacchic rites at the time of the Renaissance in the regions where they may have subsisted underground for secular, perhaps millennial, periods a much more plausible hypothesis.

Brunel (p. 150) describes the procedure of an 'Isâwîyya snake-charmer magically immunizing a client against snake-poison, in the course of which 'il lui glisse une . . . vipère dans la chemise à même la peau'. This very same ritual is known to have been practised in the cult of the Thracian Dionysos Sabazios, where a golden snake was passed through the clothes of the initiate (Arnobius, V, 21): 'aureus coluber in sinum dimittitur consecratis et eximitur rursus ab inferioribus partibus atque imis' ['a golden snake is placed in the bosom of the consecrated persons and is released from the parts below']; Firmicus Maternus, *De Errore Prof. Relig.*, 10; Clement of Alex., *Protrept.*,

II, 76, p. 11b, ed. 1688; Dieterich, *Hymn. Orph.*, 28; *Abraxas*, p. 149.)

There is a particular story (Brunel, *op. cit.*, p. 42) of how 'Ibn 'Isa, accompanied by wild animals and serpents of all kinds, went to see Moûlaï 'Abd Allah al Ghazaîmani who had to feed them in his garden. This induced (Brunel, p. 44) de Neveu (*Les Khouans, Ordre religieux chez les Musulmans de l'Algérie*, Paris, 1866, p. 85) to suggest that 'Ibn 'Isa was less of a mystic than a juggler and showman, and tamer of wild beasts. But we have, on a Babylonian boundary-stone from Susa of the early Kassite dynasty, now in the Louvre (Eisler, *Orpheus*, London, 1921, pl. III, after Father Scheil in De Morgan, *Mém. de la Délég. en Perse*, VII, p. 149, pl. XX) a bas-relief showing a female figure clashing cymbals with seven males playing a sort of banjo and leading tamed wild animals; presumably a procession of priests led by a priestess of the Great Goddess ruling the animals (πότνια θηρῶν, cf. Lucian, *Dea Syria*, 24, about the garden full of tame animals of the Syrian goddess of Bambyce). According to Aelian, *Nat. Anim.*, XII, 23, tame animals were kept in the temple of Anaîtis (the goddess clad in otter-skin, below, p. 158, note 116) in Elam whence our monument comes. Tame lions were led about by the priests of Cybele (Varro, *frgm.* 364 B.; O. Jahn, *Abh. Bayr. Akad. d. Wiss.*, VIII, 1858, pp. 261 ff.). According to Justin, VII, 14, Orpheus was the initiator of the Phrygian mysteries, that is to say the arch-priest of Cybele, the Cave-mother (Phrygian *Matar Kubile*). Strabo, VI, p. 330, makes him one of the begging servants (ἀγύρται) of the Great Mother.

In the *hizb* of Shêikh Sidi Abu Zakarîa Sidi Yahîa an Nâou-aoûi, recited by the devotees of 'Ibn 'Isa (Brunel, p. 86), God is asked to place the worshipper 'into thy clan, against any demon, potentate, unjust man, oppressor, jealous one, scorpion, serpent and lion. Thou art the master of every wild beast and disposest of its destinies.' But for the substitution of Allah for Artemis or Cybele πότνια θηρῶν and the consequent substitution of 'Master' for 'Mistress', the prayer could still be addressed to the old hunting divinity. Without any alteration it could be offered up to Orpheus or Dionysos Zagreus. This is the tradition to which 'Ibn 'Isa with his followers—not unlike Gypsy *ursari*, a bear-

and monkey-leaders' band of soothsayers and dancers—hark back. What he taught his disciples is no more than what Jesus —'Isa ibn Maryam—is said, in Mark xvi. 18, to have predicted of his disciples: 'They shall take up serpents, and if they drink any deadly thing it shall not hurt them; they shall lay hands on the sick and they shall recover.'

The most interesting of the miracles he wrought is his setting in motion by the strength of his faith *Jibl al 'Alm*, the 'Mountain of the World' (Brunel, p. 39 and p. 45). Who can read this story without being reminded of Matt. xvii. 20, 'If ye have faith like a grain of mustard seed, ye shall say unto this mountain, Remove hence to yonder place, and it shall remove; and nothing shall be impossible unto you'? Or who can read the 'Isâwîyya canticle chanted by the *moqaddem* of Miknâs (Brunel, p. 97) which says 'our shîk is like unto a vine that throws up shoots and produces fruit' without remembering the speech of Jesus in John xv.: 'I am the true vine . . . as the branch cannot bear fruit except it abide in the vine, no more can ye, except ye abide in me.' And who can fail to note the significance of this parallel who is aware of the fact that the drinking of wine is prohibited to the Moslem?

In erotic matters 'Ibn 'Isa was no ascetic, any more than was the prophet of Islam. He had a wife of resplendent beauty (Brunel, p. 38) and the whole order of the 'Isâwîyya is famous for the amatory propensities and prowess of its members. 'Sisters' (*Khuattat*) as well as 'brothers' (*Khuan*) are admitted to initiation. In the 'testament' or 'ordinance' (*ouásia*) of 'Ibn 'Isa (Brunel, p. 59) he says characteristically: 'Ne cherchez pas dans votre dévotion à faire opposition à vos âmes ni à épurer vos cœurs' . . . He quotes 'la parole suivante de Dieu: Je n'ai créé les . . . hommes que pour qu'ils m'adorent. Quiconque s'évertue à combattre son âme et à épurer son cœur, n'est pas un vrai dévôt.' This is astonishingly close to the teaching of Heraclitus (fr. 85, Diels), θυμοί μάχεσται χαλεπῶν ὅτι γὰρ ἂν θέλη φυχῆς ὠνείται; 'To fight with one's heart is burdensome, for whatever it wills, is bought at the price of one's soul' ('heart' and 'soul' are in this context the equivalent of Freud's *ego* and *super-ego*). Brunel (*op. cit.*, p. 97) says of the 'inebriating dance' (*dance grisante*) of the 'Isâwîyya: 'la danse est souvent gracieuse avec une pointe de lascivité'. This characteristic applies exactly to the sacred dances of the Dionysian orgies. The chewing of cactus leaves (Brunel, p. 98) compares with the mastication of ivy leaves by the Bacchae. The self-tormenting actions of the 'Isâwîyya masochists (Brunel, p. 98: 'ils se percent les bras, les mains, les joues de darts éfilés, s'entaillent la gorge ou le ventre avec des sabres aiguisés') have their exact parallel in the gashings and slashings which the initiates of Cybele inflicted upon themselves, so vividly described by Catullus (lxiii; see Franz Cumont, *Les Religions orientales dans le paganisme romain*, 4e éd., Paris (Geuthner), 1929, p. 47). Also in this *Oûasia* (Brunel, p. 61) 'Ibn 'Isa says: 'Ceux qui connaissent Dieu ... demandent et trouvent, voient et restent stupéfaits, étourdis.' This is as near as possible to the saying of Jesus quoted from the Gospel of the Hebrews by Clement of Alexandria (*Strom.*, V, 14, 96; M. R. James, *Apocr. New Test.*, Oxford, 1924, p. 2): 'Let him who seeks cease not till he find; when he has found he will be amazed, astonished ($\theta\alpha\mu\beta\eta\theta\dot\eta\sigma\epsilon\tau\alpha\iota$).' The *'Hizb of Virtue and Righteousness* (Brunel, p. 81), attributed to 'Ibn 'Isa, begins: 'Surely God has given proof of his satisfaction to the believers because they worshipped Thee under the tree.' We cannot read these words without being reminded of the words of Jesus to Nathaniel in John i. 48: 'When thou wast under the fig-tree, I saw thee.'

It is by no means fantastic to assume Christian survivals in the teaching of 'Ibn 'Isa, since the guiding principles of his mystic doctrine, *nîya*, 'intention', and *mohabba*, 'love' (Brunel, p. 65: *le désir du croyant doit être de posséder la divinité*), were adversely criticized by 'Abd al Ouâhid ibn Zeid (*Passion d'al Hallaj*, pp. 515–749; *Essai sur les origines du lexique technique de la mystique musulmane*, p. 176) as a survival of Jewish-Christian-Hindu mysticism (the *Nîya* = 'intention' is, indeed, nothing but the *kawana* of Jewish mysticism). A Jewish sect of 'Isawites actually existed in Persia (I. Abrahams, *Encyclop. of Rel. and Eth.*, XI, p. 332, col. b). But not enough is known of it to say whether any connexion can be established with the 'Isâwîyya of Morocco.

Perhaps the most impressive among the parallels between the Dionysian mysteries and the 'Isâwîyya ceremonies has not yet been noticed. Euripides, *Bacchae*, 700, 704–711, 758–764, tells us that one of the Maenads struck a rock with her thyrsos-staff —not unlike Moses in the desert (Num. xx. 11)—and a spring of water welled up from it; another brought up in the middle of the way a well of wine; those, however, who desired 'the white drink' 'brought forth with their fingers streamlets of milk and from the ivy leaves on their staves ran drops of honey'. In the same play (142), at the appearance of Dionysos 'the field flows with milk, wine and the nectar of the bees'. Plato, *Ion*, 534a, mentions the Bacchae drawing milk and honey out of the rivers (Eisler, *Orph.-Dionys. Myst.*, p. 330, note 2; p. 366, note 6).

Cf. with this the statement of Brunel, *op. cit.*, p. 119, about the arrival of the 'Isâwîyya procession at the tomb of 'Ibn 'Isa: 'Tantôt auprès du tombeau du Chîk, tantôt au pied d'un olivier poussant sur la terrasse de l'eau jaillit, sans qu'on s'explique la cause du phénomène. Aussitôt les pélerins se jettent à terre et boivent avidement de cette eau. Une bataille acharnée s'engage même entre eux pour atteindre le liquide' (p. 120). 'Ces jaillissements se produisent, également au pied d'un arbre gigantesque du cimetière, appellée "Tarzaza" (*micoculier, Celtis australis*) *et autour duquel campent durant le moussem les 'Aîssâoûa venant des D'khîssa* ... On y a vu également jaillir du lait et même du miel. Ces jaillissements auraient lieu tous les cinq ou six ans.' No wine is, of course, seen to spring from the earth in this fanatically Moslem country. It is easy to imagine how the miracle can be contrived by the descendants of the shêikh who control the cemetery. That it occurs is beyond doubt. It proves, incidentally, that Euripides is describing a real, not an imaginary feature of the Bacchanalia.

According to Euripides (*Bacchae*, 699 ff.; cp. Nonnos, *Dionys.*, I, 4, 361; 24, 130; 45, 304) the Maenads took to their breasts and gave suck to the whelps of wolves. See Müller-Wieseler, *Denkm.*, II, 579; Stephani, *Comptes Rendus*, 1864, p. 195; *Monum. d. Ist.*, II, 27; Roscher, *Myth. Lex.*, II, 2, col. 2262, fig. 3, showing a Maenad about to take a panther to her breast. Exactly the same story is told by the 'Isâwîyya (Brunel, pp. 216 f.): A *sba'* ('lion') and a *lbîya* ('lioness') wandered through a forest frequented by lions. They were trembling for fear of being attacked by the beasts. Suddenly they saw walking along the path they were themselves taking a lioness followed by her whelps. Bravely the *lbîya* advanced towards her and took one of the whelps to her breast. The little beast—a female—began to suck at once. 'H'a al-Bzzoûla diâl 'Ahd Allah oûa 'l Chîkh Al Kâmil.' She said to the little creature 's'ttermima nkhâf Sioûa Oûlâdî maîhafoû loladk.' 'This is the bosom of the covenant between God and the shîkh al Kamil; do not denounce me. I have no fear of thee, my children will not fear thine.' Considering that among the Bambara (Brunel, p. 238) the animal masks used during ceremonies analogous to the rites of the 'Isâwîyya include not only 'lions' (*djara*), 'hyaenas' (*souroukou*) and 'predatory animals' (*wara*), but also 'apes' (*soula*), the archetypal character of these stories is all the more evident, since to this day Korean peasant women have been observed suckling piglets and little calves after weaning their own babies. There are Babylonian representations of a female goddess (*Labartu*) with an animal head or mask, suckling various animals (Frank, *Babyl. Beschwörungsreliefs*, pl. 1; Meissner, *Babyl. und Assyr.*, II. Taf. Abb. fig. 34). The Egyptian goddess Neith is represented with a crocodile at either breast. Beliefs concerning snakes sucking women's breasts have been collected by the Rev. Dr. MacCulloch, *Encyclop. of Rel. and Eth.*, XI, p. 410, col. b, section e. All these ideas are archetypal reminiscences and actions derived from the prehistoric period before the lycanthropic mutation transforming man into a hunter and killer.

In the J'rid (Brunel, p. 199) the children who imitate the behaviour of the panther strip to the waist and disguise their faces with a covering of flour or plaster. This is an exact counterpart to the procedure of the 'Wild Men' or 'Titans' in the Orphic mysteries (Eisler, *Orph.-Dionys. Myst.*, p. 253, note 4).

106. ANIMAL MASKS OF THE 'ISÂWÎYYA

The 'Isâwîyya wear seven different kinds of animal masks: 'camels' (*jmâl*, fem. *nuwigât*), 'jackals' (*dhîâb*), 'cats' (*qtoûth*, the Berber word from which the Latin *cattus*, our 'cat', the name of the North African fallow cat, *Felis maniculata* Rüppel, is derived —the wild European cat is quite untameable); 'boars' (*hllâlf*), 'dogs' (*klâb*), 'panthers' (*nmoûra*), and 'lions' (*sboûa'*). Immediately he is introduced into the congregation, each neophyte receives an animal name and must imitate at the weekly gathering of the 'sept' (*thâifa*) or pack the behaviour of the respective animal. They do it with great skill and astonishing 'empathy'. The *shêikh* of each *thâifa* indicates to the parents of the child to be accepted the animal name 'best adapted to his natural dispositions'. This animal name is kept a secret from the outer world. Each animal pack or herd, corresponding to the *thiasos* of the Bacchic mysteries, has its own *shêikh* or elder, the neophytes being considered as his children, he as their 'father'. There is no change or promotion from one group to another, as there was, in consequence of a theory of metempsychosis, in the Mithraic mysteries (Eisler, *op. cit.*, pp. 316 ff.). On the return journey from the annual great pilgrimage (*moussem*), all these men masquerading as animals dye their hands and feet red with henna, to make them look blood-stained. A special dress is prescribed for each group, but only the 'jackals' (*dhîâb*) wear a headdress adorned with bull's horns, sheep- and jackal-tails, jackals' and foxes' claws. The 'panthers' of the region of Qairouan still wear bits of panther-skins, remains of a once ampler costume. The 'cats' are said formerly to have worn cats' pelts—adorned with hares' paws over their shoulders, and a reed-woven cap decorated with cats' paws, just as the 'Fanggen' of the Tyrol were dressed in wild cats' furs (Eisler, *op. cit.*, p. 283, note 6). In Tunis the lions' pelts, formerly worn by the *sboûa*', have been replaced by woven mats. Brunel (*op. cit.*, p. 175) explains that this is due to the extermination of lions, panthers, etc., in North Africa, which has made their furs excessively rare. The 'jackals', 'cats', 'dogs', 'panthers' and 'lions' are called *frrassâ*, because—in contradistinction to the 'boars' and 'camels'—they practise the *frissa*, the equivalent of what the Greeks called *sparagmos* and *ômophagia*, the 'tearing to pieces' of the living small cattle, thrown before them, in the towns during the five days before the *moussem*, among the tribes outside during a whole month. In Miknâs, for instance, each pack (*thâifa*) devours on an average 30–40 head of cattle as *frissa*. Each of the city's families dedicates one such animal victim. The *Mahzen*, Mulai Hassan, would occasionally give them a black ox. In the country the victims are begged for in procession, unwilling givers are cursed, and generally find that alleged real jackals or other beasts of prey make away by night with part of their herd, while the willing givers often receive nocturnal compensation in kind for their sacrifices. It would thus seem that the miserly pay in the end both for themselves and the generous givers.

The processions are headed by 'lionesses' carrying the quartered carcasses of the torn animals, just like the *Maenades* or 'raving women' of the Dionysian mystery-rites. Because the Quran forbids the eating of animals in the state known as *ḥram*, *i.e.* not ritually slaughtered, the group-leader (*moqaddem*) must give the animal a cut through the throat. He stands on a roof, to be protected from the raving *frrassâ*, excited by their dances and the magic ceaseless invocation of the names of Allah (*dhikr*), who might otherwise snatch the animal from him before he has cut its throat. The animals thus torn to pieces are oxen (rarely), goats, she-goats, rams, sheep, but never fowls. The horrible description of the procedure by an eye-witness is best reproduced in the original French of the observer: 'après avoir égorgé le mouton orienté vers la "qibla", il le prend dans ses bras, et, tandis qu'il se débat dans une agonie violente, le jette dans la cour, de façon que le sang s'écoule d'un seul jet sur les 'Aissâoûa en extase. C'est alors la ruée, on ne voit plus rien qu'une masse mouvante où émergent des têtes et des pieds. Des cris rauques se font entendre et puis, brusquement, un des pratiquants se retire et montre triomphalement sa main ruisselante de sang. La bête a été éventrée. Une odeur fade et nauséabonde se dégage, les intestins sont déchirés et trainés sur le sol. Spectacle écœurant! on croirait voir de véritables fauves se jetant sur leur proie' (p. 179). 'Très souvent, au cours de ces séances, les "sboûa'" et les "lbiât" se disputent leur victime. Le mouton étripé est enlevé par les "lionnes", qui se jettent à terre et les coudes et les genoux repliés, la tête enfouie dans le ventre de la "frissa", elles poussent des bêlements caractéristiques et se mettent en demeure de la disputer à la voracité des "lions". Ceux-ci, divisés en deux camps, font mine de se livrer un combat sans merci; ils sautent, en exécutant des bonds fantastiques, toujours en imitant de leurs mains les mouvements des fauves. Le combat peut parfois durer plus d'une demi-heure; l'assistance, très amusée par çe spectacle, suit attentivement les péri-

péties du combat. Drôle de représentation animalesque! Il est
rare que les "lionnes" aient le dessous; défendant leur proie
jusqu'au bout, la lutte se termine toujours à leur avantage.
Elles gardent alors les restes du mouton qu'elles partagent entre
elles. Les "dhîâb" sont de la fête et interviennent lorsque la
lutte est terminée, dans l'espoir de s'emparer de la "frissa". La
bête, souventes fois, surtout à Miknâs, reste intacte; seuls les
intestins ont été enlevés. Dans ce cas, la chair en est distribuée
à tous ceux qui la demandent; les malades, ceux que la mal-
chance poursuit, ceux qui veulent s'enrichir dans les affaires, les
femmes qui désirent retenir leurs époux au foyer ou avoir des
enfants, tous réclament de cette chair, qui passe pour être
chargée de "barâkâ" (*blessing*). Des "fâtihât" sont prononcées
et les lionnes, après avoir reçu les offrandes d'usage, remettent
à leurs clients ou clientes la part de viande qui leur est destinée.
Si la peau est intacte, elle est tannée et conservée en guise de
"haïdoûra". Souvent elle est donnée en cadeau aux *moqaddemin*
qui l'utilisent comme tapis de prière. Les "lbîât" répugnent à
vendre la peau de la victime rituelle, elles ne peuvent que
l'offrir en 'çadâqa (*alms*) à ceux qui la veulent. Si les ongles et
les dents des "frrâsa" l'ont mise en pièces, elle est déchirée en
une multitude de petits morceaux que se disputent les femmes
du quartier. La laine en est enlevée et très souvent renfermée
dans des coussins. A la campagne, les "fqîrât" utilisent la peau
pour confectionner des "mzoûâd" qui leur servent d'oreillers.
La dépouille est regardée comme sacrée au même titre que la
chair. On retrouve là le respect superstitieux des musulmans
et des anciens Égyptiens pour la dépouille sanctifiée par le
sacrifice.
'Parfois les "frâssas" sont entièrement dévorées par les
"sboûa". Les *lbiât* alors par orgueil se parent de leurs peaux
qu'elles portent en bandoulière ou qu'elles jettent négligemment
sur les épaules'—exactly like the Maenades wearing the *nebrides*
of the torn fawns (pp. 182 f.). 'Chez les Shâïm et les Mokhtâr on
le mange (l'animal) encore vivant, malgré l'interdiction coran-
ique'. . . . 'Le verbe "farasa", duquel dérive le vocable "frissa",
éveille l'idée de déchirer avec les mains, de dévorer, en parlant
de bête féroce. Les 'Aïssâoûa font usage, au surplus, de deux
autres verbes "chrragua" et "frra'", qui complètent heureuse-

ment le sens de celui de "farasa". Le premier exprime l'idée de déchirer, de lacérer, le second d'éventrer, d'ouvrir. Ainsi la nature du rite des '*Aissâoûa* est suffisamment précisée par le nom qu'il porte. Il consiste à dépécer, à déchirer une bête de l'espèce ovine, à la façon des fauves, lions, panthères, chacals, etc. Dans la pratique, les séides d'Ibn 'Aîsa se bornent à ouvrir le ventre de la "frissa" et à lui vider l'abdomen par l'application des doigts sur la peau. Parfois les sboûa' restent impuissants à déchirer la "frissa"; alors le *moqaddem* intervient et le frappe de sa propre main. Quand la "frissa" est ainsi déchiré, les "lbiât" s'en emparent et la gardent pour elles. Le plus souvent la "frissa" est partagée en deux, rarement elle est disséquée en menus morceaux. À Fèz, le rite semble s'être conservé dans la forme primitive. Dès que la bête est jetée, les "frrâsa" la déchirent, l'éventrent et chacun enlève un morceau de chair ou d'os qu'il dévore. Souvent les assistants demandent un lambeau de cette chair sacrée; les "frrâsa" accèdent sur-le-champ à leur désir.

'La faculté de dépecer, de déchirer les victimes du Mouloud provoquent les explications les plus diverses. Au dire des "frrâsa", cette faculté serait due à la Baraka du Chikh. Mais, très sceptiques, les rationalistes se refusent d'y croire et découvrent dans leur exercice des ruses grossières. Pour les uns, les *sboûa*' laissent pousser leurs ongles quelques temps avant le Moussem, afin de mieux déchirer le ventre de la bête. Pour les autres, ils adaptent à l'extrémité de leurs doigts de petites lamelles tranchantes, imperceptibles. L'opinion la plus répandue est que les "frrâsa" ne frappent jamais à n'importe quel endroit de la bête. Ils visent toujours la partie comprise entre les deux cuisses, partie où la peau est plus fine et plus tendre que partout ailleurs. S'ils se bornaient alors à frapper de l'extrémité de leurs doigts, peut-être n'arriveraient-ils que difficilement à mettre la "frîssa" en pièces. Dans le but d'éviter cet écueil, ils enfoncent violemment le pouce á l'endroit déterminé, puis déchirent la peau de leurs ongles et élargissent le trou pratiqué en utilisant les autres doigts.

'Évidemment, les 'Aîssâoûa supportent mal qu'on doute de leur pouvoir surnaturel. Ils se défendent avec énergie et pretendent même que ce pouvoir s'exerce à distance. En effet, la puissance s'irradiant de leurs doigts serait telle qu'il suffit de faire le simulacre d'éventrer l'animal pour le disséquer instantanément sans le toucher. Ainsi on affirme qu'Aboû Ar-râoûaîn avait coûtume de fendre d'un geste les pierres qu'il trouvait sur son chemin; on raconte également qu'une fois un membre de la Thaïfa des Ibâbra sectionna un mouton en deux, simplement en faisant le geste de le couper, à l'aide de l'index et du majeur. Nul n'ignore non plus à Miknâs la légende du Shâ'mi qui, au Dâr Makhzen, en présence de Moûlâî Hasan, frappa le ventre d'un bœuf du pouce de son pied droit et lui en sortit les viscères.'

Of the 'panthers' it is said that they dilacerate children, even their own. A. van Gennep (*L'État actuelle du problème totemique*, Paris, 1921, p. 251) reports the story of one of the 'panther-men' (*nmoûra*) of Tunis, who, dared by the Bey to do so, literally rent asunder his own child. As far as the Moroccan 'Isâwîyya are concerned, Brunel (pp. 200 f.) thinks this accusation an exaggeration, just as some Greek scholars doubt the historicity of the exactly corresponding Greek legends about the Maenads. I too used to dismiss as inventions the stories of what the Germans—some Germans, to be exact—did, even to children, in Belgium and other occupied countries. I know better now. *Homo homini lupus.*

It is, therefore, extremely serious to find that the sect of the 'Isâwîyya has spread all through Africa and beyond. Before the First World War two convents of the order were known to exist at Mecca, two at Medina. There are 'Isâwîyya in Syria, Egypt, Tripolitania, Algiers, and of course in their original home, Morocco, in Qairouan, Miknas, Fez, Tangier and in the Châouîya, in the French Sudan (Brunel, pp. 46–51). Capt. P. J. André found them along the roads of Zinder and in the Upper Volta (*L'Islam Noir*, Paris, 1924, p. 48). I have collected below (p. 152 f., note 116) a number of recent newspaper cuttings about the murderous activities of the secret society of the 'lion-men' or 'leopard-men' (*Anyotos*) in the French, Belgian and British African colonies. The most recent among them (*The Times*, 26 Feb. 1948) concerns seventeen Kikuyu committed for trial on a charge of murdering a British police inspector, Thomas Mortimer. Witnesses said that after the police were ambushed in the native village of Gatundu, when raiding the headquarters of the religious sect called 'Men of Jesus Christ', the natives implicated scattered. For several days the police combed the forests on the slopes of Mount Kenya, where they arrested many adherents, most of them wearing skin garments which were part of the sect's regalia. The police were also helped in the search by the fact that most of the members wore curious straw hats somewhat resembling the old-fashioned boater. Many were exhausted and starving and surrendered willingly. Among the men arrested in the forest was the alleged leader, still wearing his red robes. Throughout the inquiry the magistrate's court was crowded with Africans, mainly Kikuyu.

'Men of Jesus Christ' does not, of course, mean a sect of converts baptized by Christian missionaries. It is just an ignorant translation of 'Isâwîyya, based on the belief that 'Ibn 'Isa, whose followers these men profess to be, is 'Isa ibn Maryam, the Christ mentioned in the Quran and also in the prayers of the 'Isâwîyya (Brunel, p. 87: '*Aîsa*(=Jesus Christ)) *appartient à l'essence de Dieu. Que le Salut de Dieu soit sur lui'*. This is preceded and followed by similar blessings on Mûsa, *i.e.* Moses, and al Khadir, the Arab successor of the immortal Khasisatra (*Xisouthros* in Berosus), the Babylonian hero of the Deluge story. Since the 'Isâwîyya are pledged to love God above everything else and to fight against His enemies, the secret society can easily be used as a terrible weapon against all the colonial powers if they are described as infidel enemies of Allah.

107. BACCHANTES TEARING AND EATING LIVE ANIMALS

A red-figured vase-painting now in the Vienna Museum (Delaborde, *Vases Lamberg*, Suppl. II, pl. 3; Jane E. Harrison, *Proleg. to the Study of Greek Religion*, p. 400, fig. 126; *Journ. Hell. Stud.*, XIX, p. 220, fig. 6) shows Maenads brandishing and about to rend and devour snakes and fishes. The fish may be the sacred *Bakkhos*-fish, *i.e.* the red sea-mullet (Dôrion in his '*Book on Fishes*' quoted by Athenaeus, III, p. 118; Hikesiòs, *ibid.*, VII, p. 306 E), whose name indicates a connection with the Dionysian mysteries. A Maenad holding a fish while riding a panther is shown on a red-figured vase from Cumae now at Naples (Reinach, *Répertoire de Vases peints*, I, p. 488, No. 8, after

Bollettino Napolitano, N.S., V, pl. 10). The tearing to pieces and eating raw of snakes by the Maenads is mentioned by the physician Galen (*Antid.*, I, 8, XIV, p. 45 Kuhn; Prudentius, *C. Symm.*, I, 130, ed. Migne, *P.L.*, LX, col. 129). The god Dionysos is said to have eaten snakes in his madness (Aristides, chs. 9 ff., ed. Seeberg, pp. 42 ff.).

This may be compared with the 'Isâwîyya initiation rite witnessed by the German traveller H. von Maltzan (*Drei Jahre im Nordwesten von Afrika*, 2nd ed., Leipzig, 1868, IV, pp. 276 ff., Engl. trans. *Encyclop. of Rel. and Eth.*, X, p. 721): after a description of the sacred dance (*ishdeb*), consisting of rhythmic bendings and swayings of the body, the witness continues: 'The movements become more and more rapid, the bending deeper and deeper, the turnings of the head and the body more and more violent, until at length the exhausted 'Isâwîyyah are seized with vertigo, froth gathers on their lips, their eyes stand out of their sockets and roll with the shifting gaze of the insane, and the fanatical dancers fall staggering to the ground; they have attained the state of blissful ecstasy. The state of physical prostration signifies that the spirit of the founder of the order has gained control over the disciple, so making him capable of swallowing with impunity the most virulent poisons and all things that lacerate or cut. Soon the six 'Isâwîyyah are wallowing upon the ground in wild disorder, giving vent to frightful yells of an altogether unhuman character, and resembling now the snorting of the wild boar, now the roaring of the lion. Some of them, like wild beasts, grind their teeth, from which drips a whitish foam. In their disordered and threatening movements, it would seem as if they were about to rend the onlookers in pieces. A large dish is then brought forward, and is uncovered by the *muqaddam* who presides over the ceremony. It contains serpents, scorpions, toads, lizards—a jumble of loathsome and venomous creatures. Hardly has the *muqaddam* removed the cover when the six frenzied maniacs fall upon the foul mass of living things with the voracity of famished beasts of prey, and in a moment the whole is torn in pieces and devoured. No trickery here! I see the reptiles torn in pieces by the powerful teeth, while the blood of the serpents and the slimy secretion of the scorpions tinge the saliva at the corners of the mouth.'—

The phenomenon thus induced is a regression to the omnivorous diet of primitive famished mankind so disgusting to civilized man. The aborigines of North-west Central Queensland eat 'insects and grubs, ants and caterpillars, raw or dried, frogs, lizards and snakes; fish and mussels form a large item' (W. E. Roth, *North-West-Central Queensland Aborigines*, Brisbane, 1897, pp. 92–104). This is the diet that has left the extensive 'kitchen-middens' on northern European shores. Also, readers should not forget that they themselves eat their oysters alive and raw.

108. Nauck, *Fragm. Tragic. Graec.*, 2nd ed., fr. 23–25. See Eisler, *Orph. Dionys. Myst.*, Leipzig, 1925, p. 110, note 2. The word βάσσαρα, 'vixen' (above, note 98) is actually a Berber word (Eisler, *Orpheus*, London (Watkins), 1921, p. 28, note 1, and add. p. 281).

109. See my own and Wittekind's papers quoted above, note 105. The source is the *Toldoth Yeshu* manuscript of the Vienna Jewish Theological School, published by S. Krauss, *Leben Jesu nach jüdischen Quellen*, Berlin, 1901, p. 101. The Hebrew text (*op. cit.*, p. 72, line 5 from below) is quoted Eisler, *Arch. f. Relig. Wiss.*, XXVII, 1, 2, p. 178.

110. BACCHANALIA

The tearing to pieces of young fawns (Photius, s.v. νεβρίζειν...διασπᾶν νεβρούς) or kids (Hesychius, s.v. αἰγίζειν), of bulls and calves (Euripides, *Bacchae*, 138–9, trans. Prof. Gilbert Murray; Catullus 64, 256); the devouring of their raw meat (Euripides, *ibid.*, 139, ἀγρεύων αἷμα τραγοκτόνον, ὠμοφάγον χάριν) by the ὠμοβόροι θυιάδες (Apollonius Rhod. 1, 636; Lucian, *Bacch.*, 2; Clement Alex., *Cohort.*, p. 11, Potter) is the end of the wild nocturnal chase through the wood with torches and archaic, wooden pointed spears (θυρσολογχαί, Callixen. 2, see below, note 144, the Natufian spear), camouflaged, as are the hunters themselves, with twigs and leaves of ivy and wild grapes, led by Dionysos = *Dios snusos* = 'sprout of Zeus'—who is himself known as Ὠμάδιος Ὠμηστῆς, the 'raw-eater', and Ταυροφάγος 'bull-eater' (Sophocles, *fragm.* 602). He is the Zagreus or 'Great Hunter' (*Etym. Magn.*, p. 406, 46 ff.: Ζαγρεύς

... παρα τὸ ζᾶ, ἴν᾽ εἰ ὁ πάνυ ἀγρεύων; *Etym. Gud.*, p. 227, 37; Cramer, *Anecd. Oxon.*, II, 443, 8: Ζαγρεύς ὁ μεγαλός ἀγρεύων; the derivation of the name from the Elamite Mount Zagros, that is the 'lofty' or 'high mountain', *shadu zaqru* (v. Rawl. 65 b 1; *Zeitschr. f. Ass.*, III, p. 296; Sargon, *Cyl.*, 65; etc.; Muss-Arnold, *Assyr.-Engl. Deutsch. Handwörterbuch*, I, Berlin, 1905, p. 291, col. b, s.v. '*zaqru*' is quite otiose). He is the exact counterpart of the black *Grand Veneur* of Fontainebleau whom King Henry II of France is said to have seen shortly before his death. The Maenads or 'raving women' are the 'coursing bitches' (κύνες δρομάδες) of the 'hunting lord' (ἄναξ ἀγρεύς, Euripides, *Bacch.*, vv. 731 and 1189). Firmicus Maternus, *De errore profan. relig.*, ch. 6) describes the tearing to pieces and devouring of a living bull—just as the 'Isâwîyya treated the black ox given them by the *maḥzen* of Morocco: 'they tore a live bull with their teeth, recalling the savage banquet by a yearly commemoration of it. They penetrated the solitudes of the forests, uttering discordant cries and so feigning madness that the crime might be set down to lunacy not to guile' (A. B. Cook, *Zeus*, Cambr. Univ. Press, 1914, p. 662; cf. the whole chapter on 'Zeus and Bovine Omophagy' from p. 644 'the Cretan Zeus and Zagreus' to p. 665). The Mycenaean golden cup of Vaphio (after Tsuntas, *Ephem. arch.*, 1889, p. 9; George Perrot, *Bull. Corr. Hell.*, 189, p. 492; Springer-Michaelis, *Handb. d. Kunstgeschichte*, Leipzig (Seemann), 1904, p. 100, fig. 200) shows how the wild cattle were chased and driven into strong nets, strung out between trees, and attacked by a pack of naked unarmed men—the prelude to the omophagic meal. Maenads holding a severed human leg and a severed human arm of Pentheus are shown between two satyrs on the outside of a late red-figured *kylix*, now at the Paris *Cabinet des Médailles*, Bibliothèque Nationale (De Ridder, *Catal. d. Vases de la Bibl. Nat.*, II, pp. 623 f., No. 1066; publ. by Francis Lenormant, *Gaz. Archéol.*, 1879, vol. 33–37, plates 4–5; see Sir Cecil Smith, *Journ. Hell. Stud.*, XI, 1890, p. 349; A. B. Cook, *op. cit.*, V, p. 465, note 1; J. D. Beazley, *Etruscan Vase-Painting*, pl. X, 3–5; Philippart, *Iconogr. des Bacchantes*, pl. 13b). A. B. Cook, *op. cit.*, pl. XXXV, reproduces a red-figured water-jug (*hydria*) of Kameiros (*Journ. Hell. Stud.*, 11, p. 343), showing the infant Zagreus devoured by the Titans in Bacchic attire with *thyrsos*-staves, one of them with a wreath of vine-leaves or, according to Prof. Beazley, Lycurgos (below, note 112) with the body of Dryas. The monuments show Maenads with halved or quartered carcasses of the dismembered animals in their hands. Scopas, the sculptor of Alexander the Great, (Callistratus, *Ekphras.*, *b*) showed a Bacchante swinging a goat in her hand. Wilhelm Dilthey, *Archaeol. Zeitung*, XXXI, p. 90 f., was the first to see that the Thracian 'Great Hunter' Dionysos Zagreus, leading his 'raving women' as 'coursing bitches', 'fleet bitches of Lyssa' (*Λυσσῆς κυμῆς θοαί*, Eurip., *Bacch.*, 977) brandishing torches and staves through the dark nocturnal woods, presents a close analogy to the '*Wilde Jäger*', Wodan with his dogs or wolves, of Teutonic mythology (Mannhardt, *Wald- und Feldkulte*, I: *Der Baumkult*, Index, s.v. *Jagd, wilde*; Laistner, *Rätsel der Sphinx*, pp. 282 f.; Roscher, *Kynanthropie*, p. 30), the 'Wild Chase of Holda', '*la chasse du roi Arthure*', etc. As Wodan is accompanied by his wolves the Roman war-god *Mars*—as Theodor Mommsen saw, *Mars, Mavors* is only a dialectal variant of *mors*, 'death'—was represented in his sanctuary on the Via Appia standing amidst or leading a pack of wolves (Livy, XXII, 1, 12: 'signum Martis Appia via ac simulacra luporum sudasse' ['the statue of Mars on the Appian Way and the images of wolves sweated']). The Samnite war-god Mamertos—a reduplicated form of *mṛt*, 'death'—is called in so many words 'a wolf in arms' (*ὁπλίτης λύκος*), the victorious hero *Martius lupus* (Livy, X, 27, 9; cf. 21, 46); Grimm, *Deutsche Mythologie*, 3rd ed., 1079; 1074: *Iliad*, XVI, 156 ff., 352; 11, 72; Keller, *Thiere d. class. Altertums*, I, 172, on wolves ranging the battle-fields and devouring the unburied corpses of the fallen (Catullus, 108, 6; Horace, *Epod.*, 5, 99; Lucan, 6, 552) and following armies like ravens and vultures (Lucan, 6, 227; 7, 826; Beowulf, 6044 ff.).

The essential thing to know is that the primitive hunting tribes, armed only with burning torches and wooden staves, did hunt in such lupine packs through the forests and did kill and dismember their victims by the sheer fury of mass-attack with their teeth and claws. They did follow up this frenzy of coursing, rending, raw-meat eating (Porphyry, *De abstin.*, IV, 19; Euripides, Frgm. 472 Nauck, 2nd ed.) and blood drinking

(Johanna Schmidt, art. 'Ōmophagie', Pauly-Wissowa-Kroll, *Realenzykl.*, XVIII, 1, 1939, cols. 380 f.), with an equally ecstatic mating orgy between the 'raving women' and the male σειληνοὶ or 'winers'—a Thracian word derived from Thracian *zeila*, 'wine'—who had gathered strength from harvesting the ripe sugary and therefore immediately energy-providing berries of the wild vine, growing abundantly in the forests of Macedonia and Thrace—also the *Satyroi*, that is to say, ithyphallic men (from σαθὴ =*membrum virile* and τύρος, τίτυρος =*turgescens*, see Solmsen, *Indogerman. Forschungen*, XXX, 1912, p. 1, and below, note 148, on the larger sex-organs of meat-eaters). These unbridled, promiscuous drunken ruttings are shown on certain Greek vase-paintings (*e.g.* the cup of Makrôn, Furtwängler and Reichhold; also below, note 155). This is the lupine behaviour-pattern, not that of the civilized and refined Greek artists who illustrated it when it had become an archaic and attenuated ritual, but that of habitually famished stone-age man who had as much difficulty in obtaining sexual erethism as the modern, undernourished Australian black-fellow (Spencer and Gillen, *Northern Tribes of Central Australia*, 1904, pp. 136 f., on the so-called *corroboree*-festivals of promiscuity; George A. Barton, *Encyclop. of Rel. and Eth.*, XI, col. 674; Havelock Ellis, *Sexual Impulse*, pp. 209, 211). Only when gorged with the new grapes of the wild vine could the pack set out on its wild chase over the mountains; only when replete with the blood and meat of their animal victims could they mate at the end of wildly exciting erotic dances.

That their victims were not animals only is clearly visible in the Germanic traditions about the Wild Hunt chasing and rending asunder the 'little women of the woods', that is to say, the females of the helpless wood-dwelling pygmy populations, known in these isles as 'fairies' (Margaret Murray, *op. cit.*, Append. I, p. 238). In the *Eckenliet* (str. 161–201), the giant Vasolt hunts a 'wild damsel' in the forest, the Wild Hunter of Saalfelden chases 'the little moss-people'), and then throws a quarter of a 'green-moss damsel' to a peasant who has had the temerity to join in the tally-ho cries of the Wild Hunt (many such tales in Mannhardt, *op. cit.*, pp. 82 ff.). The cannibalistic myths of Romulus, the foster-child of the Roman she-wolf, torn to pieces by the Roman Senators (Livy, I, 16, 4; Plutarch, *Vita Romuli*, 27; Dionys. Halic., *Antiqq. Rom.*, 2, 56; A. B. Cook, *op. cit.*, I, p. 656, note 2), of *Pentheus*, the 'man of sorrows', who tried in vain to prevent the introduction of the Dionysian rites into Thebes, rent asunder by the raving Maenads (tragedies by Thespis, Aeschylus, Euripides, Chaeremon, Iôphôn and Lycophon, v. A. B. Cook, *op. cit.*, I, p. 679), the child Dionysos Zagreus dismembered by the Titans (Cook, pp. 65 ff.), have all a background of archetypal cannibalistic reality, overlooked or deliberately suppressed by classical scholars idolizing the Greeks and Romans and blinded by the supreme beauty of their art and poetry to the cruel strain in their mental make-up which. they shared in various degrees with all other historic nations.

III. TRIBES BEARING THE NAME OF WOLF

The cuneiform texts found at Boghaz-keui mention Luwians, (*Lu-um-na-as* 'the Luvian', E. O. Forrer, *Mél. Cumont*, p. 688),
plural
written ideographically LU^MESH UR-BAR-RA = 'men-dog-wild' (lit. 'dog-outside'), also 'goat-men' and 'lion-men' (Ungnad, *Zeitschr. f. Assyr.*, Neue Folge, I, 1923/4, pp. 2–6). The name *Luvii* must be derived from a feminine form of *lupus* (cf. French *le loup*, *la louve*), like *Lyka-îoi*, *Lyka-ônes*, while the *Luqqa* in cuneiform texts of c. 1400 B.C. (*Glotta*, 1939, p. 102) and the *Lukki*, i.e. Lycians of the Amarna tablets (Eduard Meyer, *Gesch. d. Altertums*, 2nd ed., I, 2, No. 515; R. H. Hall, *Anc. Hist. of the Near East*, 5th ed., 1920, pp. 60, 69, 270, note 2; 370, note 1), the Λνχιοι of our Greek sources, are simply the 'wolfish' people. There was still a 'Luvian village' (Λουβιον κώμη) in Iberia at the foot of the Caucasus at the time of Ptolemy (*Geogr.*, V, 11, 2), when the Greek βῆτα was spoken as a *v*, evidently the *Lu-ub-di* province of Urartu in the inscription of Assurbanipal Cyl. B., col. IV, ll. 6 ff.; Persian *Lubâmšah* (Tomaschek, Pauly-Wissowa, I, 1305, l. 40). The Ravenna geographer (11, 8) calls it *Luponissa* (Codd. *Liponissa*) with the old Luvian -*issa* ending. Pliny (*H.N.*, VI, 29) names the inhabitants of this region *Lupenii*, the *Tabula Peutingeriana* (XI, 5) *Lupones*, the Manuscripts of the Ravenna geographer (II, 12) speak of the *patria Lepon*, obviously for a Greek πατρίς Λούπων.

In Arcadia, Pausanias (VIII, 23, 8) mentions Λυκοῦντες of
Λυκοῦντα, a tribal name formed with the characteristic Luvian
plural ending -unti, -undi, -unzi. There are further the Lykaones
of Arcadia (Stephan. Byz., s.v. 'Arkadia'; Dionys. Halic.,
Antiqq. Rom., II, 1) and Lycaonia or Lucaonia (Corp. Inscr. Lat.,
III, 6818) in Asia Minor (Xenophon, Cyrop., VI, 2, 10; Anab.,
VII, 8, 25; Kroll in Pauly-Wissowa, XIII, 2253–2266), probably so called with reference to the three-coloured white, buff
and black Canis pictus Desm. or 'Hyaena-hound' (Pomponius
Mela, III, 88: 'Sunt et saevissimae ferae omni colore varii
lycaones' ['lycaones are very fierce beasts striped in all colours']),
otherwise similar to the wolf (Solinus, 30, 24: 'Eadem Aethiopia
mittit lycaonem; lupus est cervice iubatus, et tot modis varius ut
nullum colorem illi dicant abesse' ['the same Ethiopia produces
the lycaon, a wolf with a mane and so dappled that they say
every colour is represented in it']), which the Egyptians of the
Old Empire trained for hunting purposes. The name Lyca-onia,
formed like Kata-onia, Bagada-onia, Mai-onia, Pai-onia, Paphlag-
onia, with a suffix surviving in the Albanian word -ane, -ene =
'coast', 'land' is probably not Greek (cf. Halbawanaš, the man
from Halpa in cuneiform texts from Boghaz-keui, Brandenstein,
Festschr. f. Hirth, Heidelberg, 1936, p. 38). Lyka, lykê for 'she-
wolf' is not found in any Greek dialect, any more than *ἵππη for
'mare', often found, however, in composite personal names,
except in the combination μορμολύκη, the name of a 'bogy-she-
wolf'. Athenaeus, Deipnosoph., XIII, p. 567 E.F., quotes Timo-
cles and Amphis for the proper name Λύκα explained as 'harlot',
equivalent to Latin lupa; Greek λυκ-αινα is, according to Paul
Kretzschmer, Kleinasiat. Forsch., I, 17, a secondary form, modelled after λε-αινα, 'lioness'; there are an Arcadian Zeus Λυκα-ιος
and an Apollon Λυκη-γενης who have long ago been explained
(Paul Kretzschmer, Glotta, 1939, p. 102; Gernet, 'Dolon le
Loup', Mélanges Cumont, Bruxelles, 1936, p. 192, note 3, after
Meillet, Linguistique historique et linguistique générale, p. 212;
Montague Summers, The Werwolf, London (Kegan Paul), 1933,
p. 143), as due to matriarchal mother-filiation: 'he of the she-
wolf', 'born by the she-wolf', that is by Lêto, changed into a she-
wolf (Aelian, Nat. Anim., 10, 26; Aristotle, Hist. An., 6, 29, 2;
Antig. Karyst., Mirac., 61; Preller-Robert, I, 236, note 1). The

Italian, probably Illyrian, counterpart to the *Lykáones* are the *Lucani* of *Lucania* (written LYK.., LY.. on silver coins of Metapontum c. 300 B.C.), whose name was known to Heraclides Ponticus (*Peri polit.*, XX; Fragm., *Hist. Gr.*, 218) to be derived from λύκος 'wolf'. The Lucani can hardly be separated from the Roman *gentes* called *Lucanii* and *Lucceii, Lucii, Luccii, Lucilii,* especially in view of the close connexion with the foundation story of Rome and with the heroes Romulus and Remus of the Roman she-wolf (*Lupa Romana*), also known as *Luperca* (Varro, ap. Arnob. IV, 3) and of the priestly colleges or fraternities called the *Luperci* (see Appendix I below, p. 254), who sacrificed a goat every year at the entrance of the old *lupercal*, or 'wolves' den'. Nor should it be overlooked that, according to medieval texts, the Roman *insula Tiberina* was also known as the *insula Lycaonia* (testimonies coll. in Jordan-Hülsen, *Topographie der Stadt Rom*, I, 3, p. 631, 21, and Besnier, *L'île Tibérine dans l'Antiquité*, 76 ff.; Pauly-Wissowa, IX, col. 1595, lines 1–5, v. *Lycaonia insula*).

Another Samnite tribe, immediate neighbours of the abovementioned *Lucani*, were the *Hirpini*, whose name was known to be derived from *hirpus*, the Samnite word for 'wolf' (Paulus, p. 106: 'Irpini appellati a nomine lupi, quem irpum dicunt Samnite.' ['the Hirpini are so called from *hirpus*, the Samnite word for wolf']; Strabo, V, 250: ἵρπον γὰρ καλόυσιν οἱ Σαννῖται τὸν λύκον; Servius on *Aen.*, XI, 785: 'lupi Sabinorum lingua "hirpi" vocantur'). Strabo, V, 250; Festus, 106 M., record the tribal legend of the Hirpini that they had been led by the sacred wolf of their god Mars into their present settlements.

In the Faliscan region, at the foot of Mount Soracte, familiar to all lovers of Horace, lived a tribe (*paucae familiae*) known as the *Hirpi Sorani* (Strabo, V, 226; Pliny, *H.N.*, VII, 19; Solinus, II, 26; Vergil, *Aen.*, XI, 785 ff., etc.; Serv. on *Aen.*, XI, 785) or 'wolves of Sora', a Volscian city with an Etruscan name. They practised twice annually the old rite of walking barefoot over glowing ashes, which so greatly impressed the late Mr. Harry Price when a Kashmiri by name of Kuda Bux showed it in Carshalton (report with phot. *The Times*, 18 Sept. 1935; *ibid.*, 26 Sept. 1935, p. 8, a letter by Miss Rosita Forbes on the same performance witnessed in Dutch Guiana; cf. J. J. Metz, *Volks-*

stamme der Nilagiris, Basle, 1858, pp. 54 ff.; Mannhardt, *Wald- u. Feldkulte*, pp. 306 f.; and in Mysore; Tamils, in French India; G. Nanja Nath, 'Fire Walkers of India', *World Digest*, No. 87, 7 July 1946, p. 77; Mary Lady Monkswell, *A Victorian Diarist*, London (Murray), 1946, pp. 104 f., on fire-walking performed in a temple at Tokyo every 9th of April and 7th of September, and on the Hon. Eric Collier performing the exploit himself). The whole secret is that the bare feet must be washed before the ordeal in a saturated solution of ordinary salt or in sea-water and dried. If perspiring feet are stood upon a heap of dry salt, the soles will be equally well protected. This explanation was given long ago in Eisler, *Orph.-Dionys. Myst.*, pp. 149–153. The *hirpi Sorani*, who enjoyed, in return for performing annually this simple trick, exemption from all taxes and military service (Pliny, *H.N.*, VII, 19), had received an oracle (Servius, *l.c.*) to live 'after the manner of wolves', *i.e.* by banditry (*lupos imitarentur, i.e. rapto viverent*). Apparently they found it more profitable to fox their contemporaries for centuries on end by this cheap trick. Vergil, who was fooled by them, says (*Aen.*, XI, 787) that they walked 'right through the fire, confiding in their piety' ('medium freti per ignem pietate multa premimus vestigia pruna').

The *Luceres*—with the Etruscan plural suffix *-er, -ar*, before the Latin plural ending *-es*, one of the three Roman *tribus*, was believed (Cicero, *Republ.*, II, 14; Varro, *ap.* Servium *ad Aen.*, V, 560) to derive its name from the Etruscan *Lucumones*, while the grammarian Festus (120 M; 107 L) explains the *Lucumones* as 'mad people', 'homines ob insaniam dicti'. Spanish *loco* also used in English slang, Portuguese *louco* still means 'mad' and *loucura, louquice* spells 'madness' in Portuguese (Vieira, *Diccionario Portugues*, Porto, 1873, III, 134; Roque Barcia's derivation from Latin *loquax*—*Primero Diccionario General Etymologico*, Madrid, 1881, p. 468 b—is as improbable as Meyer-Luebke's derivation—*Roman. etym. Wörterbuch*, 3rd ed., Heidelberg, 1935, p. 752, No. 9038 a—from Latin *uluccus*, 'owl'), while with **lykja> lyssa*, meaning 'madness', literally 'lupine rabies' in Greek, it is possible that the Etruscan *Lucumones, i.e. 'reges'* (Servius to Verg., *Aen.*, II, 78; VIII, 65), were originally lupine were-wolves, chiefs or tyrants terrorizing the people. *Luc-umon-es* may well be the Illyrian equivalent of *lupini-homines*, 'were-wolves'.

The name of these *Luceres* (Etruscan *luxre*) has rightly been connected by Kannegiesser (*Klio*, XI, 45) with that of the *Lokroi* (Illyrian *Lucr-ista-ni*, Cassiodorus, I, 29) of Greece and the Greek colonies in Italy (see Prof. Oldfather's articles *Lokris, Lokroi, Lokros* in Pauly-Wissowa, XIII, 1136–1365). The ancestor of the Boeotian-Lelegian *Lokroi* (Aristotle, *frg.* 560) is said to have been a son of Zeus and of Maira who hunted with Artemis and was killed by the goddess for losing her virginity like Kallistô (below, note 116, p. 157). Maira appears in Dionysian legends as the name of the bitch, transferred to the sky as the constellation *Canis Maior* (Apollod., III, 192; Hygin., 130). So the mother of *Lok-r-os* was presumably believed to have been one of the κύνες δρομάδες or 'coursing bitches' in the pack of the Great Hunter god and hunting goddess.

However that may be, there lived in present-day Transsylvania and Rumania, the very region where the belief in werewolves (Slavonic *vrkolak*, see below, p. 149) and vampires (Slavonic *upir*, 'he flies away'), as described in Bram Stoker's gruesome novel *Dracula*, is still very much alive, the ancient Dacians (Δακοί). According to Strabo, VII, 304, they were originally called Δαοι. An invaluable gloss preserved by Hesychius tells us that δαος is the Phrygian word for 'wolf'. Gavril Kazarow, *Klio*, IV, N.F., 1929, p. 84 f.; P. Kretzschmer, *Einleit. z. Gesch. d. gr. Sprache*, pp. 388, 221, 214; Norbert Jokl, art. 'Phryger' in Ebert's *Reallexikon der Vorgeschichte*, Berlin, X, 1927/8, p. 146, col. a; see p. 150, col. a, cfs. old Slavonic *daviti*, 'strangle'; Nehring in Schrader-Nehring, *Lex. d. Indogerm. Altertumskunde*, II, Berlin, 1929, p. 287, left col., cfs. Greek θόας, θώς, 'jackal', also found as proper name of a mythical king. I should rather cf. Phryg. *Kan-daôn*, 'wolves' hound', 'wolfhound', an *epiklêsis* of the Thracian god Arês of Krêstonê.

In Lycia the god Hermes is called *Kan-davlas*, 'dog-strangler', he who vanquished the dog Cerberus at the entry of Hades (Eisler, *Antiquité Classique*, VIII, 1939, p. 44, notes 2, 3). There is a relief showing this dog-strangler on a Phrygian rock-tomb façade of Terelik-Kalessi (Springer-Michaelis, *op. cit.*, p. 75, fig. 160). See Gavril Kazarow, *Klio*, XXII, N.F., 1929, pp. 84 f.,

NOTES   n. 111

on the town *Daous-dava* = 'Wolfham' in *Moesia Inferior* between
Danube and Haemus (Ptolem., III, 16, 6); C. Patsch in Pauly-
Wissowa, IV, ed. 2231). On *-dava* = 'settlement', see Kretz-
schmer, *op. cit.*, p. 214; Tomaschek, *Die Thraker*, II, 2, p. 70;
Mateescu, *Ephem. Daco-Romana*, I, 208, 6.

The proper name *Daos—Davus* as a slave's name in Latin
sources—is actually found in Phrygian inscriptions (*Papers of
the American School at Athens*, II, No. 38, 81; *Bull. Corr. Hell.*,
II, 265; III, 479). Kretzschmer, *Einleit. i. d. Gesch. d. Griech-
ischen Sprache*, p. 314, compares Δάκοι > Δάοι to Γραίκοι > Γραίοι.
It follows that the Dacians called themselves 'the wolves' or
'the wolfish ones'. There are other Δάοι (Strabo, VII, 304; XI,
508, 511, 515), nomadic Scythians east of the Caspian Sea,
called *Dahae* by the Latin authors, also *Daai* by some Greek
historians (S. Tomaschek's article 'Daai' in Pauly-Wissowa,
IV, cols. 1945–1946). Their name is probably derived from the
Sakian word *dahae*, 'wolves'.

Finally there is, south of the Caspian Sea, Mazanderan,
ancient *Hyrcania*, in eastern Iranian *Vehrkana*, in western
Iranian *Varkana*, the 'Wolfland', from *vehrka*, Iranian 'wolf'. It
is inhabited by hunting tribes called in our classical sources
(Kiessling in Pauly-Wissowa, IX, cols. 454–518), *Hyrkanoi*, 'the
wolves'. In Phrygia we find an *Orka-orkoi* tribe of *rrka* with the
Luvian re-duplicated plural.

To these wolf-pack tribes on the eastern margin of the classical
world correspond *Loukentioi* and *Lucenses* in Celtiberian Calaecia,
the modern Spanish province of Galicia on the Atlantic sea-
board. Ireland, which appears to have received early im-
migrants from this coast, was known in England up to the end
of the 18th century as 'The Wolfland'. Werewolf stories abound
in .the 'wolf-land', Eire. Giraldus Cambrensis, *Topographia
Hibernica* (II, 19), tells what may well be the earliest of them:
'An Irish priest was met by a wolf in Meath and desired to
come to see his dying wife. They were natives of Ossory, whose
people had been cursed for their wickedness by St. Natalis, and
were compelled to take two by two a wolf-shape for seven
years, returning to their own form at the end of that time. The
priest was persuaded to give the she-wolf the sacrament, for the
other turned her skin down a little, showing that she was an old

woman.' Giraldus says that he was asked to give his advice on this case at the synod of Meath two years after, and that it was referred to the Pope (Giraldus, *Opera*, V, p. 119).

A citation in the *Book of Ballymote* (140b) says that the 'descendants of the wolf' in Ossory (of the race of Laighne Fylaid) had the power of changing themselves and going forth to devour people. Nennius, *Wonders of Eri* (XIV), says that the descendants of wolves still surviving in Ossory re-transform themselves into wolves whenever they bite (see below, note 230, on little girls becoming wolves when they bite). St. Patrick is also said to have cursed a certain race in Ireland so that they and their descendants are wolves 'at a certain time every seventh year, or for seven years on end' (W. Stokes, *Relig. of the Celts*, II, 1873, p. 202; *Folklore*, V, 1894, pp. 310 f.). Early English travellers in Ireland relate that the Irish took wolves as godfathers, prayed to them to do them no ill, and used their teeth as amulets. Lycanthropy ran in families. Laignech Fáelad and his family could take wolf-shape at will and kill the herds, and Laignech was called Fáelad because he was the first of them to go as a wolf. In Irish and Welsh *Märchen* transformation into wolf-form of children by a stepmother or of a husband by a wife is not uncommon.

A curious and harmless revival of these atavistic lycanthropic ideas are the 'wolf-cubs' among the Boy Scouts, suggested by the romanticized wolf-child, Mowgli, in Rudyard Kipling's *Jungle Book*, the world-wide success of which is due to the appeal it makes to 'archetypal' ideas of the human race. The numerous stories of the Romulus and Remus, *Acca Larentia* and *Lupa Romana* type (Alex. H. Krappe, 'Acca Larentia', *Americ. Journ. of Archaeol.*, XLVI, 1942, No. 4, pp. 490–499; *id.* 'Animal Children', *California Folklore Quarterly*, III, No. 1, Jan. 1944, pp. 45–52; L. L. Hanchett, 'The Lost Woman of St. Nicholas', *ibid.*, pp. 148 ff.; B. A. Bodkin, *The American People*, London (Pilot Press), 1946, No. 280 ff. 'The Lobo Girl of Devil's River') are by no means purely mythical. Some cases of exposed Hindu children having been brought up by she-wolves with their cubs, but found in a completely idiotic state, are perfectly authenticated (E. B. Tylor, 'Wild Men, and Beast Children', *Anthropol. Review*, I, 1863, 21 ff.) A more recent case was reported by the

Morning Post on 27 July 1914. See also Dr. Arnold Gesell (Yale Univ.), *Wolf Child and Human Child, The Life History of Kamala, the Wolf Girl, Based on the Diary Account of a Child reared by a Wolf and who then lived for nine years in the orphanage of Midnapore in the province of Bengal,* London (Methuen), 1941. The diary in question of the Rev. J. A. L. Singh and his wife, who educated the child, has been annotated for publication by Dr. Robert M. Zingg of the University of Denver. This wolf-child— one of two brought up by the same she-wolf and cared for in Midnapore orphanage—took years to learn to walk in the human way and could not run when she died of uraemia at seventeen. This proves that such wolf-reared children cannot have started the mutation of the original food-gathering herd of hominids into the lupine pack of hunting carnivorous *Neo-anthropus*, running down game by superior speed and encircling movements.

On the contrary, a boy brought up among the gazelles and as fleet of foot as these animals was captured in 1945 in the Transjordan region by a Ruweili chief Amir Lawrence al Sha'alan hunting gazelles in his motor-car. He was cared for by four doctors of a Baghdad hospital, appeared to be speechless and accustomed to a purely vegetarian diet (cable of M. Abdul Karîm from Baghdad, *Sunday Express,* 25 August 1946, p. 2; cf. *Daily Mail,* 22 August 1946, p. 3. Dr. Gesell mentions (p. v) other such 'feral children', notably the 'Wild Boy of Hamelin', found in 1724 and exhibited in London at the age of twelve under the taxonomic name '*Iuvenis Hannoveranus*' and ridiculed by Jonathan Swift—quite wrongly—as a fake; the 'wild boy of Aveyron', examined by the great alienist Pinel and tutored by Itard; and the boy brought up by bears and discovered in the neighbourhood of Warsaw in 1698 (*op. cit.,* p. 55). The most curious of these archetypal stories is that of Sergei Mironovich Kirov, Stalin's best friend, a member of the Russian Politburo, murdered by political adversaries. He 'was an orphan. The legend is that he was suckled by a sow' (John Gunther, *Inside Europe,* rev. ed., London (Hamish Hamilton), 1938, p. 493). The remarkable feature of this modern Romulus legend is the fact that, according to French superstition, the werewolves (*loups-garoux*) 'are men who have the power to change themselves into animals . . . most times they adopt the shape of a wolf, less frequently that of a pig' (Pierre van Paassen, *Days of our Years*, London (Heinemann), 1939, p. 234; cf. above, p. 120, the *hllalfa* or 'boars' of the 'Isâwîyya). Agathocles, *frg.* 2, Athen., 375 E; C. Mueller, *Fragm. Hist. Gr.*, IV, 289; A. B. Cook, *Zeus*, I, p. 653, note 3, cf. p. 785 to p. 660; R. C. Bosanquet on fig. 507 has preserved a Cretan legend that the infant Zeus, born in the Dictaean cave, was suckled by a sow. The 'pig' or 'sow' in question is, of course, a wild boar or sow. Another more realistic explanation of this story is, however, suggested by recent newspaper reports about a poor boy, boarded out on a lonely Shropshire farm, starved and beaten to death by his foster-parents (*e.g. Daily Mail*, 14 February, 1945, pp. 3 f.). The culprits stated in court, as an excuse for their behaviour, that the famished child 'had been sucking the red cow' . . . 'he got under a cow and sucked her teat the same as a calf would'. In a lonely, pre-revolution Russian peasant's hut, where the owner often lived in one room with the domestic animals, an orphaned child left behind by parents dying in rapid succession would very naturally try to suck a cow or sow in milk to keep alive.

112. PERSONAL NAMES MEANING WOLF

Pape-Benseler-Sengebusch's *Dictionary of Greek Proper Names*, Brunswick, 1884, p. 821 ff., and Forcellini's *Onomasticum Latinum*, have pages and pages of such Greek and Latin names. Pauly-Wissowa-Kroll's *Realenzykl.*, which lists only persons of historical importance, has on cols. 1851 f. of vol. XIII (1927) eleven men named *Lupus* and one *Louppos* in col. 1850; in cols. 2247–2252 four persons—mythical or historical—named *Lykaon*, in cols. 2393–2417 twenty-eight men, some fabulous, more of them real persons, named *Lykos*. The names *Lucius, Lukios, Lucianus, Loukianos, Loukouas* are not counted in this connection because these forms mean, in the first instance, 'the Lycian', *Lucillus* 'the little Lycian'. *Lykpeios, Lyppeios*, Illyrian for 'wolfish', is found in Paeonian inscriptions (Kretschmer, *Einleitung*, p. 247). In vol. IX, cols. 527–534, there are five kings named *Hyrkanos*, not counting one *Hyrkôdês*, 'wolf-like', a Bactrian king. Hyrkanos is the equivalent of old Persian *Warkaina*, *Wehrkaëna*, 'wolfish', recent Persian *Gurgin* (in Arabic as a loan-word, *Jorjan*). Ferdinand Justi, *Iranisches Namensbuch*, enumerates thirty-six persons of this name. Schrader (*Reallexik. d. Indogerm. Altertumskunde*, II, Berlin (de Gruyter), 1929, p. 667, col. b) lists from Sanskrit sources (*Vṛka-karman*, 'wolf's work'=Lyc-urgus, *Vṛka-bandhu*, 'wolf-kinsman', 'member of a band or pack of wolves', and Vṛka='Wolf'; Slavonic *Vuk*, 'Wolf', *Vukovoj*, 'wolf-army', 'wolf-pack'). Förstemann, *Altdeutsches Namenbuch*, 2nd ed., Bonn, 1900, says (I, p. 639): '*Vulfa* is the most frequent basic element in Old German names. In Old Scandinavian names it is *one* of the most frequent elements.' Female names composed with the word for 'she-wolf' are rarer, but there are quite a few. Hitler's name Adolf—*Aid-ulf, Atha-ulf, Aud-ulf, Az-olf*—is probably composed with the baby word *Atta, Adda*, for 'father' and means 'Father Wolf'. L. Bloomfield, *Language*, London (Allen & Unwin), 1935, p. 46, 7, explains *Adolph* as Gothic *athal-ulfs*, 'wolf of the land'. Others (Max Gottschalk, *Deutsche Namenskunde*, Munich (Lehmann), 1932, p. 124) take it to be a composite with a worn-down form of *adal-, edel*, 'noble', and to mean 'noble wolf'. The family-name of that 'fatherly' or 'noble wolf's' victim *Dollfuss* is, of course, short for Latinized *Adolphus*.

Composite names of this type are frequent among Greeks and Romans. *Lupicinus* (cf. *corni-cinus*, 'horn-blower'; *con-cinere*, 'sing together')='Wolf enchanter, 'Wolf Charmer'—the hunter who can lure the wolf by imitating his howl in addition to wearing his pelt. *Lupianus* (a *magister militum per Orientem* in A.D. 412) is the equivalent of French *louvetier*, the officer in charge of combating the plague of the wolves' depredations. *Luppianus* (a man buried in A.D. 470 at Vercellae) is only a graphic variant. Greek *Lykomêdês* (fifteen occurrences) or *Lykomidās* 'Wolf-minder'—a whole aristocratic clan of Athens—is the Greek equivalent of *Lupianus*; so is *Lykōn* (seventeen occurrences) and *Lykophontês*, 'wolf-killer'. *Lyk-andros*—one only—is the exact equivalent of 'wer-wolf' (below, note 116). *Lykios* (six occurrences) is the wolfish one, *Lykis* is an endearing form of *Lykos*, *Lykiskos*—six occurrences—feminine *Lykiska*, are diminutives for a young wolf or whelp or young she-wolf. *Lykidas* 'wolf's scion', *Lykinos*—seven occurrences—is a synonym of *Lykios* with another suffix. *Lykô*—name of a Laconian princess—is presumably a shortening (ὑποκοριστικόν) of a composite name. A gloss in Hesychius is interesting: Λυκόστρατος ὁ μοναρχὸς παρὰ ʿΙπποχάρμοι.

Lykokapras, 'wolf-boar-(kill)er,' cf. French *loup-cerrier*, is a combination like German '*Schweinehund*'; *Lykôleôn*, 'a lion to a wolf', English Lyulf[1], is, of course, a wolf-hunter's name. So is *Lyk-ôp-eus*, with two originally non-Greek suffixes, the name of an Aetolian of Calydon. *Lykophrôn* is 'he with a wolf's mind', *Lykopos* a man with a 'wolf's face'. *Auto-lykos*, 'he himself a wolf', is a synonym of 'werewolf', 'man-wolf'. Nine persons of this name are listed in Pauly-Wissowa's *Realenzyklopädie*, II, cols. 2600 ff. The earliest of them is the Homeric Autolykos, the grandfather of Ulysses, the master-thief who steals the helmet made of a boar's head brought to Ulysses for his nocturnal reconnoitring expedition by Meriones (*Iliad*, X, 267). According to *Odyssey*, XIX, 395, the god Hermes—sometimes reputed to be the father of Autolykos—gives him the gifts of successful thieving and safe perjury. According to Hesiod (Fragm. 136 Rzach) he can make all stolen goods invisible, a feature to be connected with the wolf's cap or dog's cap (*kyneê*) of 'invisible' Aïdês. Autolykos seduces Antikleia, the daughter of the super-wise Sisyphos, who becomes the mother of Ulysses, according to some commentators, not from his putative father Laërtês (Tzetzês to Lycophron, v. 344; schol. Laurent. to Sophocles, *Aias*, v. 190). There existed, obviously, a matriarchal were-wolf genealogy for the great bow-man and master of all cunning, Odysseus. *Lykourgos*—fifteen occurrences—is one who 'holds wolves at bay' (εἴργει), still another synonym of French *louvetier*. *Lykormas*—four occurrences—is the counterpart of German *Wolfgang*, he who starts or walks as a wolf. So is *Lyk-ortas*, one Arcadian, one Syrian, the 'wolf who rears' on his hindlegs. German *Wolf-wahn*, 'wolf-mad', lit. 'believing (*wähnen*) himself a wolf.' *Wulvarich*, 'wolves' king'; *Wolf-diet-rich* = *Vulfa-theodo-rix*,

---

[1] Lyulf, 4th Lord Stanley of Alderley, 4th Lord Sheffield ... inherited the baronies of Stanley of Alderley ... Eddisbury and ... Sheffield by which title he was always known (Nancy Mitford, *The Ladies of Alderley*, London (Chapman and Hall), 1938, p. xxiii and p. xxxii). 'Ly-ulf' could, of course, mean 'lying wolf',—the perjured Autolycus, above—but the Greek analogy suggests a more flattering interpretation.

'Wolf-people's-king', 'Wolf-pack-leader', Slavonic *Vluku-vlk* 'Wolf of Wolves'—all to be found in Förstemann, *op. cit.*— are other significant examples. The legendary Wolfdietrich is said to have grown up among the wolves and to have had a cross-shaped birth-mark upon his shoulder (Hoops, *Reallexik. d. Germ. Alt.*, IV, p. 564). The latter detail is explained by the Sumerian stone statue of king Lugal-kisal-si in the Berlin Museum (*Der Alte Orient*, XIX, 2, pl. I, fig. 2, after *Amtl. Berichte a. d. kgl. Kunstsamml.*, Berlin, XXXVI Jg., No. 4, Jan. 1915, fig. 28), which shows engraved on the naked shoulder of the bearded monarch the sign of a star *, in cuneiform writing the cross-shaped sign ⋈⟊ meaning 'heaven', 'god' (Christliebe Jeremias, *Die Vergöttlichung der Babylonischen Könige*, Leipzig 1919, p. 14).

There are a few such names born by Semites. Judges vii. 25 mentions a Midianite prince *Ze'eb*, 'Wolf', corresponding to the Arabic name *Dhi'b*, 'Wolf'. The 'hairy Esau', the 'cunning hunter', marries the daughter of a Hivite or 'tent-dweller' called *Zibe'on*, 'the male hyaena', the Arabic name *Duba'a* or *Dubai'a* (see above, p. 121, the *dhiba'* in the 'Isâwîyya fraternity). 1 Chron. vii. 36 mentions an Israelite of the tribe of Asher called *Shu'al*, 'Fox' or Jackal, corresponding to the Arab name *Thu'al*, the Greek personal name *Ἄλωπηξ*, 'Fox', the Persian *Rubah*, 'Fox' (Justi, *op. cit.*, p. viii).

Paul de Lagarde suggested in his 2nd edition of Eusebius' *Onomastica Sacra*, pp. 367 f., that the tribal name *Re'uben* is to be identified with Arabic *Ra'âbil*, shortened from *Ra'âbîl*, plural of *Ri'bâl*, a 'lion' or 'wolf'. According to the *Taj el-'Aruz*, the *rayâbîl* of the Arabs were those 'who used to go on hostile expeditions upon their feet and alone'—as 'lone wolves', as we should say. Miss Freya Stark, *Seeing the Hadhramaut*, London (John Murray), 1938, p. 156, speaks of a family of three generations simultaneously alive: 'the grandfather is a very fine old fighter known as "The Wolf"'.

The ritual origin of these animal names can still be observed among the 'Isâwîyya (above, note 105). Those initiated into this fraternity as 'camels', 'lions', 'jackals', 'panthers' often add this animal character to their name: 'on trouve, en effet, très fréquemment des 'Aîssaoûa se nommant Si Mohammed al Iml ba Nmr (panthère) ou Ahmad as-Sba' (le lion)' (Brunel, *op. cit.*, p. 171). But these names are rare (T. Nöldeke, *Encyclop. Biblica*, col. 3298, quoting Hammer-Purgstall, *Über die Namen der Araber*, pp. 3 f.) in comparison with the pages full of names composed with *Λύκος* in Pape-Benseler-Sengebusch's *Dictionary of Greek Proper Names* and the many pages in Förstemann, *op. cit.*

Ze'eb, 'Wolf', is a frequent Jewish name. It is the Hebrew and German-Yiddish equivalent of Benjamin, called the 'ravening wolf' in Gen. xlix. 27. No trace of the werwolf idea in Semitic folk-lore is known to me. The Berbers of Morocco who believe in war-jackals (*boudas*) are northern, fair-haired and blue-eyed Libyans who settled in North Africa in prehistoric times as the Vandals did in the fifth century A.D.

The Turks, who are familiar with the werwolf belief of their Dacian Balkan neighbours and former subjects, called their national hero and pack-leader Ata-türk, 'the Grey Wolf'. H. C. Armstrong, *Grey Wolf, Mustapha Kemal. An Intimate Study of a Dictator*, Penguin ed., 1937, p. 7, explains the nickname as derived from the Turkish tradition that the original Osmanli chief Suleyman Shah carried as his banner the head of a grey wolf, as the Roman legions marched under *signa* showing the she-wolf of Rome. This founder of the Turkish nation is said to have been exposed in his childhood and saved and nourished by a she-wolf which he afterwards married (Stanislas Julien, *Documents historiques sur les Tou-ki oué (Turcs), traduits du Chinois*, Paris, 1877, pp. 2 f. and 25 f.; Sir J. G. Frazer, *Folklore in the Old Testament*, III, Cambr. Univ. Press, 1918, p. 450, note 1). Kemal kept a great grey wolfhound as a pet (p. 126). He had stamps printed with the picture of the grey wolf of the original Turks (pp. 250 f.). It would have pleased him to know that the cuneiform tablets of Boghaz-keui mention a Hittite general *Lupakku* (Ungnad, *Zeitschr. f. Assyr.*, N.F., I, 1923, p. 3), with a name no doubt derived from a Luvian word *lupu*, 'wolf', with the *-ak* suffix so well known from Lydian *Sfard-ak*, 'a man from Sfard', *i.e.* from Sardes, a Sardian; in Thracian *Spartakos*; *Kos-ak* or *Kaz-ak*, a Kossaean or Cas-pi-an and many similar ethnic names. In the Hittite laws (Ungnad, *l.c.*, p. 4) the outlaw is addressed with the words: '*zikwa UR-BA-RA-aš ki-i-at*', 'thou hast become a wolf'. This is an exact parallel to the *'wolfhede'* (wolf head-mask) imposed on the outcast by the Laws of Edward the Confessor (about A.D. 1000): 'Lupinum enim cáput a die utlagationis eius quod ab Anglis wulfesheved nominatur. ['A wolf head, which the English call *wulfesheved*, from the day of his outlawry'.] See Henry de Bracton (A.D. 1185–1267), *De Legibus et Consuetudinibus Angliae*, ed. princ., 1569, II, 35; '... a tempore quo utlagatus est, caput gerit lupinum ita ut ab omnibus interfici possit'. [From the time he is outlawed, he wears a wolf's head, so that anyone may slay him.']

In Attica every law-court was presided over by a statue of the hero Lykos, represented in wolf-shape (Eratosthenes, περί τῆς ἀρχαιᾶς κωμῳδίας, quoted by Harpocrates, s.v. 'δεκάζων'; Suidas and Hesychios, s.v. 'Λύκου δεκάς', Apost. VIII, 49; IX, 77; X, 93; XII, 26; Zenob., V, 2; *Lex. Cantabr.*, 672, 26). Aristophanes, *Vesp.*, 389; 819, shows that he is considered as the prototype of the outcast and banished outlaw condemned to exile by the court.

113. This is the meaning of the Teutonic name 'Finns', from Norse *finna*, 'to find', given by the Scandinavians to their non-IndoEuropean neighbours (*Hirth-Festschrift*, Heidelberg, 1936).

114. RADICAL CHANGES IN ANIMAL DIET

Such a case of a radical change in the dietary habits of a species has been actually observed in the case of the Australian *kea*, a vegetarian parrot which became carnivorous with a particular addiction to the kidneys of grazing sheep, which it attacks with its powerful beak. It seems to have started the new habit by settling on the backs of sheep that had grown verminous and by feeding on their parasites, before it finally attacked the host itself (Schelderup-Ebbe, 'Social Behaviour of Birds', *Handbook of Social Psychology*, Worcester (Murchison), 1935, p. 501, note to preceding page). Conversely civilized men's domesticated cats and dogs tend to accept vegetarian food.

The most recent case of this kind has been investigated by Mr. J. Fisher of Roade, Northants, and Mr. R. A. Hinde of Norwich in the *Annual Report of the British Trust for Ornithology*,

1949, who have organized a nation-wide survey of the newly-developed taste for milk observed in tits, sparrows and other small garden birds which started opening the milk-bottles left on doorsteps by milkmen and drinking from them. Milkmen, housewives, 43 doctors and 126 ornithologists were among those who conducted observations and answered questions on the species and habits of the birds that raid milk-bottles. The organizers state that they were handicapped in their research by their research workers' lack of ornithological experience and by the fact that in many areas the milk bottle has only recently replaced the milk can. They are satisfied, however, that 'the technique used to open bottles has been extensively reported on'. Attacks are usually delivered soon after the bottles have been deposited. In some cases tits follow the milkman. In others, tin lids and stones on bottles have failed to stop the 'raids'. The spread of the habit, the organizers state, is consistent with their conclusion that 'only a small proportion of the birds make the original discovery of milk as a food and that others learn by imitation from them'. The majority of the reports refer to blue-tits and great-tits. Other offenders include coal-tits, starlings, chaffinches, sparrows, thrushes and blackbirds. The full report, containing details as to the coloured stoppers preferred by birds, will shortly be published in *British Birds*.

115. BIBLIOGRAPHY OF THE WEREWOLF PROBLEM

B. de Chauvincourt, *Discours de la Lycanthropie*, Paris, 1599; J. de Nynauld, *De la Lycanthropie*, Löwen, 1596; Wolfeshusius, *De Lycanthropis*, 1591; Jean Bodin Angevin, *De la Démonomanie des Sorciers*, Paris, 1580, livre II, ch. VI: 'De la lycanthropie et si les esprits peuvent changer les hommes en bêtes'; Boguet, *Discours des Sorciers*, Lyon, 1602; R. Andrée, *Ethnograph. Parallel. u. Vergleiche*, Leipzig, 1899, pp. 62–80; Grimm, *Deutsche Mythologie*, III, p. 409; Gruppe, *Griech. Mythol. u. Relig.-Gesch.*, p. 806; M. Bourquelot, 'Recherches sur la Lycanthropie', *Mém. de la Soc. d'Antiquaires de France*, Nouv. Ser., 1849, pp. 193–262; Wilhelm Hertz, *Der Werwolf*, Stuttgart, 1862; R. Léubuscher, *Über die Werwölfe und Tierverwandlungen im Mittelalter*, Berlin, 1850; Wilhelm Roscher, *Das Fragment des Marcellus von Sidê über Lycan-*

thropie u. Kynanthropie, Abh. d. Sächs. Gesellschaft d. Wiss., XVII, 1896, pp. 24 ff.; Sir J. G. Frazer, *Perils of the Soul*, London (Macmillan), 1911, p. 42, note 3; *Balder the Beautiful*, London (Macmillan), 1913, pp. 308–313; Eisler, *Orph.-Dionys. Myst.*, Leipzig, 1925, pp. 284 ff.; Wilh. Kroll, 'Etwas zum Werwolf', *Wiener Studien*, 1937, and Kroll's article 'Kynanthropie und Lycanthropie' in the VII. Suppl. vol. to Pauly-Wissowa-Kroll's *Realenzyklop. d. klass. Altertums*; Baring Gould, *The Book of the Werewolves*, London, 1865; E. B. Tylor, *Primitive Culture*, 3rd ed., London, 1891, I, pp. 308 f.; Rev. J. A. MacCulloch's article 'Lycanthropy' in Hastings, *Encyclop. of Rel. and Eth.*, VIII, London, 1915, pp. 206–220; George F. Black, *A List of Works relating to Lycanthropy*, New York Public Library, 1920; Montague Summers, *The Werewolf*, London (Kegan Paul), 1933; R. Trevor Davies, *Four Centuries of Witch Beliefs*, Oxford, 1933, p. 205; Richard Preston Eckels, *Greek Wolflore*, Philadelphia, 1937, pp. 33–48. The most recent example is recorded by Pierre van Paassen, *Days of our Years*, London (Heinemann), 1939, p. 235. 'We had a werewolf scare in the winter of 1930 through the disappearance of a farmer named Richard who had a bad reputation as a sorcerer, blighting the corn through his evil eye. He prepared love-philtres. Upon his death there were found in his cabin bottles, various herbs, magic stones, amulets with "druidic" inscriptions, the head of a calf, assorted powders, waxen manikins labelled with the names of various persons in the neighbourhood long deceased, dried salamanders, a pair of leather gloves. There was one statuette with the name of a prominent landowner with a pin traversing its throat from end to end. The landowner died of a cancer of the larynx. Other manikins had pins stuck in the stomach, backs, heads. He had been paid for these magic practices by estranged relatives of the prospective victims. The man was believed to walk by night in the shape of a wolf'. There is not much difference between this lycanthrope of Bourg-la-Reine in 1930 and the Moeris of whom Vergil's Alphesiboeus sang in 39 B.C., nearly 2,000 years ago (*Ecl.*, VIII, 95).

> *has herbas atque haec Ponto mihi lecta venena*
> *ipse dedit Moeris (nascuntur plurima Ponto)*

his ego saepe lupum fieri et se condere silvis
Moerim, saepe animas imis exire sepulchris
atque satas alio vidi traducere messis.

['These herbs and these poisons, culled in Pontus, Moeris himself gave me—they grow plenteously in Pontus. By their aid I
have oft seen Moeris turn wolf and hide in the woods, oft call
spirits from the depth of the grave, and charm sown corn away
to other fields.']
Propertius (IV, 5) mentions spells that will transform a human
being into a wolf. The most circumstantial account is given in
Petronius (*Satyricon*, 61): 'Niceros tells how his soldier friend
stripped off his clothes and addressed himself to the stars. Then
he *circumminxit vestimenta*, and all at once became a wolf, which
ran howling into the woods. Niceros next heard from a widow
whom he visited that a wolf had been worrying her cattle, and
had been wounded in the neck. On his return home he found
his friend bleeding at the neck, and knew then that he was a
versipellis.'

A good example of werewolf belief among the American
Indians is found in Alberta Hannum's book *Spin a Silver Dollar*
(condensed in *Reader's Digest*, July, 1946, p. 86); 'There was a
Navaho man in the vicinity of a neighbouring trading post
whom the other Navahos feared with a fear almost worse than
that of death. He was called the werewolf. He was believed to
turn himself into a wolf at night and raid their flocks. Worse
than that, it was believed that he also killed human victims and
devoured them—and the victims of the werewolf were usually
women.'

116. ETHNOLOGY OF THE WEREWOLF

Gervase of Tilbury, *Otia Imperialia*, 895 (beginning of the
13th century): '*Anglice* werewolf *dicunt*, were *enim anglice virum
sonat*, wolf *lupum*' ['In English they say *werewolf*, for in English
were means man, and *wolf* wolf]. The Norse counterpart to
'werewolf' is *vargulfr*, literally 'rogue wolf', Norwegian and
Swedish *varulf*, Danish *vaerulf*, medieval Latin *guerulfus*, 12th-
century Norman *garwalf* (Mogk, *Reallexik. d. Germ. Altertumskunde*, vol. IV, pp. 500 f.); Norman-French *loup-garou*, Picard

loup-varous, Portuguese *lobarraz* (<*lobo-barraz*), also *lubis homems* (Bourquelot, *Mémoires de la Soc. d. Antiqu. de France,* N. Ser., IX, p. 233), Italian *lupo-manaro,* Calabrian *lupu-minare,* Molfettian *lę̨pomęne,* Neapolitan *lupu menare,* Sicilian *lupu-minaru,* Aquileian *lupe-panaru,* Abruzzan *lope-kummari* (Meyer-Lübke, *Romanisches etymolog. Wörterbuch,* 3rd ed., Heidelberg (Winter), 1935, p. 426, No. 5173). The numerous dialect forms show that it is a popular concept and not a learned technical term, borrowed from some common source. In modern Greek werewolves are called *Λυκο-καντζαρι* (J. C. Lawson, *Modern Greek Folklore,* Cambridge, 1910, pp. 208 and 254), a dialect form of **λυκο-κένταυροι,* 'wolfish bull-prickers' (Eisler, *Orph.-Dionys. Myst.,* Leipzig, 1925, p. 287, note 5; *κένταυρος* is explained by the Byzantine grammarian Tzetzês as *κεντο-ταύρος,* 'bull-baiter', from *κεντεῖν,* 'prick with the spear-point', as the mounted *picadores* do it in the Spanish bull-fight (*corrida de toros,* Eisler, *ibid.,* p. 263, note 4).

In the Slavonic languages the werewolf is called *vlukodlak* in ancient Bulgarian, meaning literally 'wolf-haired' or 'wolf-skinned'; Slovenian *volkodlak,* Bulgarian *vulkolak,* Polish *wilkolak,* White Russian *volkolak,* Russian *volkulaku,* Serbian *vulkodlak,* whence modern Greek *brukolakas* or *bourkolakas* (*bêta* being pronounced *vêta*) for the 'vampire', an originally Slav word for him who 'flies away' (*upir*), that is a 'fly-by-night'. The explanation of the Slavonic composite word can be found in the Serbian tradition (MacCulloch, *op. cit.,* p. 208, note 4; Baring-Gould, *op. cit.,* p. 115 f.; J. Grimm, *Teuton. Mythol.,* p. 1095) that the *vulkodlak* have annual gatherings when they hang their wolfskins on trees. Should such a skin be taken and burnt, the owner retains human form. According to Norse tradition the transformation into a werewolf is effected by donning the *ulf-har* (='wolf's hair'), a belt of wolf's leather, evidently representing the wolf's pelt or *ulfhamr* or 'wolf's skin' (MacCulloch, *op. cit.,* p. 208; Baring-Gould, *op. cit.,* p. 56). In the *Völsunga Saga,* ch. 5–8, King Völsung had ten sons and a daughter, Signy, who was married to King Siggeir. Siggeir later slew Völsung and bound his sons in the stocks. There nine of them were devoured by an old she-wolf—the mother of Siggeir, who had taken this form. Through Signy's craft the tenth son, Sigmund, overcame this werewolf and went into hiding. Signy exchanged form with a sorceress, and had a son by Sigmund, called Sinfiötli. He and Sigmund took to a wandering life and, on one occasion, came to a house where two men were sleeping, with wolfskins hanging above them. For nine days they were wolves and on the tenth day came out of their skins. Sigmund and Sinfiötli donned the skins and became wolves, and each went his way, after agreeing that neither should attack more than seven men without howling for the other. In the sequel Sinfiötli slew eleven men without Sigmund's aid. The latter, hearing of this, flew at his throat and wounded him. When he was healed and the day had come for doffing their wolf-skins, they agreed to lay them aside for ever, and burned them in the fire. Godtmund says in this story to Sinfiötli: 'Thou thyself hast eaten wolves' meat and murdered thy brother. Thou hast often sucked wounds with cold mouth, and slunk, loathsome to all men, into the dens of wild beasts' (Vigfusson-Powell, *Corpus Poetic. Boreale*, Oxford, 1883, I, p. 136).

Among the North American Indians there are secret societies of wolfmen. (See below, note 117, on a werewolf among the recent Navahos). The Nootkas relate that wolves once took away a chief's son. They became his friends (see above, p. 138, note 111, on 'feral children') and ordered him on his return home to initiate the other young men into the society, the rites of which they taught him. In the ceremony a pack of 'wolves', that is, men with wolf masks, appears and carries off the novice; next day they bring him back apparently dead (presumably drugged) and the society has to revive him (J. G. Frazer, *Golden Bough*, 2nd ed., III, pp. 434 ff.). A similar recruiting system is practised by the African leopard-men discussed below, p. 152.

The Slavonic words describing the werewolf as 'wolf-haired' or 'wolf-skinned' have their exact counterpart in the Norse words *Ulfhedhnar*, 'wolf-clothed,' and *ber-serker*, German *Bärenhäuter*—the title of a forgotten opera by Siegfried Wagner —from Norse *ber* = 'bear' and *serk* = 'raiment', 'clothes', applied to the dreaded Northern war-mad fighters 'running amuck' (see for a recent case below, App. V)—*amog* in Malay—whose 'berserkers' fury' was considered an obsession similar to canine or lupine rabies (Vigfusson-Powell, *op. cit.*, I, p. 425; Baring-Gould, *op. cit.*, pp. 36 f.).

In the *History of Hrolf Kraka*, Björn—this frequent Norse name means 'bear'—is transformed into a bear by his stepmother who shook a wolf's-skin glove at him (one would expect a bear-skin glove, but there it is!). He lived as a bear and killed many of his father's sheep, but by night he always became a man, until he was hunted and slain (Sir W. Scott, *Minstrelsy*, London, 1839, p. 354).

In order to assume the crest of the *Lulem*, the Bear, the Carrier Indian took off all his clothes and spent some days and nights in the woods. On his return he joined in the Bear Dance, in which he was dressed as a bear (Frobenius, *Die Masken und Geheimbünde Afrikas*, Halle a.S., 1898, p. 69).

A counterpart to the employment of these Norse *berserker* as life-guards at the Byzantine court (the reader will remember the bear-skin helmets of the English Royal Life Guards) are the *lykopodes* or 'wolves' feet' employed as a body-guard—probably of Thracians—by the tyrant of Athens, Pisistratus (Aristophanes, *Lysistrata*, v. 664, and the ancient lexicographers quoting the word *lycopodes*), who owned big estates in Thracia. The hitherto unexplained word is a counterpart to the Westphalian word *Büksenwolf* (Hoops, *Reallexik.*, *l.c.*) for the werewolf. The word means 'trouser-wolf' and refers presumably to trousers made of wolf's pelts with the claws still attached to the legs (cf. Greek βασσάρα, 'fox', for the fox-fur boots of the Thracian hunters (*Etymologicum Magnum*, s.v.). The African Anyoto or Leopard-men use specially carved sticks—now in the Ethnographical Museum of Tervueren—possibly as stilts—to impress a leopard's spoor into the soft ground and iron claws to lacerate their victims (report from Slain's Farm in the Vienna *Neue Freie Presse* of 20 June 1937). The *lykopodes*-guard of Pisistratus might very well have used a similar device to leave the traces of wolves' feet on the ground whenever they perpetrated some nocturnal abduction or murder. In one case, in Central Africa, where the Makanga believe that a bewitcher (*mfiti*) can turn himself into a hyaena, leopard, crocodile, etc., tracks of a hyaena and of human feet were seen together, when a goat had been carried off (A. Werner, *Natives of British Central Africa*, London, 1906, pp. 84 ff., 241; MacCulloch, *op. cit.*, p. 212a, note 8). The animal tracks could easily have been imprinted into the soft soil by means of the cunningly carved sticks above-mentioned.

Therioanthropy, the metamorphosis of men into animals, is not confined to the change-over into wolves. The Berbers of Morocco believe in '*boudas*', men who can turn into hyaenas at nightfall and resume their human shape at the dawn of the morning (Pierre van Paassen, *Days of our Years*, London (Heine-mann), 1939, p. 278 f., quoting the native chauffeur who drove him in 1934). The belief in *boudas* is found equally in Abyssinia, where blacksmiths are believed to be such were-hyaenas trans-formed by a mysterious decoction of herbs (N. Pearce, *Life and Adventures . . . with Coffin's Visit to Gondar*, ed. J. J. Halls, London, 1831, I, 287; H. Salt, *Voyage to Abyssinia*, London, 1814, p. 427; W. C. Plowden, *Travels in Abyssinia*, London, 1868, pp. 300 ff.; MacCulloch, *op. cit.*, p. 212, note 1).

The same belief occurs from the Sudan to Tanganyika.

In many parts of Africa the belief in men who can transform themselves into lions and leopards and kill their enemies in this state is ineradicable (P. B. du Chaillu, *Wild Life under the Equatro*, London, 1869, p. 254; *Adventures in the Great Forests of Equatorial Africa and the Country of Dwarfs*, New York · (Harper), 1890, p. 129; Albert Schweitzer, *Mitteilungen aus Lambarene*, Bern, (Haupt), 1925). There are quite recent reports of their con-tinued activities: *Wiener Tagblatt*, 3 May 1934 (execution of nine Negro members of the sect of 'leopard-men'); *Neue Freie Presse*, 16 May 1936 (execution of eight Anyotos in Stanleyville, Belgian Congo); *Neue Freie Presse*, 20 June 1937, '*Menschliche Leoparden*' by 'Africanus', dated 'Slain's Farm, Equatorial Africa, end of May', describing the masks of the men as made of brown tree-bark, painted with black and yellow spots, with a real leopard's tail attached to the back. The Anyotos in ques-tion dragged young people, chiefly women and girls, by night from their huts, lacerated them with knives shaped like leopards' claws, pierced the heart with a trident knife [probably repre-senting forked-lightning.—R.E.] and devoured the bodies. *Sun-day Times*, 6 April 1947; *Sunday Express* of same date: 'Twenty-six African natives have been arrested in Tanganyika in connec-tion with murders and suspicious deaths—28 of which have been conclusively proved to be the work of "lion men". "Lion men" are natives who believe in ritual murders to obtain such blessings as good weather, and they leave wounds resembling the marks of a lion's claws.' *Daily Telegraph*, 9 April, 1947: 'Sixty-one native men and women have been arrested during inquiries into alleged murders by "lion-men", or witch-doctors, in the Singida district of Tanganyika, it was officially stated here to-day. The police said they expect to bring the total to 70. Many of those arrested will be brought before the Tanganyika High Court for trial on murder charges.' 'Murders of natives have been reported from the Singida district in the last few months. According to some accounts the "lion-men", wearing lion skins, stalk their victims and attack them with knives. Thirty-five killings have been reported to the police. Six are proved to have been done by man-eating lions' (Reuter). *The Times*, 25 Sept. 1946, records the execution in Lagos of 18 members of the dreaded Leopard Society, following a series of murders which terrorized the native community in Calabar (Nigeria). *The Evening Standard*, 10 Jan. 1948, reports from Dar-es-Salaam (Tanganyika): 'Three women have been hanged in Tanganyika for the first time in the country's recorded history. They died, with four men, for their part in the "lion-men" murders in the Singida district last spring, when more than 40 natives were slaughtered by people dressed in lion skins.' These 'lionesses' are, obviously, the exact counterparts of the 'lionesses' taking part in the gruesome *farissa* ritual of the 'Isâwîyya (above, note 106) and of the Maenads of the Thracian Dionysos clad in panther skins (above, note 105). The murders for which they were executed show that the Roman Senators were not necessarily misled by spurious evidence when they condemned for murder the participants in the Roman *Bacchanalia* celebrations (Livy, XXXIX, 8–13, etc.; Georg Wissowa in Pauly-Wissowa's *Realenzyklop.*, II, cols. 2722 f.). It is perfectly conceivable that somebody playing the role of 'Pentheus', the 'man of sorrows' torn to pieces, was actually rent asunder in the process and a testament of his faked in favour of the murderers (the forging of testaments was one of the counts of the indictment).

The hero of the great national epic of the Georgians, *Shota Rustaveli*, is 'The Man in the Panther-skin'—a knight named Tariel on a black horse, wearing over a long cloak the skin of a panther (*vep'hkhvi, i.e., felix pardus*) 'with the hair outside'. This archetypic story is explained in the introduction as 'the story of man enveloped in passion' (Mary Scott Wardrop, *The Man in the Panther Skin*, London (R. Asiatic Society), 1912, ch. II, p. 15).

In China, especially in the North, people believe in were-foxes who dwell in the borderland between the earth and the underworld. In their human form they appear as young and pretty girls—sometimes betraying their real nature by the possession of tails. Male were-foxes mate with women, were-vixens with men. In either case a morbid state results resembling that caused by the medieval *incubi* and *succubae*. Their animal shape becomes visible when they sleep or are under the influence of drink, of which they are as fond as the Maenads of Dionysos (H. A. Giles, *Strange Stories from a Chinese Studio*, London, 1880, I, pp. 32, 85, 163; N. B. Dennys, *Folklore of China*, London, 1876, pp. 61, 70; L. Wieger, *Folklore Chinois Moderne*, Sienhsien, 1909, pp. 11, 111, No. 56; p. 116, No. 57; pp. 147 ff., No. 79; p. 153, No. 81; p. 114, No. 86; p. 217, No. 114; p. 270, No. 151; p. 315, No. 175; J. M. de Groot, *Religious System of China*, Leyden, 1892, IV, pp. 188 f.).

The Jesuit father Leon Wieger (*Folklore Chinois Moderne*, Paris (Librairie Orientale Geuthner), 1908, No. 65, p. 126; No. 67, p. 128; No. 166, p. 127; No. 68, p. 128), has collected a number of Chinese stories concerning were-wolves: for instance, of a woodcutter attacked in the evening in a wood by a big wolf, who mounts a tree and hits the wolf's forehead with a cut of his axe. The wolf remains lying on the ground until dawn, then disappears. His traces lead to the door of the hut of a peasant, who is found with a cut across his forehead. His sons kill the peasant, who while expiring transforms himself again into a wolf.—A youth of twenty years falls ill and loses weight, because he sends out his soul night after night in the shape of a wolf devouring many village children. When his father kills him, he is transformed into a wolf.—The mother of General Wang-hau of Tayuan (Shansi), a fierce virago, rides on horseback, bow and arrows in her hand, through the forests, shooting bears, stags and hares. At the age of seventy she confines herself to her apartment and becomes subject to attacks of ungovernable rage.

One night the servants see a she-wolf emerging from her bed-room, which returns in the morning. Her husband is informed and has her watched. She asks for a stag to devour. She hears the servants guarding the locked door and disappears, breaking out through the trellis of the window (from a 9th-cent A.D. record). A man married a widow. She is found out to be a were-wolf (from a 10th-cent. record). In the province of Kwang-tung at Ye-chu the septuagenarian mother of a peasant changes into a were-wolf. Hair grows first on her arms, then on her body, which assumes vulpine curves; a tail appears, and finally a white she-wolf runs away from the house.

In Japan the were-fox superstition can be traced back to the 11th century A.D. *Nogitsone*, the 'wild fox', can assume any shape, but its reflexion in water is always that of a fox. The *Ninko-* or *Hoto Kitsune* fox prefers the shape of a beautiful girl. Men possessed by fox-demons run about yelping and eat only foxes' food, but the possessing fox-goblin may be exorcized (A. B. Mitford, *Tales of Old Japan*, London, 1871, *passim*; Lafcadio Hearn, *Glimpses of Unfamiliar Japan*, London, 1894, I, pp. 312 ff.; B. H. Chamberlain, *Things Japanese*, London, 1890, s.v. 'fox'). The Japanese term for lupinomania is *Kitsune-tanki* (H. B. Chamberlain, *op. cit.*).

The Chinese and Japanese were-vixen is an exact counter-part to the Thracian βασσάρα or 'vixen' of Dionysos (above, note 105) and to the Roman and Greek term *lupa* and λυκή, English 'bitch', for 'a harlot'; see Prudentius, *Contra Symmachum*, I, 107, 'rusticolae lupae intersalicta et densas sepes obscoena cubilia ineuntes' ['the country wenches couching obscenely among the willow-groves and thick bushes'].

Lupanar, 'she-wolves' den', 'she-wolves' earth' for a 'brothel' (Lactantius, *Div. inst.*, I, 20, 1 and Livy, I, 4, 7, say that the she-wolf who gave suck to the exposed twins Romulus and Remus was really a harlot. See Ovid, *Fasti*, ed. Sir J. G. Frazer, III, London, 1929, p. 14, note 1; E. S. MacCartney, 'Greek and Roman Lore of Animal-nursed infants', *Papers of the Michigan Academy of Arts and Letters*, IV, 1924, New York, 1925, pp. 50-60; A. H. Krappe, 'Acca Larentia', *Americ. Journ. of Archaeol.*, LXVI (1942), No. 4, p. 490; Eisler, *Orph.-Dionys. Myst.*, p. 400, note 3). In Longus' delightful novel *Daphnis and Chloë*, the innocent shepherd-boy is taught the *ars amandi* by a good-looking town-bred hussy, married to a peasant neighbour. The poet gives her the significant name *Lykainion*, 'little she-wolf' (Loeb ed., trans. George Thornley, rev. by J. M. Edmonds, London (Heinemann), 1916, p. 151—book III, ch. 15). The Athenian comic poet Kratinos (*Cheirones, Fragm.* 241; *Comic. Attic. fragm.*, ed. Kock, I, 87) called Pericles' famous, highly cultivated mistress Aspasia 'a bitchfaced harlot' (παλλακὴν κυνόπιδα).

In the Babylonian *Gilgamesh Epic* (tabl. II, col. III b, line 41) the Sun-god says to the hero Engidu, who has been lured away from his happy life with the beasts of the wild into the city and mourns his fate: 'Why, Engidu, dost thou curse the harlot? the harlot I have made to carry from thee' (that is to say she has become pregnant by seducing Engidu). 'I have clothed her with the pelt of a lion' (or 'dog'—the line is broken and the syllable -*bi* could be supplemented either [*lab*]-*bi* or [*kal*]-*bi*) 'and she is chasing across the desert.' Here too the harlot becomes the 'lady in the fur' and a homeless, nomad outcast. If the pelt is dog's skin, she becomes a kynanthropic 'bitch', if it is a lion's pelt, she becomes a lioness like those of the 'Isâwîyya brotherhood (above, p. 122, note 106).

The coarse Latin word *scortum*, 'pelt' for 'harlot', corresponds to the Dutch title '*het pelsken*', 'the peltlet', for Rubens' portrait of his wife in the nude wrapped in the fur, discussed above, note 26, p. 84.

In Attica the young maidens, or later a selection of them, had to serve in Munychia, in Brauron or in the Brauronian sanctuary of the hunting goddess Artemis—called Λυκεῖα 'the wolfish one'—in Troizênê (Pausan. II, 31, 4, 5)—a period of initiation or probation before their marriage known as ἄρκτεια (sc. δουλεία), 'bearish service' (*Schol.* Aristoph., *Lysistr.*, 646; Harpocrat., s.v. ἄρκτευσαι; Pausan. *Lex.* ap. Eustath., *Iliad*, II, 732, p. 331, 26 ff.; Apostol. VII, 10), during which they wore a special saffron yellow dress (κροκωτίς), said to represent the bear's pelt (*Schol.* Aristoph., *l.c.*; Suidas, s.v. ἄρκτος), in the same way as the woven and painted πάρδαλις of the Maenads represented the panther-skin or the surrogate painted dresses of the 'Isâwîyya stand in stead of the formerly worn, now unobtainable leopards' skins. During this period the girls are

known as the ἀρκτοί or 'she-bears' of the goddess and have to
assist at the sacrifice of a goat (Poll., VIII, 107). This sacrifice
too is called ἀρκτεύειν, 'act as a bear', and evidently symbolizes
the slaying of a goat by the she-bears of the goddess. The duty
of these virgin 'she-bears' may be compared with the obligation
of the twenty Λυκηάδες κόραι or 'wolfish maidens' who had to
carry—presumably according to a rota—the water needed in
the Athenian sanctuary of Apollo Lykeios in the Ilissos valley
(Callimachus, *Fragm. anonym.*, 197, p. 745, Schneider; Hesychius
s.v. Λυκηάδες κόραι). The obligation for the maidens to serve as
female *ber-serker* the two lupine hunting divinities Artemis
Lykeiê and Apollo Lykeios is a survival of the primeval state of
affairs when the females of the hunting tribe joined the males
in the chase until they became mothers, bound to the home by
the burden of childbearing and the duties of motherhood (see
the quotation from Chaucer below, p. 158). The 'nymphs' hunting with Artemis are these as yet unburdened maiden 'brides'.
The story of Kallistô, that is the 'most beautiful' of these nymphs
of Artemis, daughter of the wolf-hero or werewolf Lykaôn
(above note 112) (Hesiod *ap.* Eratosth., *Catast. relig.*, ed. Robert,
p. 50) and mother of Arkas, the bear-hero and ancestor of the
Arcadians, the bear-tribe, changed by Artemis into a she-bear
as a punishment for having lost her virginity to Zeus who
seduced her in the shape of Artemis (Eratosthenes, *Catast.*, 1,
pp. 50 ff. Robert), is most revealing. Evidently the service to
Artemis of the maidens dressed up as she-bears, which had to
be performed 'before marriage', was interpreted in a later age
as an atonement to the virgin goddess for the loss of virginity
in the period of unbridled licence and promiscuity allowed in
many primitive societies to the unmarried young girls. (Herodot., V, 6, on the Thracians; many parallels are given by
Thurnwald, art. 'Promiskuität' in Ebert's *Reallexik. d. Vorgesch.*,
X, p. 320, col. b, 3; Malinowski, *Argonauts of the Western Pacific*,
London, 1922, p. 53). According to Apollodorus (3, 8, 2, 3;
Tzetzês to Lycophr., 478, ed. Franz, p. 343; Charon Lampsac.,
ibid., p. 480) the seducer of Kallistô and father of Arkas is not
Zeus but Apollo, probably the Apollo *Lykeios* to whose *Lykeion*,
Lyceum or 'wolf's den' the Λυκηάδες κόραι or 'maiden she-wolf
daughters' had to carry the water.

As to Artemis herself, the 'virgin goddess' and the 'Persian Artemis' Anaïtis (*Anahita*), called 'the she-wolf' by the Magi (Porphyry, *De abstin.*, IV, 16), described in the *Avesta* (*Yasht*, V, 126–129) as wearing an otter's pelt, they are the ancestral prototypes of the barren women, hunting with the male hunters, *berserker* or werewolves, because they are not burdened with childbearing and tied to the home by the task of rearing the young of the pack.

> *I am, thou woost, yet of thy company*
> *A maide, and love hunting and venerye*
> *And for to walken in the wodes wild*
> *And noght to ben a wyf and be with child*
>
>   (*Chaucer*).

The strange assertion of Dr. S. Zuckerman, *Functional Affinities of Man, Monkeys and Apes*, London, 1933, p. 159: 'Hunting as an occupation of women is practically non-existent among the peoples of the world', must have caused a good deal of amusement, at least among English readers of this otherwise excellent book. To the quotations from Sir Osbert Sitwell's and Miss Nancy Mitford's books printed below, pp. 220 ff., in note 200, I should like to add here the following lines from a letter of the Hon. Edward Stanley to his wife, dated Black Mount, 30 Sept. 1847 (Nancy Mitford, *The Ladies of Alderley*, London (Chapman and Hall), 1938, p. 166, No. 200): 'We had a splendid day yesterday and killed ten stags; three of them were brought to bay by the hounds and the Duchess (of Montrose) shot them all with her rifle, which has made a proud woman of her and a famous paragraph in the papers when Her Grace will probably find some observations on her dress as well as her pursuits.' (See *ibid.*, p. 165, No. 199, Black Mount, 28 Sept. 1847: 'The Duchess wears plaid trousers and short petticoats about half way down below her knees.') 'She seems good-humoured and unaffected, but I fear may cause that worthy man the Duke some uneasiness as she is quite at home amongst the hornéd beasts of the forest.'

Xenophon, *Cyneg.*, XIII, 18, gives a list of famous hunting-women such as Procris, Atalanta and others. Dido rides out hunting with Aeneas (Vergil, *Aen.*, IV, 130 ff.). The Spartans sent their boys and girls hunting at early dawn, with but little provision, so that hunger should make them eager to kill their quarry (Justin, *Hist.*, III, 3). Since early pregnancies would obviously incapacitate the girls for this and all other sports, they were expected to preserve their virginity and kept away from the boys by their female pack-leader. This is the real prototype of the mythical virgin hunting-goddess and her virgin 'nymphs' or 'brides'. Lesbian relations within this pack of hunting maidens explain the story of Zeus or Apollo seducing Kallistô, 'the fairest' among them, after assuming the shape of the hunting goddess. All these features presuppose the chastity taboos and marriage rites of the later patriarchal society. In the original matriarchal pack, ignorant of the part played by the male in the procreation of offspring, the hunting 'she-wolves', 'vixens' or 'she-bears' or 'bitches' were simply the barren females hunting with the males.

It is not generally realized that the word 'harridan', now used for a haggard, shrewish woman, meant originally 'vixen'. On 12 April, 1945, Lord Geddes wrote to *The Times* about certain cruel old women maltreating children who were once 'charming and delightful characters and understanding mothers'... 'It was observation of this change of character that convinced earlier generations that some women had sold their souls to Satan and become witches. The truth about such old sadists is that the supra-granular cortex of the cerebrum has regressed. Hotels in safe areas have for the last years housed hundreds of these harridans. (Note well this ancient word indicating the immemorial recognition of the type!) The word is just like 'bitch' (above p. 155), the expression of an archetypal reminiscence. The Armenians who believe in werewolves (*mardagails*) know these 'harridans'. They say that sinful women are sometimes forced by a spirit to don a wolf-skin and become wolves. Soon the wolf-nature grows in them, they devour their children, then those of relatives, then those of strangers. Doors and locks fly open before them by night. In the morning the skin is doffed (A. F. L. M. von Haxthausen, *Transcaucasia*, London, 1854, p. 359). About twenty years ago the *Théatre du Grand Guignol* in Paris ran a gruesome play, *L'Étrangleuse*, dramatizing the court proceedings against a nursery-maid who had strangled babies under her charge in such a way that no evidence could be brought against her.

The Rev. Dr. MacCulloch has shown conclusively that the werewolf belief is found all over the world, just as we should expect, if it goes back to a mutation in the *modus vivendi*, Greek δίαιτα, our 'diet', of a part of mankind in the palaeolithic period.

117. LYCANTHROPY AS A MENTAL DISEASE

The term *folie louvière* was introduced by J. de Nynauld, *De la lycanthropie*, Louvain, 1596, as a translation of the Greek λυκανθρωπία or κυνανθρωπία, described by Marcellus Sidêtês in the poem discussed by Roscher, *op. cit.*, above, note 110; Robert Burton, *Anatomy of Melancholy*, ed. princ., Oxford, 1638; ed. London, 1836, pp. 88 f.; L. F. Calmeil, *De la folie*, Paris, 1845, I, p. 74; E. Parish, *Hallucinations and Illusions*, London, 1897, pp. 40 f.; D. Hack Tuke, *Dictionary of Psychol. Medicine*, London, 1892, I, p. 434; vol. II, p. 752; Leonardo Bianchi, *A Textbook of Psychiatry*, trans. Macdonald, London, 1906, pp. 323, 597, 689. Ancient physicians (Galen, *Peri melancholias*, ed. Kühn, XIX, p. 719, derived from Marcellus of Sidê; Oribasius, VIII, 10; Förster, *Physiognomonici Graeci*, II, p. 282; Aëtius, ed. Venet. 1534, p. 104 B; Paulus Aeginetês, ed. Basil, 1538, p. 66; Joannes Actuarius, ed. Ideler, *Physici et Medici minores*, II, p. 387 and p. 282) insist on dryness of the tongue and inordinate thirst as among the symptoms. This, of course, is well known as a feature of *rabies canina* in human beings bitten by rabid dogs or wolves, and driven themselves to bite others. But a similar inhibition of salivation and lacrimation can also be produced by small doses of hyoscyamine (henbane) or stramonium, known to have been used by witches to drug themselves and produce soaring and flying dreams (MacCulloch, *op. cit.*, p. 215, col. b). The statement that the lupinomaniacs walk by preference in February (Bourquelot, *op. cit.*, p. 209) and haunt the cemeteries at that time must be compared with the fact that the Roman feast of the *Lupercalia* was celebrated by the *luperci* (below, p. 254, Append. II) in February.

A recent case is recorded by Alberta Hannum, *Spin a Silver Coin*, London (Michael Joseph), 1947, p. 76: 'There was a Navaho man in the vicinity of the neighbouring trading post at

Klagaton whom the other Navahos feared with a fear almost
worse than that of death. He was called the Werewolf. He was
believed to be able to turn himself into a wolf at night, and raid
their flocks. Also he was supposed to do the horrible and dig up
dead bodies and rob them of their jewels. And it was true that
he was unaccountably rich in sheep, and it probably also was
true that he robbed graves, for he possessed a great amount of
silver and jewellery, some of which was unique and recogniz-
able by the family hall-mark. But since the fear of the werewolf
goes back as far in the Navaho tribal tradition as the fear of
witchcraft itself, any white person could understand how a local
witch could exploit that fear indefinitely and unbeatably.

'But the fear of this particular witch, that increased now with
Mary in mind, was worse than that. The real terror of the
nocturnal wanderer was an unshakable notion that he killed his
human victims and devoured them—and the victims of the
werewolf were usually women.

'The belief in the werewolf is a common and ancient one
with the Navahos—the belief in a human wolf, in a man disguised in animal skins who goes about at night practising witchcraft. Witchcraft, anywhere that it is believed in, feeds upon
human fears and contentions. And sexual pathologists put down
this particular idea of a man changing himself into an animal
for cannibalistic purposes to the desire to devour both the loved
and the hated objects, and see in the werewolf's lust the symbolism of repressed sexual regression.

'And in the mad, wild way that thought of the worst seems to
spring involuntarily to the human mind, horror tales began
springing up like wildfire around the trading post—of werewolves and were-bears meeting in the night and travelling so
fast none can catch them but leaving tracks like paws, and looking down into hogan roof-holes and knowing how to make
people sick. Sometimes the wolf would knock four times, or
sometimes the people inside the hogan would only hear the
mud falling from the roof and know it was the wolf there. But
always, with or without warning, the wolf appeared with
paralyzing slowness to its victims—peeping around the corner
of the door blanket, or letting just its eyes show for a while over
the hole in the roof, and then slowly the rest of him. Wolves

caused sickness. That was the way tuberculosis came. A wolf would throw something down on to the hogan fire to make it flare and stink, and the evil fumes would get into the lungs.

'If they caught their victims out in the open they would throw a powder on them, which would kill them slowly. It was a powder made from digging into graves or the tongue of a girl and the finger of a man.

'Usually the young traders tried to help straighten out the problems around the post without offering any radical changes in the way of Navaho natural life. But this time, because Joe was so distraught, they tried to tell him that there was no such thing as witchcraft—that if people died from such practices it was their own fear which killed them. That might be so. But there was no arguing the fact that the man from Klagaton *did* sometimes dress himself up in skins at night and attack women —and that it was a screen for sexual abnormality was no less reason to worry about the missing Mary.'

118. LYCANTHROPY IN LITERATURE AND LORE

In Webster's *Duchess of Malfy* one of the murderous brothers goes mad and imagines himself to be a wolf:

> *... Two nights since*
> *One met the duke 'bout midnight in a lane*
> *Behind Saint Mark's Church, with the leg of a man*
> *Upon his shoulder; and he howled fearfully,*
> *Said he was a wolf, only the difference*
> *Was, a wolf's skin was hairy on the outside,*
> *His on the inside.*

Wier, *De praestigiis daemonum*, lib. IV, c. 23, describes the case of a peasant near Padua who in A.D. 1541 became a *lupo manaro* (above, p. 149, note 116), stating that he had grown 'wolf's hair', but 'turned inside under the skin'. See Montague Summers, *The Werewolf*, London (Kegan Paul), 1933, p. 175, note 91, on Norse *hamrammr*, 'skin turned inside out', and Latin *versipellis*, 'werewolf'.

In Dan. iv. 25–33 it is said that king Nebuchadnezzar '. . . was driven from men and did eat grass as oxen and his body was wet with the dew of heaven, till his hairs were grown like eagles' (down) and his nails like birds' (claws)'. There is no reason to doubt the historicity of an access of melancholic madness in the life of this king, since his own inscriptions (*Keilschr. Bibl.*, III, 2, pp. 10–70) politely record a four years' suspension of interest in public affairs (Hugo Winckler, *Altorient. Forsch.*, II, p. 214; Stade-Holzmann, *Gesch. d. Volkes Israel*, II, 324 ff.; C. H. W. Johns, *Encycl. Bibl.*, 3771; Schrader, 'Die Sage vom Wahnsinn Nebukadnezars', *Jahrb. f. prot. Theol.*, VII, 1881, pp. 618 ff.).

As Wilhelm Roscher (*op. cit.* above, note 110, pp. 15 and 30) has shown, this bovine form of therioanthropy is not without parallels in ancient tradition. Ovid, *Metam.*, VI, 363 f., with the commentary of Lactantius Placidus, *ad loc.*, mentions the transformation of the ladies (*matrones*) of Cos into cows as a penitence for having exalted their own beauty above that of the goddess Aphrodite. Similarly, the daughters of king Proitos of Argos roam the country naked, believing themselves to be transformed into cows (Aelian, *Var. hist.*, III, 42), according to Hesiod, because they had refused to be initiated into the mysteries of Dionysus (Apollod., II, 2, 2). To cure them, the prophet and healer Melampous (='Blackfoot', probably one of the priests of Dodona who are called in Homer ἀνιπτόποδες, 'never washing their feet', so as not to remove the earth of the country settled by them from their soles) had them chased by the strongest young men, roaring and dancing after them over mountains and valleys, until they fell down exhausted and came to their senses, with the exception of the eldest among them who died from the effect of the cure. This mimetic chase can now be seen to be a close parallel to the whipping of the Roman matrons by the *Luperci* (below, p. 256, Append. II).

According to Hesiod (*Catalogues frgm.* 41, 12 Marksch.) the madness of Proitos' daughters was nymphomania. According to this version their bovine therioanthropy has to be compared with the story of the Cretan queen Pasiphaë who entered a wooden cow so as to be raped by the bull with which she had fallen in love (Apollod., III, 1, 4; Diod., 4, 77; Libanii *Narr.* 15 (Westermann, 379, 30); *Schol.* Eurip. *Hippolytus*, 887; Hygin., *Fab.*, 40; *Mythogr. Vatic.*, 1, 43; Philo, *De spec. leg.*, 7; Dio Chrysost. *De philos.* (71), p. 626 M.; Philostephanos in *Schol.* to

Iliad, 2, 145; Agatharchides, *De mare Erythr.*, frg. 7; .Vergil, *Bucol.*, 6, 46–60; Ovid, *Ars amandi*, 1, 289–326). In this story the bull-lover is no less a human masquerading as a bull than Pasiphaë is a woman taking her place, for the purpose of the magic union, in a wooden cow, such as the surviving idols of this shape representing the Egyptian goddess Hat-hôr (*Gazette des Beaux Arts*, Paris, 1907, 2ᵉ sem., p. 269; Ranke, *Altorient. Texte u. Bilder*, Tübingen (Mohr), 1909, fig. 108). The combination of nymphomania and bovine therioanthropy of the daughters of Proitos—said to have infected all the other women of Argos (Serv. on Virg., *Ecl.*, VI, 48; Pausanias, II, 18, 4; Herod., 9, 34)—is easily understandable. Women restrained in their former matriarchal erotic liberty by the possessive restrictions of the patriarchal family would subconsciously envy the freedom of the cows in the roaming cattle-herds. I was told only a few years ago by a girl of sixteen who had developed neurotic symptoms under the over-affectionate attentions of a dreaded father trying to keep her away from the society of all young men, that she had dreamt of 'waking up one morning as a white heifer grazing with the famous pedigree cattle on a neighbour's estate' and enjoying the idea that 'now she could stray as she pleased'.

A. von Schrenck-Notzing, *Die Suggestionstherapie bei Krankheitserscheinungen des Geschlechtslebens*, Stuttgart (Enke), 1892, p. 9, reports the case of a female patient who imagined in the course of her auto-erotic activities that she was being served by a stallion. This may explain the horse-tails worn by the otherwise naked Sileni and Satyres in the Bacchic orgies.

There is, finally, the story of the daughters of Pandareus, mentioned in Homer's *Odyssey*, XX, 66 ff., of whom the scholiast (Roscher, *Lex. d. Mythol.*, III, 1, col. 1500; *id. Kynanthropie*, pp. 3 ff., 62 ff., 1500 ff.;) says that Zeus afflicted them with the disease known as κύων, 'the dog', because their father had stolen the golden dog of Zeus. According to Roscher this is not the facial spasm (περὶ τὸν γνάθον σπασμώδης πάθος, Simplic. *ap.* Hesych. ed. Schmidt, s.v. κύων; τὸ κατὰ προσῶπον πάθος, Galen, 8, p. 573 Kühn; *ibid.*, 18 B, 930; Aretaeus, pp. 85 and 90 Kühn; *ibid.*, p. 459; cf. *Rhein. Mus.*, 1898, pp. 169 ff.), but the terrible kynanthropic or lycanthropic melancholic mania, known to the

Arab physicians Ali ibn Abbas and Ibn Sina (Avicenna), l.
III, p. 315, as *kotrob* (Roscher, *op. cit.*, p. 20).

In the case of king Nebuchadnezzar, the great warrior-king
—said in Dan. ii. 38 to have ruled 'over the beasts of the field
and the fowls of heaven wherever the children of men dwell'—
it is perfectly conceivable that he suffered from a cyclothymic
manic-depressive psychosis, the elation of a 'Caesarian' megalo-
mania of the divinized world-ruler being succeeded by a
depression in which he developed a sense of guilt and responsibility for all the blood shed at his behest and wanted to return
from the accursed state of a blood-stained predatory werewolf or
lion-man to the innocence of the grazing cattle. The case is quite
analogous to that of the neurotic individualist intellectual who
dreams of restoring 'the gibbon' (above, p. 44, and note 205).

If only there were a reliable eye-witness account of the story
of Hitler 'biting the carpet' in his accesses of rage, the problem
would arise whether these carpets represented for him the hairy
coat of the living animals into which the 'Isâwîyya 'lions' put
their teeth or the grass which the despondent king Nebuchadnezzar ate. If the stories about Hitler's rages are true, they
would appear to have been manic lycanthropic states and not
melancholic bouts of repentance as were the depressions of
Nebuchadnezzar. If the accounts are both invented, they have
both sprung from archetypal depths of the storytellers' unconscious race-memory and not from the archetypal minds of the
doubtless paranoic subjects of the stories in question.

119. Hack Tuke, *op. cit.* (note 117), II, p. 754, left col.: 'a
typical case in the asylum of Maréville under the care of
M. Morel', reported *Études Cliniques*, II, p. 58: 'He trembled and
exclaimed: "See this mouth, it is the mouth of a wolf, these are
the teeth of a wolf. I have cloven feet, see the long hairs which
cover my body" (see below, note 158), 'let me run into the woods
and you shall shoot me."' The man's insistence on his—real or
imaginary—wolf's teeth is most revealing in view of the change
from a taurodont to a cynodont denture which has actually
occurred in the course of evolution. See J. R. Marett, *Race, Sex
and Environment, A Study of Mineral Deficiencies in Human Evolution*,
London (Hutchinson), 1936, p. 205.

Simon Gontard, *Histoires admirables*, I, p. 80, tells the case of a naked man covered with hair, found near Compiègne crouching over the remains of four animals he had torn to pieces, emitting bestial sounds. Brought into the presence of king Charles IX he attacked the king's dog with his teeth—presumably the case Lord Northcliffe had in mind when he said, 'If a dog bites a man, it is not news. But if a man bites a dog it is news.'

120. *Dictionary of Psychological Medicine*, London, 1892, I, p. 434; II, p. 752.

121. Leonardo Bianchi, *A Textbook of Psychiatry*, trans., Macdonald, London, 1906, pp. 323, 597, 689. See also L. F. Calmeil, *De la folie*, Paris, 1845, I, p. 74.

While this lecture was being prepared for the press the Rome Correspondent of the *Daily Telegraph* (15 July 1949) cabled: 'Howls coming from the bushes in gardens in the centre of Rome last night brought a police patrol to what seemed a "werewolf." Under the full moon they found a young man, Pasquale Rosini, covered in mud, digging in the ground with his finger-nails and howling. On being taken to hospital Rosini said that for three years he had regularly lost consciousness at periods of the full moon and had found himself wandering the streets at night, driven by uncontrollable instincts. He was sent to a clinic for observation.'

122. See above, note 117, on the thirst characteristic of human hydrophobia attributed to lycanthropes.

123. Terrible outbreaks of canine rabies may be and have been caused by rabid wolves biting tame dogs. See Colin Mathews, *Antiquity*, XVII, 1943, pp. 13 f. In Puy de Dôme in Dec. 1839, 28 persons were bitten, 12 died of hydrophobia. In 1866, 18 persons were bitten in Carmarthen, most of whom died. In 1866 Pasteur treated 19 Russian peasants from the Smolensk district who had been bitten by a rabid wolf, saving 16 of them.

The Evening News of 17 Sept. 1947 printed a Reuter cable:

'Foxes, maddened by thirst owing to the drought in Poland, attacked people on the roads near Cracow, said Warsaw radio to-day.'

124. The *Völsunga Saga* relates how Sigmund and Sinfyotl find two men fast asleep, wearing magic golden rings; suspended above them are two wolves' pelts, which they take off every fifth day, putting them on again by means of the said rings. The two Völsungs don the wolves' pelts, become werewolves and kill numerous people until they succeed in shedding the skins and burning them. Sometimes a mere belt of wolf's skin, wolf's hair or leather works the transformation.

125. This is what Dolôn—a name equivalent to 'the cunning one'—does before starting on his nocturnal spying prowl in the 10th book of the *Iliad*, v. 334, known as the *Dolôneia*. On his head he puts, curiously enough, not the λυκείη or 'wolf's head helmet', but an ἰκτιδείη or 'marten's head cap' (*Iliad*, X, 335, 458). See Gernet, 'Dolon le Loup', *Mélanges F. Cumont*, Bruxelles 1939, pp. 189 ff.; also Pausan., 6, 7, 11, on Lykas (codd. *A-lybanta*), the evil hero of Temesa: λύκου δὲ ἀμπισχετο δέρμα ἐσθητα ['he put on a wolf's pelt as his vestment']. In French the word *loup* denotes not only 'the wolf', but also a black velvet vizor worn over the upper part of the face by masqueraders.

126. See the Rev. S. A. MacCulloch, *Encyclop. of Rel. and Eth.*, XI, p. 590, col. b, No. 5 'Vampire and Werwolf'.

127. THE GERMAN WEREWOLF ORGANIZATION, AND THE MAFIA
According to *The Times* and *Manchester Guardian* News Service from Stockholm, 3 April 1945, quoting a Berlin report, the 'Werwolves' were organized by a certain Fritz Klappe at Halle in 1923 on the model of the Sicilian *Mafia*. Statistics of their exploits were compiled in Dr. E. J. Gumbel's books on political murder in Germany between the two wars (*Zwei Jahre Mord*, Berlin (Verlag Neues Vaterland), 1921, Preface by Prof. G. F. Nicolai; *Vier Jahre politischer Mord*, Berlin (Malik), 1922; *Verschwörer*, Vienna (Malik), 1924, p. 65, on the *Stahlhelm*—the

nationalist war-veterans' organization—and the 'Werewolves' intended to absorb civilian conspirators under the black flag adorned with the white skull and crossbones; p. 73 on the corresponding youth-leagues of 'Eagles' and 'Falcons'; cf. below p. 223, note 213, and see *op. cit.*, p. 56, on a number of group-portraits of the male and female members of these organizations taken together in the nude, found when one of their leaders, a bookseller Grenz in Oldenburg, was arrested by the Weimar Government; cf. below, note 233, on the German nudist movement). These 'Werewolves' were resuscitated by Dr. Goebbels (*The Times*, 28 May, 1945, p. 5, last col., by 'Military Correspondent lately in Germany') as an underground resistance movement after the Second World War. They operated a 'secret' broadcasting station of their own in 1945. They murdered Franz Oppenhoff, anti-Nazi Roman Catholic Mayor of Aachen, and four other burgomasters, and boasted of other political assassinations, even in U.S.A. prison camps. Their chief was Otto Skorzeny (Curt Riess, *The Leader*, 26 May 1945) leader of the airborne commando raid which liberated Mussolini, under the supreme command of the journalist Pflugk-Harttung, a son of the well-known historian of that name. With or under him served General Dalüge, successor to the assassinated Heidrich in Bohemia, Dr. Ernst Kaltenbrunner, former head of the Nazi security police intelligence office, Gauleiter Frank and a déclassé Count Bassewitz (*Daily Mail*, 5 April 1945 from Stockholm). According to Walter Farr, *Daily Mail*, 20 April 1945, their badge was a black armband with skull and crossbones and S.S. in silver. According to the *News Chronicle* of 19 April 1945 a band of female werewolves with the same badge and a *W* below the skull and crossbones was organized in Leipzig to pour scalding water from the windows on troops passing below them. A considerable number of soldiers of the French occupation army were killed by 'werwolves' in the Grand Duchy of Baden (*Daily Mail*, 29 August, 1945). *Picture Post*, 18 May, 1946, printed a letter from W. E. Lawrence of Gateshead reporting that a wreath of flowers recently laid on the 'secret' grave of Mussolini bore the inscription 'We shall avenge you. The wolves are awaiting their chance to spring'. Some further details on the German 'werewolves' are published in H. R. Trevor

Roper's *The Last Days of Hitler*, London (Macmillan), 1947, p. 50. Their central office was controlled by one Prützmann, 'vain, idle and boastful'. . . . At Nuremberg Speer and Fritzsche said the 'werewolves' were under Bormann's ultimate control (p. 51, note 1). In Austrian Tyrol the Americans had trouble with 'werewolves' down to May 1945 (*The Times*, 26 May 1945). The Führer's address at Rastenburg was, until 20 Nov. 1945, '*Wolfsschanze*' (Diary of Hitler's personal servant Heinz Linge, quoted by Roper, p. 57). Speer feared they would murder him (p. 123).

Lützow's 'Free Corps' raised against Napoleon I in 1813 at the start of the wars of liberation—a 'resistance organization' as it would now be called—in which the German poet Körner served and met his death, was known as *Lützow's wilde verwegene Jagd*' ('Wild Hunt'), in transparent allusion to the nightly host following the '*Wilde Jäger*', Wodan, hunting by night with his wolves. The black uniform of the National Socialist S.S. (*Schutz-Staffeln*), the skull and cross-bones on their caps—taken from the regimental badge of the Prussian Black Hussars (*Totenkopf-husaren*)—are all reminiscent of the nightly terror of the 'wild hunt' and of the skeletons of the dead following in the wake of the 'Wild Hunter' in the clangour of stormy nights.

128. Rauschnigg, *Hitler Speaks*, London (Thornton Butterworth), 1939, p. 247. The authenticity of these words—widely discussed in Germany at the time—is beyond doubt. The Führer simply gloated on what he loved to call the 'brutal', *i.e.* inhuman animal character of the political measures he was going to carry through or had already resorted to. The very title 'Führer' denotes the leader of the hunting lupine pack of his followers.

The title of M. van Blankenstein's little book *The Wolf as Neighbour*, London, 1944, alludes only to the Aesopian fable of the wolf and the lamb. See also W. R. Inge, *End of an Age*, London (Putnam), 1948, 'Philosophy of the Wolf State'.

129. This is, of course, impossible by definition. But there is the phenomenon of enjoying one's own suffering, known as *algolagnia*, discussed above, p. 76, note 5.

130. INDEPENDENCE OF THE WOLF

As to the 'independence' of the wild wolf and its alleged contempt for the tamed dog, see Alfred de Vigny's poem, *La Mort du Loup, de deux grands Loups-cerviers et de deux Louvetaux*, easily accessible in the *Oxford Book of French Verse*, ed. St. John Lucas, Oxford (Clarendon Press), 1907, pp. 299 f., No. 233, especially p. 301:

> . . . *sa louve et ses fils qui tous trois*
> *Avaient voulu l'attendre et comme je le crois*
> *Sans ses deux louvetaux, la belle et sombre veuve,*
> *Ne l'eut pas laissé seul subir la grande épreuve.*
> *Mais son devoir était de les sauver, afin*
> *Du pouvoir leur apprendre à bien souffrir la faim,*
> *À ne jamais entrer dans le pacte des villes,*
> *Que l'homme a fait avec les animaux serviles,*
> *Qui chassent devant lui, pour avoir le coucher,*
> *Les premiers possesseurs du bois et des rochers.*

> *Hélas, ai-je pensé, malgré ce grand nom d'Hommes*
> *Que j'ai honte de nous, débiles que nous sommes!*
> *Comment on doit quitter la vie et tous ces maux,*
> *C'est vous qui le savez, sublîmes animaux!*
> *À voir ce qu'on fut sur la terre et ce qu'on y laisse,*
> *Seul le silence est grand, tout le reste est faiblesse.*
> *Ah, je t'ai bien compris, sauvage voyageur,*
> *Et ton dernier regard m'est allé jusqu'au cœur.*
> *Il disait: si tu peux, fais que ton âme arrive*
> *A force de rester studieuse et pensive*
> *Jusqu'à ce haut degré de stoïque fierté,*
> *Où naissant dans les bois j'ai tout d'abord monté.*
> *Gémir, pleurer, prier est également lâche.*
> *Fais enérgiquement ta longue et lourde tâche*
> *Puis, après, comme moi, souffre et meurs, sans parler.*

131. See above, p. 152, note 116.

132. THE MAENADS AND THEIR FUR ATTIRE

The Maenads, Lyssades, 'rabid' or 'raving women', or 'cours-

ing bitches' (κύνες δρομάδες) in the *thiasos* of Dionysos Zagreus—
the equivalent of a *thaîfa* of the 'Isâwîyya, above, note 105—
wearing panthers' pelts—the παρδαληφόρος Μαινάς of Sophocles
(*fr.* 16; *Schol.* to Aristoph., *Aves*, 943)—are first represented on
the vase-painting by Amasis, an artist with an Egyptian name,
once in the collection of the Duc de Luynes (reprod. after de
Luynes, *Vases*, No. 3 in Roscher's *Myth. Lex.*, II, 2, col. 2259,
fig. 1). The panther was never native to Greece in historic times.
Oppianus (*Cyneg.* 4, 305) says in so many words that the tradition about the metamorphosis of the Maenads into panthers is
Libyan. In other words, it comes from the African regions
where we still find the ritual masquerade of the 'panther-men'
(*nmoura*, above, note 84). In Egypt statues of priests clad in
panthers' skins have been found in Heliopolis (Erman-Ranke,
Aegypten, 2nd ed., Tübingen (Mohr), 1923, p. 337, note 9;
Eisler, *Weltenmantel*, Munich (Beck), 1910, p. 106, fig. 30,
reprod. of a statue now in Turin). 'Leopard-men' or 'wer-
leopards' are still a plague in various regions of Africa (see
above, p. 152, note 116). The original native costume of the
'raving women' was presumably the pelt of the lynx from
the Othrys mountains (Aristophanes, *Ploutos*, 732 ff.), from the
Pangaios and Kittos (Xenoph., *Cyneg.*, 11), still found in the
Greek mountain fastnesses and known there as ρῆσος (Held-
reich, *Faune de Grèce*, Index s.v.). This explains, by the way,
the tradition recorded by Philostratus (*Heroic.*, p. 680) of the
mythical Thracian hero Rhêsos: 'when he hunts, wild boars,
gazelles and other game hurry voluntarily to his altar and offer
themselves as sacrifice'. Pliny (*N.H.*, VIII, 70) describes the
northern lynx as similar to a wolf, but with panther's spots
(*effigie lupi pardorum maculis*). The spotted furs worn by the
Maenads shown on pictorial representations may very well be
meant for the pelt of *Felis pardina* Oken or *Lynx pardella* Miller,
the pard-lynx, still found in southern Europe (Steier in Pauly-
Wissowa, *Suppl.* III, Stuttgart, 1927, col. 2476, lines 33–38).
The 'raving women' called *bassarae* or *bassarides*, 'vixens' or
'vixens' daughters' (above, note 116), were obviously clad in
fox-pelts just as their leader Dionysos *Bassareus* (below, note
133) was wrapped in and wore boots made of or lined with
fox-fur (*bassarae*). The pelt of the wild cat which lived in ancient

Greece as well as in Italy (Pauly-Wiss., XI, col. 53, line 14) was worn by the wild *'Fanggen'* or *'Wildfanggen'* ('game-catching' hoydens) of the Tyrolean forests (Mannhardt, *Antike Feld- und Waldkulte*, pp. 140–152), whose name is paralleled by that of the Maenad in hunting dress *Thêrô* on a polychrome vase (*Mon. del Istit.*, 10, 23). These fur-wraps are a typical Greek hunters' costume, as we can see on the so-called François vase (*Wiener Vorlegeblätter*, 1888, pl. II, Roscher's *Myth. Lex.*, II, 2, col. 2610) where some of the heroes chasing the Calydonian boar—inscribed *Meleagros* and *Asmêtos*—are seen in this attire. It should, finally, be noted that the Maenad is also poetically called λυσσάς (Eurip., *Herc. fur.*, 1024; Manetho, 5, 338; Plutarch *Mor.*, p. 22 A and elsewhere), the woman affected by λύσσα, 'madness', a word meaning originally lupine rabies (*lykja, see Lagerkranz, *Zur griech. Lautgeschichte*, pp. 88 f., where previous literature is given; Eisler, *Orph.-Dionys. Myst.*, p. 288, notes 1–3). The donning of the wolf's, lynx's or fox's pelt and the 'right raving' (ὀρθῶς μανῆναι, Plato, *Phaedr.*, 244 D, explained Eisler, *l.c.*) followed by the shedding of the wild animal's fur was considered a magic purification from rabies and paranoiac lycanthropy, not clearly distinguished from one another by ancient medicine.

Conversely, personified rabies and lupine madness *'Lyssa'* is said to celebrate the ecstatic Dionysian rites (Λύσσα βαχχεύει Eurip., *Herc. Fur.*, 899). Sophocles (*Fragm.*, 844, 4) speaks of Lyssa as a Maenad (Λύσσα μαινάς).

133. See above, p. 128, notes 108 and 110.

134. See above, p. 151, note 116.

135. A. B. Cook, *Zeus*, Cambridge Univ. Press, pp. 63 ff., 654. Kruse's art. 'Lykaion' in Pauly-Wissowa-Kroll, XIII, 2, cols. 2235–2246. Representations of this god with a wolf's pelt after Overbeck, *Kunstmythologie*, II, 1, 266.

136. THE WILD HUNT
Jakob Grimm, *Mythol.*, p. 872, *Wörterbuch*, IV, 2, 2205, *Das wütende Heer*, 'the raging host'—analogous to Greek *Mainades*—

French *Mesnie Furieuse*; Mannhardt, *Baumkultus der Germanen*, Berlin (Bornträger), 1875, pp. 82 ff., 105, 112, 115, 116, 121, 122 ff., 137, 145, 149, 150, 151, 251, *ibid.*, p. 85, about Frau Gode, Holla and Perchta's 'wild hunt'. The silliness of the old mythological theories explaining the descriptions of the 'Wild Hunt' as imaginative interpretations of the noises of the storms blowing through the forests, passes belief. As if country-bred country-dwellers would ever mistake the familiar sound of high winds in the trees for those of hounds and hunters chasing their game through the woods! No anthropologist will doubt for a moment the far more realistic explanation that, in defiance of the strictest game laws, poachers' gangs drove their quarry by night with torches and hounds in the old primitive way through the forest, closing in upon it before dawn and feasting in the gruesome archetypal way. The fact that they would not hesitate to chase and kill human beings who got in their way, spread a terror through the countryside, which the members of the 'wild hunt' were but too glad to exaggerate by the most horrible tales they helped to spread. Like the witches assembling in their covens, these nightly poachers naturally consisted of people who had remained addicted to their ancient pagan cults. Whether they were known as 'Wodan's hunt' or 'Arthur's chase'—ἀρκτοῦρος from Homeric οὖρος 'watcher', 'guard', 'he who watches the bear', 'the bear-stalker'—makes very little difference. *Perchta* is but 'she with the beard'; the *Perchten*, '*schöne*' or '*schiarche*' (fair or ugly) are just poachers disguised with false beards and other masks and not 'personifications of storm- and thunder-clouds', as the armchair mythologists imagined.

137. *De primo frigore*, 18; *De mulierum virtute*, 13, p. 249e.

138. See the *stela* of Melnik now in the Museum of Brussels. It shows the Thracian hunter-god spearing a boar in the midst of a tangle of wild vines, such as can still be seen growing in the valley of the Vardar. The grapes are harvested by *Sileni* ('wine-men' from Thracian *zilai, zeilai, zelas*, Lagercrantz, *Indogerm. Forsch.*, XXV, 363; Kretzschmer, *Glotta*, II, 398; IV, 351; X, 61. Reprod. after Perdrizet, *Revue Archéol.*, 1904, I, 20,

pl. I; *id., Cultes et Mythes du Pangée*, p. 21, pl. II; Eisler, *Orpheus*, London, 1921, pl. VI). Perdrizet has acutely observed that the god here called by his barbaric name *Asdoulês* (Clermont-Ganneau, *Recueil d'Archéol. Orientale*, VI, 214) is none other than Dionysos Zagreus. This name is explained as ἄναξ ἀγρεύς, 'hunter Lord', by Euripides, *Bakkhae*, 1189 ff. As to *za-* = 'great', 'very much', see *Etym. Magn.*, p. 406, 49, Gaisford; *Etym. Gud.*, p. 227, 40; Cramer, *Anecd. Oxon.*, II, 443, 8. As to the name Asdoulês, *astwat(s)* is the Armenian, non-Indo-European word for 'sky' and 'god'. (Schrader-Nehring, *Reallexikon der Indogerman. Altertumskunde*, Berlin (de Gruyter), 1923, I, p. 406, left col.) *Aswad* is the name of a hunting god of the Swanetians in the Caucasus (Nic. Marr, *Izvestiya of the Russ. Academy of Sciences*, 1911, p. 759; 1912, p. 827: Eisler, *Orph.-Dionys. Myst.*, p. 100, note 3). ''*Aztuwadi*, king of the *Danuna*,' has just been found in a 9th-century B.C. Aramean inscription at Kara-Tepe near Adana (R. D. Barnett, *Iraq*, X, 1948, pp. 58 f.). It is the exact equivalent of Greek *Dio-genês, Dios-kouros*, etc.

139. Mannhardt, *Der Baumkult der Germanen und ihrer Nachbarstämme*, Berlin (Bornträger), 1875, p. 137; *ibid.*, p. 138, on king Oden (Wodan) hunting at the head of a pack of wolves, not hounds.

140. See the testimonies above, p. 152, note 116.

141. Prof. W. E. LeGros Clark, 'Pithecanthropus in Peking', *Antiquity*, XII, 1945, No. 73, pp. 1 ff.

142. Franz Weidenreich, *Palaeontologia Sinica*, No. 327, 1943.

143. G. H. Koenigswald, *Early Man*, 1937, p. 31; Sir Arthur Keith, *Essays on Human Evolution*, London (Watts), 1946, p. 178.

144. VIOLENT DEATHS IN EARLY MAN

Sir Arthur Keith, *op. cit.*, p. 179: 'In 1939 Dr. T. D. McCown and I published an account (McCown and Keith, *The Stone-Age Men of Mount Carmel*, II, 1939, p. 373) of people who were buried in the caves of Mt. Carmel during the last (Riss-Wurm) interglacial period, which, on the Zeuner scheme of chronology (*Geol. Magaz.*, 1935, 72, p. 350), gives them an antiquity of 140,000 or 150,000 years. In one man, a tall fellow of lusty build, we found the left hip-joint shattered by a wooden spear which had been driven with such force that its point had entered the pelvis, where it became snapped off. Before the wooden point had decayed, lime salts had collected round it, forming so perfect a mould that we were able to take from it a cast showing in all its details the pointed form of this ancient weapon of war. The warrior who inflicted that wound must have had a strong arm and a fierce, passionate, and violent temper. Three sites in Europe, all of them of about the same degree of antiquity as that at Mt. Carmel, have yielded evidence of murderous or cannibalistic practices; at all three sites the fossil remains were of men of the Neanderthal breed. Near the ancient hearths of the Krapinians, of Croatia (Prince Kropotkin, *Mutual Aid: A Factor in Evolution*, 1914, p. 197), there were found the limb-bones of animals, now extinct, split open for the removal of their marrow. Some human bones seem to have been treated in a similar manner. The skull of the Ehringsdorf Man, found deep in a limestone quarry near Weimar, had been split open by five powerful blows while still in a fresh state (Sir A. Keith, *New Discoveries*, 1931, p. 319). The third site is at Monte Circeo, a coastal bastion of the Pontine Marshes... This site was visited in legendary times by Ulysses; but more to our present purpose is the visit paid to it by Count A. C. Blanc in 1938 (*Rend. R. Acad. Naz. de' Lincei*, 1939, 17, p. 205). He made his way into a virgin cave to find within it the fossil skull of a Neanderthalian. In Dr. Weidenreich's opinion this skull had been mutilated at death in the same manner as that practised by the *Sinanthropus*.'

145. *Race, Sex and Environment, A Study of Mineral Deficiency in Human Evolution*, London (Hutchinson), 1936, p. 160.

146. This is why the goddesses of agriculture are the female Dêmêtêr and Korê, 'Mother Earth' and 'Maiden Earth', also called *Proserpina* the 'leading sickler' (Varro *ap.* Augustine, *Civ. Dei*, VII, 20: '*a proserpendo Proserpina dicta*'). Agriculture with

dibble-stick and hoe is a purely feminine occupation. Only when the plough is yoked to the tamed bull is the superior strength of the male drover, who did the taming, harnessed to the service of agriculture and mixed farming brought into existence, originally still on a nomadic basis, abandoning the land when the soil is exhausted and clearing ever new land by burning the bush. (V. Gordon Childe, *What Happened in History*, Harmondsworth (Penguin Books), 1942, p. 51. Moritz Hörnes, *Natur- und Urgeschichte des Menschen*, Vienna (Hartleben), 1909, I, pp. 536–538).

147. See below, p. 216, note 194, on the Sabine women raped by the sons of the *Lupa Romana* being the females of the 'vine-yarders'. There is a close parallel in Judg. xxi. 21: 'Behold, if the daughters of Shiloh come out to dance in dances, then come ye out of the vineyards and catch you every man his wife of the daughters of Shiloh and go out to the land of Benjamin.' The tribe of Benjamin thus addressed are exhorted in the Blessings of Jacob, Gen. xlix. 27 (time of Solomon): 'Benjamin shall raven as a wolf, in the morning shall he devour the prey and at night he shall divide the spoil.' 'Divide the spoil' has an ominous ring if read in connection with the horrible story in Judg. xix. 25 of the mass rape of a woman by these Benjaminites (that is 'sons of the Right Hand', which means Southerners or 'Yemenites') and the fact that the woman killed in this way is 'cut up into twelve pieces' (xix. 29) by the very man who threw her to the wolves to save himself (xix. 25).

148. Gen. ii. 19 f.

149. Gen. ii. 9.

150. Gen. ii. 16, cf. i. 29.

151. Gen. vi. 11; ix. 2. f.

152. Gen. ix. 2 f. 'Like the green herb' has a close parallel in the Sumerian story of the Fall of Man (Edward Chiera,' 'A Sumerian Tablet of the Fall of Man', *Americ. Journ. of Semit.*

Languages and Literature, XXXIX, 1922, pp. 46 ff.). The broken tablet (ed. Lutz, I, p. 2, Univ. of Pennsylvania Series No. 103) begins with the accusation... 'Like vegetable food'... 'to do that with malice he has'... 'he has not been obedient to thee'... This is apparently explained by the curse line 20: 'to my ox for leading it, as an outcast thou shalt not return, to my garden thou shalt not return'. It seems clear that the culprit has treated some animal from among the god's cattle 'like vegetable food', that is to say, he has eaten it.

153.   See above, p. 167, note 125.

The whole history of protective armour—the helmet, which the Greeks called λυκεία or κυνέη—the *caput lupinum* or *wolfshede* of the Anglo-Saxon laws, the *houndscull* or *hundsgugel* of the Middle Ages, the shield, the cuirass (from *cuire*, corium, 'leather', 'skin')—distinguishing the Greek ὁπλίται, the *gens d'armes*, from the γυμνῆται, 'stripped' or 'naked' light auxiliaries, can be traced back in the last instance to Dolon's λυκέη δορά, the 'coat of skin' of the primitive 'werwolf', 'berserk', 'leopard-man' or 'lion-man' whose idealized memory survives in the Greek Herakles, the man 'famous through his ancestress' (*Hêra* is the feminine of *herôs*, glorified 'ancestor') clad in the lion's skin and battling against the big saurians of the prehistoric age with the heavy wooden club of the Stone Age hunter and the bow and arrow first encountered in the African Stone Age civilization.

According to Propertius (V, 10, 20), Romulus, the foster-child of the *Lupa Romana*, wore a 'wolf's-helmet' (*galea lupina*). Cf. Vergil, *Aeneid*, I, 275: 'Inde lupae fulvo nutricis tegmine laetus Romulus excipiet gentem...' etc. ['Then Romulus, proud in the tawny hide of the she-wolf, his nurse, shall take up the line', etc.]. According to Polybius (VI, 22) the Roman *velites*, lightly-armed soldiers, wore a λυκεία, a dog's or wolf's head helmet (κυνῆ or λυκῆ in other authors). See also Herodotus, VII, 75; Xenophon, *Anab.*, VII, 44, on the fox-pelts the Thracians wore over their heads with the animals' paws knotted round their necks.

154. V. Gordon Childe, *What Happened in History, supra cit.* (note 146), p. 34.

155. Gen. iii. 7.

156. LEAF CLOTHING

In the western islands of Torres Straits the women wear a tuft of grass or split pandanus leaves; for dancing a short petticoat of shred pandanus leaves is worn over this (Haddon, *Journ. of the Anthropol. Institute*, XIX (1890), 368, 431). In Samoa the only necessary garment was, for men or women, an apron of leaves (Turner, *Samoa*, 1884, p. 212). According to G. Brown, *Melanesians and Polynesians*, 1910, p. 315, they wear girdles of *ti*-leaves (*Condyline terminalis*) gathered when turning yellow. The Nyam-Nyam Negress wears a leaf tied to a girdle (Ratzel, *History of Mankind*, Engl. trans. 1896–8, I, p. 94). Palyan women are sometimes dressed in a leaf-girdle only. Gond women wear bunches of twigs around the waist. The Kolarian Juangs of Chota Nagpur are famous for their leaf-dresses (Sir Rich. Burton, *Goldmines of Midian*, London, 1878, p. 141). When dry and crackly they are changed for fresh leaves (W. Crook, *Things Indian*, 1906, pp. 156 f.). The Semangs of the Malay peninsula wear girdles of leaves, adorned on festal occasions with flowers. The Sakai wear a waist-cord from which leaves depend in a fringe (Skeat-Blagden, *Pagan Races of the Malay Peninsula*, 1906, I, pp. 53, 142, 364; II, pp. 118, 124, 136 f.). This is retained even under the sarong adopted at a later stage of civilization. The dancing dress of the Jakun is made of the leaves of the serdang-palm and consists of an elaborate fringed head-dress, a bandolier and belt. Leaf-aprons are still worn by the Kōragar women (J. M. Campbell, *Indian Antiquary*, XXIV, 1895, p. 154). In tropical countries the use of leaves as occasional or permanent garments is common. Several peoples, such as the Indonesian islanders, in Ceram for instance, and the Polynesians, elevated the practice into an art (E. A. Crawley, art. 'Dress', *Encyclop. of Rel. and Eth.*, V, pp. 44 f., from whom the preceding quotations are taken). Moritz Hörnes, *op. cit.*, II, 309, cf. I, p. 516, on the Veddas wearing among themselves a kilt of leafy branches of aromatically smelling plants held by their waist-cord. This is worn for dances and ceremonial visits. The Andamanese bestow such a leaf-skirt on their young men at the age of puberty when they have to perform a dance, holding leaves in their hands. The girls get this skirt of leaves when they marry. The Hindus of the Madras district wear it at certain festivals. The members of a Melanesian secret society in the north-east Gazelle Peninsula are clad in leaf-dress for the performance of masked dancing. See R. Parkinson, *Dreissig Jahre in der Südsee*, hg. v. Dr. B. Ankermann, Museum f. Völkerkunde, Berlin; Stuttgart (Strecker u. Schröder), 1907, p. 784, pl. 50 (masked men of Lihir with palm-leaf, fern and reed aprons); pl. 46 (*Sisu*-masque of men from the Sulka tribe made of long narrow leaves); pl. 4 (spirit-dances on the Gazelle Peninsula performed by men wearing leaf-kilts); pl. 43 (Tubuans entirely wrapped up in leaf-cloaks); p. 575, fig. 103; and p. 693, fig. 115. See Georg Buschan, *Illustrierte Völkerkunde*, Stuttgart (Strecker u. Schröder) 1910, pl. IX; Hörnes, *op. cit.*, II, p. 309, note 1. The reader will remember the story in the *Odyssey* (VI, 128 f.) of the naked shipwrecked hero emerging from the thicket in view of princess Nausicaa and her maids, covering himself modestly with a leafy bough broken from a tree: ἐκ πυκινῆς δ' ὕλης πτόρθον κλάσε χειρὶ παχείῃ φύλλων, ὡς ῥύσαιτο περὶ χροῒ μήδεα φωτός ['With his stout hand he broke from the thick wood a leafy branch, that he might hold it about him and hide his nakedness therewith.'].

This kind of primitive vegetable clothing survives in certain fertility rites. At times of prolonged droughts in Serbia young girls march through the villages singing songs, to elicit rain from heaven. One of them, called *Dodola*, takes off all her clothes and covers herself with reeds, boughs of willow, grasses, leaves and flowers. She dances a round before every house with the other maidens circling and singing around her until some-one emerges from the house to throw a sacrifice of the precious water over her (Ami Boué, *Die Europäische Türkei*, I, p. 656, quoted by Hörnes, *op. cit.*, II, p. 309). Quite similar is the Rumanian Paparuda dance executed by stark-naked Gypsy girls wearing a skirt of dwarf elder or dane-wort boughs and a pelerin of the same plants over their shoulders. They too are soused with water by the villagers in order to produce rain (E. Fischer, *Arch. f. Anthropol.*, 1908, N.S., VI, p. 3; Hörnes, *l.c.*; Mannhardt, *Baumkult*, pp. 329 f.).

Baronga women, to make rain, strip themselves of their

clothes and put on instead leaf-girdles or leaf-petticoats and head-dresses of grass (H. A. Junod, *Les Baronga*, Neufchâtel, 1898, pp. 412 ff.). A Gujarāt mother, when her child is ill, goes to the goddess's temple at night, naked or with only a girdle of *nim* (*Melia*) or *asopato* (*Polyalthea*) leaves (Ward, *Hindoos*, 3rd ed., I, p. 72, cf. p. 130; J. M. Campbell in *Indian Antiquarian*, XXIV, p. 265; E. A. Crawley, *op. cit.*, p. 60, col. b).

157. CAPRIFICATION

Mesopotamian leaf-dresses are represented in Bruno Meissner, *Babylonien und Assyrien*, I, Heidelberg (Winter), Tafel-Abb., 9, statue of Lugaldalu (Banks, *Bismaya*, 193); Tafel-Abb., 11, family-portrait relief of Urnina (de Sarzec, *Découvertes en Chaldée*, Pl. 2 *bis*, No. 1); Taf.-Abb., 21, Statue of an archaic ruler of Ma'er (King, *Hist. of Sumer and Accad*, p. 102) and Taf.-Abb., 22, statue of an archaic ruler from Assur (phot. Berlin Museum). See also Heinrich u. Andrae, *Fara*, Berlin, 1931, pl. 27 D; reprod. also in Ebert, *Reallex. d. Vorgeschichte*, VII, pl. 146, fig. a).

Meissner, pp. 50, 80, 316, calls these leaf-skirts *Zottenröcke*, 'coats of hair-tufts'. H. R. Hall, *Ancient History of the Near East*, 5th ed., 1920, p. 172, says they look 'as if made . . . of palm-tree leaves'. Their nature has been hotly debated, indeed to such an extent that Prof. Henri Frankfort, 'Archaeology and the Sumerian Problem', *Oriental Institute of Chicago University, Studies in Ancient Oriental Civilization*, No. 4, 1932, p. 12, note, laments: 'The problem of Sumerian dress is exasperatingly difficult'. W. Reimpell, *Gesch. d. babyl. u. assyr. Kleidung*, p. 24, describes the material as made of coarse wool with loose loops (*Schlaufen*) similar to crocheted woollen blankets. Eduard Meyer, *Sumerer und Semiten*, p. 76, is reminded of a long-haired multi-coloured woollen kind of mohair. Léon Heuzey, *Revue Archéologique*, 1889, reprinted in his *Origines Orientales de l'Art*, pp. 120 ff., thinks these skirts are what the Greeks called the καυνάκης, *i.e.* the Assyrian *gaunakku*, 'frilled and flounced cloak'. (Aristophanes, *Wasps*, 1137; a purple καυνάκης, Menander, 972; said to be of Persian or Babylonian make, Arrian, *Anab.*, 6, 29, 5; Pollux 7, 59, cf. *Schol.* to Aristoph., *l.c.*; Semus, 20; *Papyr. Cair.*, Zenobius 48.3, 3rd cent. B.C.; καυνακή, fem. *Papiri Greci e Latini*, Publ. d. Soc. Ital. p. 1. ricerca dei Papiri,

Firenze, 1912, vol. VI, 605 (3rd cent. B.C.); γαυνακή in codd. of
the *Periplus Maris Rubri*, 6; dimin. *χαυνακιόν* in Zonaras; Lat.
gaunacum; Léon Heuzey, *Rev. arch.*, 1887; Jean Przyluski, 'Une
étoffe Orientale, le kaunakês', *Journ. R. Asiat. Soc.*, 1931,
pp. 339–347, quoting J. Charpentier and E. Schwyzer on Old
Persian **gaunaku*, Pâli *gonaka* or *goṇaka*, 'long-haired woollen
stuff', Skr. (Buddhist) *gonika*, Iranian *gaona*, 'hair', Pehlvi
gaunaka). Similarly Bruno Meissner, *Atlantis*, 1929, p. 318,
thinks of a flakily woven material (*flockig gewebter Stoff*). Mrs.
E. Douglas van Buren, *Liverpool Annals of Archaeology and Anthropology*, XVII, 1930, pp. 39–56, speaks of a 'flounced dress of
sheepskin', but admits (p. 46) that this tasselled skirt cannot be
meant for a fleece, because this looks quite different when represented, although Prof. Frankfort thinks of two different styliza-
tions of the same thing. But Victor Christian, *Wiener Zeitschr.
f. Kunde d. Morgenlandes*, XXXIII, p. 229, in a review of Eck-
hard Unger, *Sumer. und Akkad. Kunst*, Breslau, 1926, pp. 13 and
15, had already explained this peculiar dress as an apron of
leaves, and pointed out that Eannatu's 'Stele of Vultures'
clearly shows a cape of fur worn with this leaf-apron. Walter
Andrae, *Die Archaïschen Ischtartempel*, pp. 12 ff.; *Kunst d. alten
Orients*, p. 141; 2nd ed., p. 151, speaks of 'tufts of reed-leaves'
(*Zotten von Schilfblättern*) stitched on to a piece of cloth. In his
book *Das wiedererstandene Assur*, p. 74, Andrae has rallied to the
opinion that these flounced skirts are sheepskins, possibly
treated like modern astrakhan lamb skins. Dietrich Opitz
has published a monograph, 'Womit kleideten sich die alten
Sumerer?' in Prof. Weidner's *Arch. f. Orientforsch.*, VI, Berlin,
1930/31, pp. 19 f. He describes this peculiar dress as a structure
comparable to a tiled roof (*dachziegelartiges Gebilde*), but forgets
that there are actually such roofs thatched with palm-leaves.
He thinks of a particular kind of frieze or curl-weaving (*Schlau-
fengewebe, Friesgewebe*) and believes that the question has now
been decided by Sir Leonard Woolley's discovery of the statue
of a goat with golden legs and an alleged body-fleece of carved
shells and, on the shoulders, lapis lazuli, exactly in the style of
the Sumerian 'flounced skirts' (L. Woolley, *The Development of
Sumerian Art*, London (Faber), 1935, colour-plate 36 facing
p. 78). Not illogically, Dr. Opitz argues that it would be

unlikely for a goat to be clothed in a curly woven textile costume, let alone in a leaf-coat. But he has forgotten that this goat is shown mounting, that is fertilizing, a golden fig-tree. The biblical title 'the ram caught in the thicket' which Sir Leonard Woolley gave to this figure (*op. cit.*, p. 77) is unfortunate. The sculpture symbolizes the *caprificatio* of the fig-tree, considered, no doubt, as a magic or ritual action. If Dr. Opitz had ever seen the reproduction of the Austrian so-called *Weinbeergoas* or 'grape-goat' wine-harvest idol covered with fruit of the season and the equivalent of the *Dionysos Botrys*, an idol of the god Dionysos made entirely of grapes (Eisler, *Orph.-Dionys. Myster.*, pl. XVIII, fig. 105 to p. 227, note 7, and 104, to p. 227, note 3; also Eisler, *Orpheus*, pl. LXIX, p. 281, note 2, after *Jahrb. d. deutsch. arch. Inst.*, XXXII, 1917, p. 35, fig 12), he would not have thought it improbable that a goat representing the spirit of the male wild fig-tree (*caprificus*, τράγος ἐρινεός) should have been represented in a ceremonial coat or caparison made of leaves exactly like the aprons worn by human beings. The leaves of which they were originally made look very much like those of *Ficus elastica* Roxb. I do not want to exclude the possibility that the garment represented by the Sumerian sculptures may have been made in historic times of some textile material, but the shape of it is beyond doubt intended to look like an 'apron of leaves' (Eisler, *Le Monde Oriental*, XXIII, 1–3, Upsala, 1929). The decisive proof of this assertion is the lines 15 f. in the Sumerian '*Story of the Fall of Man*'—overlooked by all the authors above-quoted (Chiera, *op. cit.*, p. 46): 'From my place go into the desert. To me for ever, for having taken the tree which establisheth clothing (*giš-gi-tug-ga*), as an outcast thou shalt not return'. This shows clearly that Sumerian dress was made from something taken from a sacred tree, the tabu on which was supposed to have been broken by a man living in the garden of his god or gods and driven out from it to man's present abode in the midst of the desert. Taken in connection with the monuments referred to earlier, this proves that the Sumerian aprons were leaf-skirts. The 'tree that establisheth clothing' has its close parallel in the 'shirt-tree' of Brazil, a *Lecythis*, the pliant bark of which is easily stripped. From a length of the trunk a cylinder of bark is taken and beaten soft.

two armholes are cut and it is ready for wear (Ratzel, *Hist. of Mankind*, Engl. trans., I, p. 96, see below, p. 184, on the 'dress of trees' of Banous).

In another Sumerian 'Legend of the Fall of Man' (Langdon, *Le Poème Sumérien du Paradis, du Déluge et de la Chute de l'Homme*, Paris, London, New York, 1919, pp. 133 ff.; considerably revised and improved edition in Langdon, *Semitic Mythology*, vol. V of 'Mythology of all Races', Boston, 1931, pp. 190 ff., *The Sumerian Legend of Tag-tug and Paradise*) which may quite well be the initial part of that published by Lutz and translated by Chiera or a local variant of it, the hero or heroine is Tag-tug, the gardener (there is a female goddess Tag-tug, *Journ. of the Americ. Orient Soc.*, LXIII, No. 3, 1943, p. 190, note 5); it may be an androgynous being such as the Biblical Adam from whose 'side', not rib, Eve was cut (see Eisler, *Plato*, London, 1951). The name of this 'gardener'—closely comparable to Adam and Eve in the garden of Eden which they were ordered 'to dress and keep'—is written TAG-TUG and may be read *tibir* (Deimel, *Sumerisches Lexikon*, III, 1209). This is all the more likely since it is followed (Langdon, *Poème du Paradis*, p. 137, note 2) by the syllable *-ra*, so that it could be read *tibirra*. This means in Sumerian 'smith', 'metal-worker', and would closely correspond to the Biblical Cain (*qayin* = 'metal founder', 'smith') who is called in Gen. iv. 2 a 'tiller' or 'serf of the earth'—a term that could denote a gardener as well as a ploughman and miner of the ore he smelts (Eisler, *Monde Oriental*, op. supra cit., pp. 58–64). What interests us in this context is the fact (Deimel, *op. cit.*, III, 1, 203) that the signs TAG and TUG can be read (Deimel, 204, 14) *rakâsu*, 'bind', and *ṣubatu*, 'clothing', 'cloth' (207). So the ideographic writing TAG-TUG for Tibirra may be taken to indicate the gardener who 'bound together the clothing', presumably from the leaves of the 'tree that establisheth clothing'. TAG-TUG =Tibirra seems to have broken the tabu of the sacred tree and been banished from the garden in consequence. But in the end the god EN-KI (='Lord of the Earth') says ('Legend of the Fall of Man', II, Langdon, *Sem. Mythol.*, p. 199): 'I have decreed for

ever the fate of the plant, My King has spoken of the same . . .
he may cut therefrom and eat . . .'

It is interesting to note in this context the efforts of certain
Rabbinic commentators to explain away the 'coats of skin'
(*kethoneth 'or*) made by God for man in Gen. iii. 21, so as not to
imply that the Creator had, for this purpose, killed one of the
animals, at that time still all supposedly in the state of innocence.
Some of them say these garments were made of the fallen-out
or gently plucked camels' hair or sheep-wool still used by
Beduin women for spinning and weaving purposes. The Christian Syrians (*Cave of Treasure*, ed. C. Bezold, p. 7; Solomon of
Basra, *Book of the Bee*, ed. Budge, p. 24) say that these clothes
were made from the 'skin of trees', that is bast or bark (see
above, p. 182, on the Brazilian 'shirt-tree' and the Sumerian
'tree that established clothing'). The hermit Banous, that is 'the
Baptist', with whom the young Flavius Josephus (*Vita*, ch. 2)
dwelt in the desert, wore 'a dress of the trees' (ἐσθῆσι ἀπὸ δένδρων
χρώμενον; see Eisler, *Jesous Basileus*, etc., Heidelberg Univ.
Press (Winter), 1930, II, pp. 34 f., and vol. I, p. 120). A Coptic
hermit, hairy all over his body, clad only in an apron of leaves,
is mentioned in the *Peregrinatio Paphnutiana* (C. A. Williams,
Oriental Affinities of the Legend of the Hairy Anchorite, Univ. of
Illinois, Studies in Lang. and Lit., XI, p. 83). In the *Vita Pauli
Eremitae* of St. Jerome (Williams, *op. cit.*, p. 95), this saint too
makes himself clothes of palm leaves. A plate in *Acta Sanctorum*,
May, I, after p. xxx, No. 12, shows the saintly hermits St. Peter
of Mount Athos and St. Onuphrius in a Russian illuminated
manuscript.

158. GREEN MEN

In Lower Austria the watchmen who guard the vineyards
against nocturnal depredations when the grapes are ripe, wear
a heavy rustling cloak made of reeds, allegedly to keep them
warm in the chilly night (Arthur Haberlandt, 'Aus dem Weinge-
birg', in *Festschrift zum zehnjährigen Bestehen der Jugendbundes-
gruppe Germania des Deutschen Schulvereins Südmark*, s.a., p. 7).
This is, however, nothing but the traditional 'grass-coat' worn
by the Thracian *Sileni* or 'vintners' who follow the Thracian
'Great Hunter' god. (Pollux, IV, 118: χορταῖος χίτων δασύς ὃν

οἱ Σιληνοί φέρουσιν; cf. Dionys. Halic., VII, 72: μαλλωτοὶ χίτωνες οὓς ἔνιοι χορταίους καλοῦσιν, 'the shaggy, fleecy coats which some people call "grass clothes" '.) An illustration shows young Negroes of Angola in the primeval jungle-hunters' camouflage made of creepers, lianas, etc., and still worn during the puberty initiation ceremonies. Cf. the costume of the 'Wild Men' so often used as heraldic supporters (*écuyers*, esquires, shield-bearers) of coats of arms, *e.g.* on Dürer's portrait of Oswald Krell in the Pinakothek at Munich dated 1499. The shield on the left side is supported by a man clad in tufts of moss, armed with a club, the one on the right by a man with fair hair all over his body. See also Georg Leidinger, *Einzelholzschnitte des 15. Jahrhunderts in der Staatsbibliothek München*, I. Serie, 1907, pl. 46, showing a dance of these shaggy 'Wild Men', or P. Lacroix, (*le bibliophile Lacroix*) *Mœurs, Usages et Costumes du Moyen Âge*, Paris, 1871, p. 263, fig. 185. The latter illustrates a manuscript of Froissart's *Chronicle* (IV, 52, ed. Paris, 1574) telling the story of the *Ballet des Ardents* dramatized by Goethe in the second part of his *Faust* (Act I, sc. 3). Charles VI of France arranged on 29 Jan. 1393 in the Hôtel Royal de Saint-Jean a fancy-dress ball in honour of the second marriage of a lady of the bed-chamber of queen Isabel of Bavaria. The king and four of his equerries danced as *hommes sauvages*. For this purpose Charles VI ordered 'six cottes de toile couvertes de delié lin en forme et couleur de cheveux'. 'Ils furent vestus de ces cottes, qui estoient faites à leur point et ils furent dedans cousus et ils se monstroient être hommes sauvages; ils estoient tous chargez de poil depuis le chef jusqu'à la plante du pié.' The Duke of Orléans in-advertently touched one of the dancers with a burning torch and set them all aflame. The king was saved by the Duchesse de Berry who recognized him and threw her mantle over him, and the others were all burnt to death. On the Twelfth Night of 1515 a pageant was produced at Greenwich for King Henry VIII. There . . . 'came out of a place lyke a wood 8 wyldemen, all apparayled in grene mosse' . . . (Thos. Hall's *Chronicle*, ed. princ., 1548; ed. London, 1809, p. 580). In 1575 Queen Elizabeth, arriving at Kenilworth, was received by the poet Thomas Gascoyne emerging from the wood as a 'wild man', entirely covered with ivy and carrying a little uprooted tree in his hand (see plates in Strutt, *The Sports and Passetimes of the People of England*, London, 1841, pp. 377 f., cf. 375; 253; XLI).

'The Green Man', 'Jack in the Green', 'Green George', *Vir Viridis*, or the 'Wylde Man' depicted as covered with 'green hair', that is grass and leaves, is the archetypal hunter camouflaged so as to get as near as possible to the animals of the wood and jungles by hiding not only his visual appearance but also his scent. Cf. above, p. 178, note 156, on the Veddas using sweet-smelling leaves for their leaf-aprons. Leaf-skirts and leaf-pelerines worn over the shoulders (see above, p. 179, note 156 on the Rumanian Gypsies) are worn instead of complete leaf-coverings because the strong scent of the unwashed human animal emanates mainly from the armpits and the excretory organs.

159. GREEN MAN AS A CAMOUFLAGED OUTLAW

That the 'wyldeman's' leaf-and-moss-costume is originally a hunter's camouflage is proved by the fact that the 'Green Man' is known as *le Loup Vert* at Jumièges (Normandy) where the 'green wolf' of the year dances at the head of the other members of the *Confrérie du Loup Vert* around the St. John's bonfire. A pretence is made of throwing the 'Green Wolf' elected for the next year into the bonfire. Mannhardt, *Antike Feld- und Waldkulte*, Berlin (Bornträger), 1877, pp. 323 ff., after *Magazin Pittoresque*, Paris, 1840, pp. 287 ff.; Liebrecht, *Gervasius von Tilbury*, pp. 209 and 192; Cortet, *Essai sur les fêtes religieuses*, Paris, 1807, p. 221; Sir J. G. Frazer, *The Golden Bough*, 2nd ed., III, p. 282). The 'Green Wolf' or 'Grass Wolf' or 'Corn Wolf', 'Rye-wulf', 'Pea-wolf' 'Bean-wolf' (Mannhardt, *op. cit.*, pp. 318 ff.; *id.*, *Roggenwolf und Roggenhund*, Danzig, 1865; 2nd ed. 1866)—thus called because he is wrapped in corn or rye straw, pea or bean stalks—of Germany, Lower Hungary (an ancient Illyrian region), French Burgundy, Flanders, Nivernais, Champagne, Brittany, Estonia and Latvia, Poland, etc.—is by no means a creature of mythical imagination, but the archetypal figure of the disguised outlaw and werewolf hiding and feeding in the ripe cornfield, as he hides and feeds in the vineyards when the grapes are ripe. Walking over the Cotswolds with an Alsatian wolf-dog, I have seen her time and again, running—completely hidden by the high stalks—through the ripening cornfields to chase the hares and rabbits attracted to the furrows by the succulent grain. This is exactly what the wolves must have done when they were still plentiful in those regions where people still say 'the wolf runs through the corn', 'the corn-wolf hunts over the field', the corn-wolf has arrived', 'the she-wolf is cubbing in the corn' whenever the wind blows through the waving cornfields. The French in the Dordogne did not speak of a 'vegetation-spirit' when they said '*le loup est dans les blés*', but of the real wolf who used to haunt the cornfields. Escaped prisoners of war and fugitives from the law who have hidden for days on end in the ripe cornfields, where they could not only hide in a place un-likely to be walked through, but sustain themselves by munch-ing the ripening or ripe grain, peas or beans, will easily under-stand why hungry outlaws and werewolves of old would go into and hide in the fields at this season and why the harvesters would expect to find them there, cunningly camouflaged against detection by covering themselves with wheat-, rye-, bean- or pea-stalks bound round their bodies. If Westphalians in the neighbourhood of Osnabrück called trampled-down or wind-laid spots in their cornfields 'werewolves' nests'; if the Eastern Frisians said of such places in their fields 'Zei, da het de Wulf vernacht slapen' ('See, the wolf has slept there overnight'); if the French of the Seine-et-Marne *département* warned their children against the *loup-garou* crouching in the corn; if it is said in the Limousin (Corrèze) 'lorsque les blés se trouvent couchés, on dit que c'est le béroux' (*loup garou*); in Loire-Inférieure 'c'est le loup qui se roulait là' (Mannhardt, *Wald- und Feldkulte*, p. 322; J. G. Frazer, *Golden Bough*, 2nd ed., II, pp. 264 ff.), there was a time when this was not a superstition. At no time did these sayings refer to a 'corn-spirit', a 'pea- or bean-spirit' to be preserved in the last sheaf, but always to a dangerous camouflaged outlaw to be caught in the fields, if possible slain and burnt by the harvesters. If a man with a wolf's head—the Greek λυκείη, the *wolveshede* of the Anglo-Saxon outlaw—ran along with the 'wilde man' and his 'wilde wife' in the Nuremberg butchers' Carnival procession (Mannhardt, *Baumkult*, p. 334; *Wald- u. Feldkulte*, p. 323); if the Zürich butchers carried on the same occasion an image of 'Isengrim' (*Baumkult*, p. 433;

Wald- u. Feldkulte, p. 323); if the Hessians and Thuringians led about in procession one of their gang, entirely covered in green leaves, representing 'the wolf' and collecting a tax for this procession, it is because originally the werewolf outlaw and 'wyldeman' found it expedient to use such a hunting-dress of leaves and other plant material taken from the vegetation of wood and field where he intended to hide, hunt and harvest.

160. Laws of Edward the Confessor (about 1000 A.D.), *Lupinum enim caput a die utlagationis eius quod ab Anglis wulfesheved nominatur.* Cf. above, p. 145, note 112.

161. See above, p. 151, note 116; p. 162, note 118.

162. See on this phenomenon known as hypertrichosis the monograph by F. Houssay, *Les Velus*, Paris, 1912.

163. TRADITION OF ADAM'S SHAGGY SKIN

G. Megas, 'Das Chirographon Adams', *Zeitschr. f. Neutest. Wiss.*, XXVII, 1928, pp. 305 ff., a story recorded by the author in Didymoteichon of Thrace from the mouth of an illiterate, 75-year-old man. A Rumanian parallel is to be found in Princess Bibesco, *Ishvor, le Pays des Saules*, Paris (Plon), 1921, I, p. 173; M. Gaster, *Literat. Popul.*, pp. 282 f. (*Versul lui de Adam*), p. 206, lines 1 f. German version, *l.c.*, p. 308: 'They began to go with one another, to amuse themselves, but they do not know how to generate children. "Of all fruits shalt thou eat, but from the fig-tree thou shalt not eat a fig."' 'And they were then hairy. As a bear they were' (καὶ αὐτοὶ ἴταν τότε μαλλιαροὶ ἀρκοῦνδα ὁπῶς, ἴναι ετσ᾿ ἴταν). The 'wild men' of Tyrol, Vorarlberg and Switzerland are described as very strong, with bodies 'shaggy with hair all over', wearing animal pelts (Mannhardt, *Wald- u. Feldkulte*, p. 149; *ibid.*, p. 147, as the Hessian woodmen. The *Salvegn* (=*silvani*) of Fassa are said to look 'like big apes, strong with hairy bodies' (*ibid.*, p. 127). Those of Mantua (*ibid.*, p. 126) are even said to have tails like monkeys.

164. Tablet I, col. II, lines 34–37: 'the goddess Aruru (the Earth) washed her hands, pinched off clay, cast it on the field.

She (made) Engidu, created a mighty one; a great offspring, a host of Ninurta. (Covered with) hair his whole body, he is [provid]ed with hair on his head like a woman, the locks on his head stretch out as long as those of the Corn-goddess' (the corn-goddess *ilu Nidaba* is represented by a sheaf of corn). The myth refers to an aboriginal race which the scientists following the army of Alexander the Great still encountered on the coast of Gedrosia (modern Mekran and Baluchistan) and described (Arrian, *Indica*, 24, 9) as 'hairy all over the body' and wearing their hair felted (τρίχωμα πεπιλωμένον ἐῶσι). They were (Diod. Sic., III, 15; XVII, 105, 1 f.) ἔθνὸς ἀξένον καὶ παντελῶς θεριῶδες ['an inhospitable and wholly beast-like tribe']. Strabo, *Geogr.*, XVI, 746, mentions such tribes surviving in Assyria also.

165. Hörnes, *Natur- und Urgeschichte des Menschen*, Vienna (Hartleben), 1909, I, p. 258, cf. p. 530; Stuhlmann, *Mit Emin Pascha im Herz von Afrika*, p. 445.

166. Hörnes, *op. cit.* (note 165), I, p. 259, note 1.

167. Moritz Hörnes, *Der Diluviale Mensch in Europa*, Braunschweiʒ, 1903, pp. 35, fig. 1–3, p. 36, figs. 10a and 10b. E. Piette, 'La Station de Brassempouy et les statues humaines de la période glyptique', *L'Anthropologie*, VIII, pl. I., figs. 1–3.

168. It can hardly be a mere coincidence that the Greek term for a disease of the scalp resulting in baldness is ἀλοπῆκια (Latin *alopecia*) 'fox-mange' (Sophocles, *frg.* 419; Galen, 12, 381; Aristotle, *Probl.*, 893b, 38), since ἀλωπεκίς means 'fox-fur-cap' and one can still hear people attribute their baldness, rightly or wrongly, to the habit of wearing caps, hats or helmets most of the time. The Japanese were-foxes are said 'occasionally to shave men's heads, making them look like tonsured monks' (Henry L. Joly, *Legend in Japanese Art*, London, 1908, p. 71.

169. This is quite compatible with Marett's explanation (*op. cit.*, pp. 8 and 160 ff.) of man's loss of hair through 'the need to economize iodine and adapt an anthropoid body to a life on the treeless alp of a young mountain system' (heavy rainfalls in the

pluvial period caused soil acidity and an accumulation of iodine which is reduced through increasing aridity; iodine deficiency is known to cause lack of body-hair in domesticated animals). But Marett's theory fails to explain why the animals grazing on this alp deficient in iodine and the other predatory beasts preying on them did not shed their hair.

170. Gen. xxv. 25, 27: 'and the first (of the twins) came out (from the womb of his mother) red, all over like a hairy garment (*addereth*) and they called his name Esau' (which means the 'hairy' or 'shaggy one') . . . 'and Esau was a cunning hunter, a man of the field' (read 'steppe') cf. *ibid.*, xxvii, 16; 23; 'Rebecca . . . put the skins of the kids of the goats upon his (Jacob's) hands and upon the smooth of his neck . . . and he (Isaac) discerned him not, because his hands were hairy as his brother Esau's hands'. See pl. XX in Eisler, *The Messiah Jesus*, London (Methuen), 1931, p. 238; *id.*, *le Monde Oriental*, XXIII, 1929, facing p. 80. Werner Pieper, *ibid.*, XVII, 1923, facing p. 8, after M. v. Oppenheim: *Vom Mittelmeer z. pers. Golf*, Berlin, 1899, facing p. 220. The reader will notice how the gazelle pelts cover most of the hands like mittens, and compare this fact with the Biblical story.

171. USEFULNESS OF A REMOVABLE HAIR COAT

The advantage in terms of energy saved by a movable haircoat is undeniable. Gerald Heard, *Pain, Sex and Time*, London (Cassell), 1939, p. 44, tries in vain to discount it. 'To guard against cold', he says, 'we wear layers of clothing' . . . 'All that this does for us is to make the body's "vaso-motor," heat-controlling system cease to work. We have then exchanged for a natural automatic defence against the pain and misery of cold, a clumsy, "economic", inaccurate defence. We are therefore only the worse off for our progress. How much we have actually lost our power of protecting ourselves by so depending on clothes, *et cetera*, is shown by the children in Dr. Rollier's sanatorium at Leysin, in Switzerland. These children have all been tubercular, but by re-training their bodies' natural capacity to stand cold, they are made so healthy that not only is the disease itself cured but they go out regularly skiing and need

wear nothing but their skis! Nor is this the limit to which
natural resistance to the pain of cold can be developed. Reliable
anthropologists (Dr. W. Y. Evans Wentz, *Tibetan Yoga and
Secret Doctrines*, Oxford Univ. Press) now confirm the report
that in the Himalayas there are men who train themselves to
be able so to hold off the intense cold that they can sit in the
snow for hours, wearing nothing but a cotton robe'. Granting
this to be true, for the sake of the argument, it is obvious that
the energy used up to maintain the body temperature at the
right level is not available for other purposes. I myself have had
to stand in *ersatz*-cotton clothes without overcoat for many
weary hours on the Buchenwald parade ground at tempera-
tures far below freezing-point. No doubt some people can
survive such exposure, as the ascetics practising their austerities
in the Himalayas do. Dr. Rollier's sanatorium children go
naked in the still sunshine of Leysin; they are not exposed to
snow-storms and wet fogs as the inmates of Buchenwald were
and the Fuegians still are. It is certain that the Eskimo could not
live their strenuous life without their fur coats, and that the dark
inhabitants of the tropics profit from their ability to go naked
in their hairless skin.

172. 'Though manners make, yet apparel shapes' (John
Florio, *Second Frutes*, 1591, p. 115; 'The hood makes not the
monk, nor the apparel the man' (Robert Greene [d. 1592],
Works, vol. IX, p. 19); David Hume, *Essays*, 'The Epicurean':
'Art may make a suit of clothes but nature must produce a
man.' All these quotations remind us of the current proverb
'*Clothes make the man*'.

173. Charles Allyn Williams, 'Oriental Affinities of the
Legend of the Hairy Anchorite', Urbana, Ill., 1925–26 (Univ.
of Illinois, Studies in Language and Literature, X, 13 sqq.,
XI, 57–138; *Nieuw Theol. Tijdschift*, 1928, pp. 282 ff.

174. NUDITY A CONSEQUENCE OF CLOTHES
Moritz Hörnes, *Scientia*, XI, 1912, pp. 81 ff.; summary in
Ebert's *Reallexikon der Vorgeschichte*, VI, Berlin, 1926, p. 382, §2,
art. *Kleidung*, said: 'As long as the preliminary question is not

resolved, whether the first man (*der erste Mensch*) was hairless or hairy, it is not even possible to decide whether the introduction of clothing is a consequence of nudity or whether the natural hair-covering was lost through the wearing of artificial clothes.'

I give a *verbatim* quotation of these words with their exact date, to exemplify the confusion prevailing in the minds even of prominent anthropologists on a question of such basic importance. Those who profess or pretend to believe in 'the first man' can be referred to a credible, albeit extracanonical tradition (above, note 163) that he was hairy. Those who accept the theory of a continuous evolution of man from subhuman Primates know that the few naked mammals such as the present tropical elephant (the mammoth was hairy), the whales, dolphins and other cetaceans are not in the ascendant genealogical tree of *Homo sapiens*. If all the Primate apes are hairy, and if there are still men as hairy as the Ainu and Wambuttu dwarfs, if there are hairy throw-backs even among present men (notes 162 and 237), primeval man must have been shaggy and can only have become naked at some time in the course of evolution to *Neoanthropus*. The only question is, how and why.

175. See above, p. 110, notes 103 f.

176. *Καθαρμοί* (='Purifications') *fragm.* 139, Diels, quoted by Porphyry, *De abstin.*, II, 31, σχέτλια ἔργα βορᾶς, paraphrased by Porphyry as 'the sin connected with our food' (περὶ τῆν τροφήν ἁμαρτία; see Eisler, *Orph.-Dionys. Myst.*, pp. 31 and 353). According to Empedocles, *frg.* 154, this crime was committed by the first men who made out of bronze or copper (ἐκαλχεῦσαντο) a sword and first ate the cattle that helped them to till the ground, just as the Book of Genesis attributes the first murder to Cain, that is *qayin*, the 'metal-smelter'. They could not know that animals were already killed with stone weapons and fellow human beings murdered with the wooden spear of the Natufians (see above, note 144).

177. The god who walks in his garden amidst the desert is a divinity of the tree—an '*El* (a 'god') of the '*elah* (fem. 'tree') —such as the Syrian *Ba'al* or 'Lord' holding a grape-vine and

corn-ears represented in relief on the rock-face of Ibriz, a divinity of primitive gardeners and orchard dwellers like Venus —originally a patroness of the fruit and vegetable garden— *Pomona* or the Illyrian apple-god Apollo (*Apalliunaš*), *Liber Pater* or Dionysos *Phleus* or *Phloios*, the god of the drink drawn from the bark (Latin *liber*, Greek φλοῖον) of certain trees and subjected to fermentation. See Eisler, *Orph.-Dionys. Myst.*, pp. 247, note 6–252 on the origin of tragedy out of these rites of atonement.

178. Gen. ix. 4 . . . 'but flesh with the life thereof (which is) the blood thereof shall ye not eat'. By allowing the ghosts in Hades to drink the sacrificial blood Odysseus in the Underworld enlivens them temporarily so that they get the λόγος again and are enabled to speak. Loss of blood in haemorrhage is known to kill even to the primitive savage, whence his dread of suffering and causing loss of blood.

179. Gen. iv. 11: 'the earth hath opened her mouth to receive blood from thy hand'. The later practice is to pour out the blood at a sacrificial stone or altar (1 Sam. xiv. 32 ff.; cf. Lev. xvii. 3 ff. (see George K. Moore, *Encycl. Bibl.* col. 4217, No 43, 'Blood of Victim').

180. PLANTS AND THE FEELING OF PAIN
The distinction was, so far as I know, first established in *The Notebooks of Leonardo da Vinci* (trans. by Sir E. MacCurdy, London (Cape), 1939, I, p. 77 (From the manuscript in the library of the Institut de France, H 60 (12)): 'Though nature has given sensibility to pain to such living organisms as have the power of movement—in order thereby to preserve the members which in this movement are liable to diminish and be destroyed—the living organisms which have no power, consequently do not have to encounter opposing objects and plants, consequently do not need to have a sensibility to pain; and so it comes about that, if you break them, they do not feel anguish in their members as do the animals.' Whether or not this plausible argument can still be upheld, in spite of the famous experiments of the Nobel Prize winner Sir Jagadis Chandra Bose of the Botanical Research Institute of Bombay, I leave to

be decided by biologists more competent than I can claim to be. I remember before the War sitting in a London cinema beside a lady, unknown to me, who burst into silent tears when a German documentary film was shown, illustrating the geotropic, hydrotropic and heliotropic movements of plant-roots and flowers. To my whispered enquiry what was the matter, she replied in an agonized voice: 'But they are alive as much as you and I, can't you see? I am an ethical vegetarian. What can I eat now, after seeing this?' I could not, there and then, embark on an explanation of Pavlov's theory of 'conditioned reflexes'. Also it would have been disingenuous to overlook the fact that our own most terrible pains are actually concomitant with our corresponding 'conditioned reflexes'. As to Leonardo da Vinci, he seems to have been an 'ethical vegetarian'. At least there is in *Quaderni d'Anatomia*, II, 14 r°, Royal Library of Windsor (ed. MacCurdy, I, pp. 89 f.), the following sketch for a speech, possibly inspired by a passage found in the *Life of Apollonius of Tyana* or in the *Martyrdom of Matthew* (M. R. James, *Apocr. New Test*, p. 460) addressing the Anthropophages: 'Let such as these remain in the company of the beasts and let their courtiers be dogs and other animals eager for prey . . . ever pursuing whatever takes flight from them. They follow after the inoffensive animals who in the season of the snow drifts are impelled by hunger to approach your doors, to beg alms from you as from a guardian. If you are, as you have described yourself, the king of the animals—it would be better for you to call yourself king of the beasts since you are the greatest of them all!—why do you not help them so that they may presently be able to give you their young in order to gratify your palate for the sake of which you have contrived to make yourself a tomb for all the animals? Even more I might say, if to speak the entire truth were permitted me. But do not let us quit this subject without referring to one supreme form of wickedness which hardly exists among the animals, among whom are none that devour their own species except for lack of reason (for there are insane among them as among human beings, though not in such great numbers). Nor does this happen except among the most voracious animals as in the lion species and among leopards, panthers, lynxes, cats and creatures like these which sometimes eat their young. But not only do you eat your children, but you eat father, mother, brothers, and friends, and this even not sufficing, you make raids on foreign islands and capture men of other races and then mutilating them in a shameful way you fatten them up and cram them down your gullets. Say, does not nature bring forth a sufficiency of simple things to produce satiety? Or if you cannot content yourself with simple things, can you not, by blending them together, make an infinite number of compounds, as did Platina and other authors who have written for epicures?'

181. Eisler, *Orph.-Dionys. Myst.*, pp. 234 ff., 236, 270, 278. See now the earliest text of this type, Dussaud, *Découvertes de Ras Shamra*, Paris, 1937, p. 78.

182. See above, note 135, and Eisler, *Orph.-Dionys. Myst.*, pp. 226–279.

183. VEGETARIANISM
In reality, there is no 'absolute necessity' for a carnivorous diet. The following letter appeared in the *Sunday Express* of 7 April 1946: *The simple life*: 'My age is 35. I am a fruitarian. I am a housewife with a man to feed, and recently gave birth to a daughter. I never took advantage of the "extras" allotted to expectant mothers, yet we are all happy and healthy. We wear the minimum of clothes, so that clothes rationing presents no problems. My husband wears a thin shirt with no undervest, and I only one silk or substitute undergarment winter and summer alike. No support, no stockings, both before my confinement and since. We never have colds.'

Vegetarians never tire of asserting that it is a wasteful process to pass vegetable food through animal bodies and then to absorb the meat thus produced, and that the earth could support a larger population of strict vegetarians than of omnivorous meat-eaters. Of the total weight of 1·60 lb. of an average Englishman's pre-war diet 0·80 consisted of beef, 0·30 of veal and mutton, 0·20 of pig products. At the Brighton meeting of the British Association of 9 Sept. 1948 Professor A. Fleisch of Lausanne, President of the Swiss Federal Commission for Nutrition, spoke of six years' experience of war rationing and its results on the 4 million inhabitants of Switzerland. Statistics had shown the large amount of calories, proteins and fats, formerly considered as the optimum, and attained in such countries as America, Britain, and Switzerland, to be utterly unnecessary. To-day, said Professor Fleisch, when the great nations were suffering from shortages, if the world converted large quantities of wheat into eggs, thus losing 90 per cent. of the nutritive value, and used a tremendous amount of maize and barley as fodder, with a loss of 75 per cent. of calories and proteins, we must call that waste—a waste without any value for health (*The Times*, 10 Sept., p. 6, col. 5). Mr. Henry Bailey Stevens of the University of New Hampshire sent me in 1947 a typewritten summary of a book, *The Recovery of Culture*, to be published by Harpers, trying to demonstrate that a return to a frugivorous diet is entirely possible: 'The shift in food demands would reduce by at least 80 per cent. the amount of land plowed for food purposes. Provided fiber demands were also met from tree crops, as can most efficiently be done, then tillage could be confined to the level areas of the Class I and Class II types approved by soil conservationists. Other types of land could be devoted to tree culture. Soil erosion would be practically stopped.' 'In modern orchards under the sod-mulch system no plowing is required, but the cuttings of grass are spread each year under the branches. To remove the hay is to rob the trees. Many growers even add materials such as refuse, manure, seaweed, sawdust or finely chopped bushes in order to maintain a good supply of organic matter.

'Several million farmers would be relieved of their present confining routine of service to animals 365 days a year. Agriculture would tend to shift back to a way of life in which families had their own gardens, small orchards and ornamental plants. The unhealthy concentration of people in large cities would be greatly reduced. With the disappearance of livestock the total human population would be greatly increased, but more important, it would spread out over the land; for with the emphasis on small holdings industry would find it profitable to decentralize. Village culture in the arts, religion and government would be stimulated. Skill in horticulture and forestry would be an important feature of our education. Substitutes for leather and other by-products of animals would have to be found, but the industrial chemists have already practically accomplished this step. Any such difficulties would be more than offset by the elimination of those diseases which have been circulated through meat and livestock products. The effect would be marked on tuberculosis, high blood pressure, typhoid fever, undulant fever, kidney diseases and probably cancer, insanity and poliomyelitis. But the greatest of all would be the effect upon our ethical and esthetic culture if we made ourselves consistent with that primate nature which was built over long ages into our very genes. It has been hard to have a church and a schoolhouse at one end of the street and a slaughter-house at the other; to fill our minds with kindness and our stomachs with tortured flesh; to teach peace and eat like beasts of prey. There is a story that after Diomedes inveigled his horses into carnivorous habits they went mad and tore him to pieces. This is what each generation has done to us in return for the ugly lies we have taught them; for we have whispered in the ears of the children that it is necessary to kill animals for food and people for military objectives. Workers for peace have been afraid hitherto of the extra burden involved in attacking a deeply rooted food habit. But the truth is that they would be greatly strengthened by the integration; for there is something in the human mind that likes consistency. Furthermore, the roots of the flesh-eating habit are not deep. We can safely challenge any parent to present a young child with a lamb and a bag of almonds, to explain impartially the process of getting protein from each source and to let the child choose his food accordingly. If we were to grow children again in the environment of the temple garden, the number of sad faces would begin to decrease; happiness would become the rule; and art would have a chance to develop. Since the time of the Essenes most Christians have refused to face this situation, have not been concerned that people should train their babies to a repulsive and perverted diet. Supposing the pulpit spoke out and connected daily food with redemption! The result in moral strength would be immeasurable. If violence were no longer at the center of daily diet and of land use, it would soon cease to be the foundation of our public affairs where at present it requires nine-tenths of the national budget. It is true that modern industry has greatly intensified the competition for mineral resources. The deposits of coal, iron, gold, oil, tin, copper, etc., have been prizes of trade and close to the roots of war. But they have never been the shibboleth that excited men to kill and die. Control over land *per se* has been the rallying cry. Fight for your homes! Fight for your freedom! Such have been the slogans that have caused people to accept conscription, without which modern war would be impossible. A reduction in the pressure for land would ease that extreme nationalism which is the danger point in our world situation. And a purified diet would stiffen our intellectual and moral fiber and send the unclean spirits of war over the cliff with the swine even as in the Gadarene legend.'

The magazine *Time* of 6 Sept. 1948, p. 13, col. B, reports that the American Vegetarians are running a candidate of their own for that year's Presidential election, one John Maxwell, an eighty-four-year-old Chicago doctor of 'naturopathy'. 'The party advocates extermination of all cattle and conversion of their grazing lands to food production.' This vegetarian party is apparently not animated by ethical motives and Dr. Albert Schweitzer's respect for the sanctity of all life, but by purely practical motives. Far from being impossible, the advocated 'extermination of all cattle' was very nearly achieved in Soviet Russia when the *muzhiks* slaughtered and devoured the live stock they did not want to see nationalized. The consequences were not such as to recommend the procedure as exemplary.

Although not myself a vegetarian, I am sufficiently moved by archetypal emotions to feel that, given an all the year round abundance of really good fruit and cereals, I should not too much miss all the rest of my food. What I cannot imagine is how propaganda, however effective, could succeed in reversing the trend of dietary evolution from 'The Fall' to the present time.

I do not believe with Dr. Louis Berman, *Food and Character*, London (Methuen), 1933, p. 158, in 'natural vegetarians' and 'natural carnivorous varieties of human beings'. These 'varieties' described by Goldthwaite, Bryant, Berman and others are beyond doubt products of human history, that is of human choice leading to climatic adaptation, vegetarianism in the tropics, carnivorous diet in the cold northern regions.

I am not a hunter of any kind. I have, as a boy, shot a roe-buck but, having looked into the beautiful eyes of the dead animal, gave up this sport for ever. But I also know that over-preservation of wild life and not shooting any of the lovable creatures of the wild is absolutely impossible. It would ruin not only agriculture and orchardry, even if fields and gardens were fenced, but the forests themselves. There was in my country a great forest-owner, Count Überacker, who enclosed a large deer-forest and stopped all shooting. A completely ruined forest with the bark rubbed off the ghostly white, dead trunks of the finest trees used to stand there as a monument of well-meaning human folly. I do not know what became of it after the Nazi invasion of Austria. Nor are sacred cows in India, dying a 'natural death' with carrion crows and vultures feeding on their emaciated bodies while they are still alive but too weak to defend themselves a very edifying spectacle.

Cf. in this context the opinion of Thomas Day, the author of *Sandford and Merton*, quoted by Hesketh Pearson in his biography of Erasmus Darwin (*Doctor Darwin*, London (Dent), 1930, pp. 51 f.). Day 'would willingly have been a vegetarian, if he had not decided that "the practice of rearing and killing animals for food was productive of more happiness than pain to them; as the existence of most of them is owing to this practice, and their lives, though shortened, are rendered comfortable by the indulgence of their appetites, while no fear of the deaths to which they are destined disturbs their repose"'. I do not think that Hesketh Pearson is right in saying: 'This seems about as good an excuse for eating *pâté de foie gras* as anyone has come upon,' because the forceful overfeeding of closely-caged geese necessary for producing the artificially enlarged livers means torturing the geese, while cows, bulls and oxen, sheep and goats on their pastures do enjoy their lives as much as they are able to, until they are killed by man in a more 'humane' way than the bear or wolf killed their wild forebears. If the killing of animals—in the 'humanest' possible way, of course—is apparently unavoidable, meat-eating would seem to be at least excusable. Anyhow, this book is concerned with 'description, not prescription.'

184. See Eisler, *Orph.-Dionys. Myst.*, p. 234, note 4, the quotation from Plutarch, *Convivium Septem Sapientium*, 16, 159 c; Kern, *Orph. Fragm.*, p. 62, No. 215, on 'the flight from the unjust actions connected with our food' where Orphic vegetarianism is called 'a sophism rather than a real avoidance of these wrongdoings'. As to the Manichaeans forbidden to kill animals, the Elect or Perfect ones among them abstained not only from both flesh and wine but also from picking fruit. Only spontaneously fallen fruit (αὐτόματοι καρποί), collected for them by their 'hearers', could be eaten by them (see Eisler, *ibid.*, pp. 231, note 2; 235, note 2; and 249).

185. THE HYMEN AND HONOUR

There is a touchingly delicate description of the young lover's fear of the loss of blood and the pain that defloration will inflict upon the beloved maiden in Longus' immortal Greek novel *Daphnis and Chloë* (III, 19, 2—III, 20, Loeb ed., George Thornley and J. M. Edmonds, London (Heinemann), 1916). But it is worth pointing out that the virgin's hymen seems to be a late acquisition of human females, presumably produced by the sexual selective action of the possessive jealous male attaching particular value to the demonstrably intact virginity of his female mates. No hymen is ever encountered in adult Chinese females owing to the deep-cleansing methods applied to female babies by their mothers at the earliest age and continued by Chinese girls taught to do so as soon as they can wash themselves. A rudimentary hymen is found in female elephants, horses, donkeys and bitches, bears, pigs, hyaenas and giraffes, but not in apes (see Hyrtl, *Anatomie*, II, p. 189; G. Gellhoen, 'Anatomy and Development of the Hymen', *Amer. Journal of Obstetrics*, August 1904). The phrase 'bridegroom of blood' (*hathan dam*) used in Exod. iv. 25 in connection with a Hebrew legend concerning the institution of circumcision shows that this widespread rite was originally a puberty ceremony intended as an anticipatory atonement for the blood shed in the process of defloration.

The feeling of guilt so widely connected among certain people with the sexual act in itself must have spread from this experience of shedding a virgin's blood. It cannot have existed in the matriarchal stage before the jealous and possessive patriarch had succeeded—by returning to her parents, who will often kill the rejected girl, as the Beduin do to this day, the bride not bleeding at the first penetration—in breeding from a highly-prized accidental mutation a pure strain of maidens provided with a hymen, an anatomical characteristic analogous to webbed feet or hands, which has since then been identified with 'a woman's honour, residing in her vagina whence it could be, with or without her consent, removed' (Doris Langley Moore, *The Vulgar Heart*, London (Cassell), 1945, p. 187). She might have quoted as an illustration of this perfectly correct statement the 'maiden's prayer' in the twenty-first of Pietro Aretino's *Sonnetti Lussuriosi* published in *Dubbii Amorosi e Sonnetti Lussuriosi*, printed at Paris about 1774 'chez Grompé aux dépens de Corbie, intendant du Duc de Choiseul et de Moëtte' (Bodl. Lib. Φ, f. 48):

> The girl: *stà sù, non mi far male, ohimé!*
> *stà sù, crudele! se non, moriró, stà sù!*
> *Lasciami stare perch'io griderò!*
> *Ahimè, qual dolor, ohimé non posso più!*
> The boy: .   .   .   .
>   .   .   .   .
> The girl: *Ohimé, crudel! ohimé, lascia mi andar!*
> *Guarda che fai, deh non mi tor l'honor!*
> *Se mi vuoi ben, deh non mi fa gridar!*

Answering the girl's pitiable complaint, the lover makes a coarse but simple proposal to the effect

> *che no havrai*
> *Doglia si grande e l'honor tu salverai.*

The meaning 'hymen' for *honore* is actually listed in the largest and most complete Italian dictionary by Tomaseo and Bellini. It no longer appears in Guglielmo Volpi's large *Vocabulario della Lingua Italiana*, Firenze (Barbera), 1945, p. 801, col. a, s.v. *onore*, No. 7 ='pudicizia, castità delle donne'. That certainly marks some progress.

I gather from stationery and leaflets that there is in Great Britain an 'Alliance of Honour', 'a specialist society in the field of sex-education, marriage and the family, founded in 1903, the name of which appears to be dedicated to the preservation and propagation of this patriarchalist idea.

The local proximity between the excretory and the reproductive organs—which, Bernard Shaw said, he would certainly have avoided, if he had been the Creator—is responsible for the sexual guilt-feelings of the modern fastidious worshipper of that cleanliness which is 'next to godliness'. See about this type, Hesketh Pearson, *Bernard Shaw: his Life and Personality*, London, (Collins), 1942, p. 108. 'W. T. Stead was a Puritan who had brooded so intensely on sex that his brain had got maggoty' (p. 111). 'He often told Cecil Chesterton... that the sexual act was to him monstrously indecent and that he could not understand how any self-respecting man and woman could face each other in the daylight after spending the night together' (*viz.* under the merciful cover of darkness). Unfortunately, this type, creating a great deal of unnecessary misery for itself and others, is not self-eliminating because the 'purer than thou brother' does succumb to the temptation of 'sin' as frequently as unredeemed man. See Harvey O'Higgins and E. H. Reede, *The American Mind in Action*, New York, 1924; also Heywood Broun and Margaret Leech's, very fair, illustrated biography of *Anthony Comstock*, New York (Boni), 1927. The remedy against the damage done by the Puritan attitude to sex was found by a much earlier sect, split off from the disciples of John the Baptist, known as the Hemerobaptists and described by Herbert G. Wood, *Encyclop. of Rel. and Eth.*, II, p. 391, note *, as an 'obscure sect'. This creed, which has now conquered, in a secularized form derived from the Roman devotion to the use of the public baths, the whole upper classes of the Western civilized world, is based on the theory attributed by Tertullian (*De baptismo*, c. 15) to his Jewish contemporaries: 'Israel Judaeus quotidie lavat quia quotidie inquinatur', ['Israel the Jew washes every day because every day he is defiled'], cf. *De oratore*, c. 14: 'omnibus licet membris lavet quotidie Israel, nunquam tamen mundus est' ['Although Israel washes all his members every day, yet he is never clean']. 'Clean living' does not, indeed, consist in a neurotic, hysterical fear to touch what is deemed unclean, but in washing as often and as thoroughly as possible. The documents about the Jewish *tob'lêi shaharith* or 'morning bathers' who insisted on a full immersion bath every morning because of the possibility of night pollution (*Tosefta Yadayîm* II *c. fin.: Jer. Talmud Berakhot*, fol. 15, I–III, 6 c; *Babyl. Talm. Berakh.*, fol. 22a) are discussed by Wilh. Brandt Suppl. XVIII to the *Zeitschr. f. alttest. Wissenschaft*, Göttingen, 1910, pp. 48 ff., sect. 15; *ibid.* on the Christian Hemerobaptists (Justin Martyr, *Dial. c. Tryph*, p. 307; Hegesippus, quoted by Eusebius, *Hist. Eccl.*, IV, 22; *Constit. Apost.*, VI, 6; Epiphanius, *Haeres.* XVII, 1, cf. *Epitome*, 17; further sources Brandt, *op. cit.*, p. 2, especially the testimony of 'Ebion', that is of the Ebionite 'Gospel of the Poor,' that St. Peter took a daily bath before touching his bread, a very plausible thing for a fisherman living on the lake-shore to do. See Brandt, *op. cit.*, pp. 90–122, on the daily bathings in the Jordan and Euphrates of Ebionites, Elkhasaites, Mazbothaeans, Mughtasilas, Sabaeans, etc.; also the ample literature on the Mandaean Gnostic 'bathers' (W. Brandt, *Encyclop. of Relig. and Eth.*, VIII, pp. 380–393; E. S. Drower, *The Mandaeans of Iraq and Iran*, Oxford Univ. Press, 1937). The psychological effects of this now secularized and common practice are of the greatest importance.

The basic fact underlying all our valuations is the biological metabolism. 'Good' in this fundamental sense—the very word 'good' is a click expressive of oral satisfaction—is that which we can and must eat, that is incorporate, to sustain life; 'bad' is what we have to reject, spew out or excrete through the organs developed for the purpose. These excrements, including the irritating deposits of dust and perspiration on the skin, must be removed from the body as thoroughly as possible and the animal has to get away as quickly as possible from the places where it has dropped excrements, carriers of disease and sources of smells which betray his presence to dangerous enemies. The excretions are that which is essentially 'bad' for him (Greek κακά, 'the evil things', is the universal baby-word for what must be excreted and avoided). To call all sexual and erotic phenomena 'dirt' and 'filth'—even Prof. C. G. Jung does not quite refrain from this equivocation when he criticizes Freud (*Modern*

Man in Search of a Soul, London (Kegan Paul), 8th impr., 1945, p. 52, where he speaks of a 'swamp' and 'mud puddle')—is wholly unscientific. 'Dirt' and 'filth' are just 'matter in the wrong place' and the 'wrong place' is simply where *we* do not want it to be and therefore excrete and remove it from ourselves or *vice versa* ourselves from it. The Hemerobaptist habit of washing daily, or many times daily, because we are constantly and unavoidably contaminated, removes not only undesirable matter and its scent from our skins, but also the depressing feeling of being 'unclean' and therefore as objectionable and hateful to oneself as one may be in this state to whatever invisible ancestral powers and spirits there may be. This is the subjective psychological meaning of the feeling of 'guilt', or 'sin' or 'sinfulness'. In this sense, 'sin' can really and easily, at that, be washed away in water, and there was no reason for Juvenal (I, 520–523) to be so satirical about the 'superstitious' Roman washing away his sins by dipping his head three times in the waters of the Tiber. The 'moral' valuations of the 'great unwashed' will, therefore, gradually come in line with the more latitudinarian ideas of those who do not allow themselves to become 'defiled' by any contact whatever with the equally clean bodies of their fellow-creatures. The adage 'To the pure everything is pure' is true in this sense. On the basis of the biological explanation given above of 'the bad' (*κακά*) as the 'execrable', the only 'perversions' are those of a coprophilic character, running counter to the metabolic need of removing the inassimilable and incorporating only what we can profitably assimilate. But even such 'perversions', inverting the general metabolic trend that must be followed if the species and the individual are to survive, are not 'against nature' (see above, note 4, on the meaning of this term). Anyone observing the behaviour of his dogs and cats cannot fail to observe that they bury their excrements so as to prevent them from betraying their presence to their enemies. They use them, however, equally instinctively for signalling to their own kin, thus enabling them to follow their track. The annoying tendency of cleanly kept pet-dogs to roll themselves in cattle- or sheep-dung, or even on carrion lying in the fields, must be an atavist survival of a lupine practice designed to camouflage their own characteristic scent by applying these alien 'perfumes'. It is evident that the smells thus distributed all over their hunting-grounds are erotically attractive to the members of the herd which they are intended to attract. Such *prima facie* strange human 'perversions' as 'undinism' are easily understandable as archetypal survivals from the behaviour of our animal ancestors. This ancestral behaviour need not even be subhuman. That excellent anthropologist Geoffrey Gorer (*Africa Dances*, London, 1938, Pelican ed., 1946, p. 100) records a 'disconcerting habit of pissing while engaged in conversation' of the Cabrai, both sexes of whom walk about completely naked. These are, of course, atavistic habits perpetuating the usual dog-courtesies, so well known and often so embarrassing to the owners of canine pets when meeting those of strangers so evidently annoyed by the spectacle. Since the tame dog is certainly descended from some wild lupine or vulpine ancestor, these dog-courtesies must be originally wolf- or fox-habits. Since nothing similar is recorded by observers of ape and monkey behaviour, they would seem to be habits acquired together with the hunters' werewolf-mask by men who became 'naked savages' in the process and transmitted coprophilic and undinist (ureticophilic) habits to their descendants.

There is no doubt that, among the unwashed people or classes, the sensitivity of the sense of smell is dulled against the ever-present weaker body-scents and that the more pungent of them act as aphrodisiacal incitements for them (Krafft-Ebing, *op. cit.* note 6 above, p. 77). In the throes of the 'hangover', such people will naturally be inclined to connect their feeling of guilt with the natural customary abhorrence of 'dirt' or 'filth', momentarily overcome by the invincible erotic urge. On the other hand a *nostalgie de la boue* is quite often found among the more 'refined', habitually washing classes.

The anthropologist and the psychologist can do no better than follow strictly and unrelentingly Spinoza's advice: 'non ridere, non flere, intellegere' ['Neither laugh nor weep, but understand']. They will certainly be considerably helped in this task by reading the lecture on 'The Significance of Smell: some Speculations on the Phenomenology of Olfaction' delivered by Dr. F. A. Baker before the Royal College of Science on January 18, 1935 (*Journal of the R. Coll. of Science*, V, 1935, pp. 84 ff.) 'The profound differences in external habit and internal tempo', said this lecturer, 'which distinguish the Age of Reptiles from the Age of Mechanized Humanity, are emergences whose vehicles have been, whether mono- or polyphyletically, acts of sexual union culminating in birth. In this way and through these channels the life eternal of the Germ is canalized in the lives of its mortal Somata and the Past, persisting in the Present, debouches upon a Future towards which perpetually it is drawn; so that Reproduction, whose span embraces the extreme terms of Duration, is the medium, simultaneously, of Heredity and Variation.

'If smell is, therefore, as we are supposing, in contradistinction to sight, the *organon*, not of actualities extended in Space, but of unlocalized potentialities enduring in and emergent through Time, then we should expect to discover, *inter alia*, an intimate physiological relation between the organs of reproduction and those responsible for the production of odoriferous substances. Facts are not lacking which give countenance to this assumption. It is conspicuous, for instance, how in the higher vertebrates, the organographical locus of the reproductive organs includes olfactory glands. I recall the so-called *perineal glands*, familiar to everyone who has dissected a rabbit, and the homologous organs of the skunk, civet, musk-rat, and muskdeer; together with the functional relation of these organs to periods of intense sexual activity. Nor are these reciprocities confined to mammals or vertebrates. In insects, though more particularly in the Lepidoptera, similar relations are apparent. Thus, in moths and butterflies, olfactory attraction determines, if I may use in this connexion a happy phrase of Dürken, with *multiple assurance*, the association and union of the sexes. Fritz Müller, for instance, long ago noticed the presence, exclusively in the male, of well-developed organs of scent-production—the modified, erectile scales or androconia. So, also, he observed the characteristic odour produced by such structures in *Pieris napi* and *rapae*, *Papilio Grayi* and *Morpho Adonis*, the last smelling strongly of vanilla. These observations were later confirmed by Longstaffe and by Dixey, whilst the relation, long suspected, between scent production and sexual union was established by Carpenter who, in 1914, was "able to watch the mating of one of the African butterflies, and observed the male hovering over the female alternately protruding and withdrawing its plumy and conspicuous scent brush, and apparently scattering over her a perfumed dust composed of the débris of the scent scales" (Hampton). With regard to these phenomena, it is clear, direct aphrodisiacal stimulation of the female by the male is primarily in question. In addition to and reassuring this, however, we have the long-range attraction of the male by the female, early remarked by Delpino in the case of *Bombyx pavonia minor*; whilst to Fabre we owe a wonderful and lucid account of the same phenomenon in *Pavonia major*, "the Great Peacock". Observation shows, he tells us, that the guests at this nuptial feast do not make straight for their object, as they would if they derived their information from some kind of luminous radiation, whether known or unknown to our physical science. It is something that apprises them from afar, leads them to the proximity of the exact spot and then leaves the final discovery to the airy uncertainty of random searching. It is very like the way in which we ourselves are informed by hearing and smell, guides which are far from accurate when we want to decide the precise point of origin of the sound or the smell.

'In the case of Bombyx there are, it is true, certain facts which still await explanation. The odour is imperceptible to the human nose. The males, furthermore, reach the females over a distance of several miles, against a contrary gale. Nevertheless, albeit that a certain mystery is attached to the *mode* of perception, that it is *smell* which is *perceived* both general analogies and additional facts clearly indicate. Pieces of material, such as wool, for instance, that have been in contact with the female acquire the capacity for attraction. Again, in a hermetically sealed vessel the attraction ceases. "To give these" (*i.e.* the males) "a free passage", says Fabre, "one condition is indispensable: the receptacle in which the female is contained must be imperfectly closed, so as to establish a communication between the inner and the outer air." It remains to note that, in other insects, the smell produced by the female may be quite conspicuous to the human nose. The female of *Dacus zonatus* smells of citronella, whilst the male is odourless. Moreover, the essence of citronella is a powerful source both of attraction and stimulation to the latter, so that they will "almost cover a handkerchief scented with it, sitting on the scented surface and rocking to and fro in their characteristic courtship movement" (Hampton). Through such facts, it is clear, our hypothesis, this time reference to extrospective analysis, gains a further credibility.

'In speaking of the relation of Smell to Memory, we have ignored a revelation that is no less relevant to our discussion— I mean its directly perceived aphrodisiac quality, in which we observe, subjectively, that same relation of smell to sexuality which, objectively, is disclosed through the physiological connexion between the reproductive organs and the olfactory glands.

'The oblation to Aphrodite—whether as Urania or Pandemos —which from every perfume perpetually ascends, indicates, to our more prosaic inquiry, that the organological relations we have been discussing are in nowise superficial or contingent. Rather do they constitute something of one piece with the final nature of olfactory perception. Nor should this, now, be altogether hard to understand. For, if reminiscence, the nostalgic emotion, is the feeling of things past, then is every erotic emotion, and above all the sexual feeling, a portent of things to come, since, as Schopenhauer crisply observes, "That which is decided by it, is nothing less than the composition of the next generation. The *dramatis personae* who shall appear when we are withdrawn, are here determined, both as regards their existence and duration, by these frivolous affairs." ' The speaker then proceeds to discuss 'certain connexions established between the olfactory qualities and the chemical composition of odoriferous substances. Consider, for instance, the extreme terms of olfactory perception as exemplified in the Stench and Perfume respectively. Now, a stench is the odour of corruption and of death; whilst a perfume we might call, by reason of its aphrodisiac connotation, the smell of life itself. But, as Schopenhauer has it, "Birth and Death are the projection of the same line in opposite directions"; and, if physiologists prefer, rather, to speak of Anabolism and Katabolism, that is only, *bien entendu*, the familiar impulse of the scientist to exorcise the ghosts of metaphysics by verbal incantations. If, therefore, smell relates throughout to the potentialities of organic metamorphosis enduring in Time, it should relate, simultaneously, to Birth and Death, and this dual reference to the terminal moments of Generation should be capable of demonstration, *inter alia,* in the chemistry of perfume. This almost appears to be the case. Smell, I mean, discerns, in the chemistry of substances, their physiological relation to the ascending phases of metabolism. Now, the smell of corruption, as witnessed in the disintegration of protein, is intimately associated with the production of indole and its methyl derivative scatole; a fact variously observable through the activities of bacteria (such as the colon group) the higher fungi, such as the stinkhorn (*Ithyphallus impudicus*) or of aroids (such as the English *A. maculatum,* the Mediterranean *A. Italicum,* or the giant exotic species *Amorphophallus*). Mark now a significant point. It is precisely the same indole derivatives, which we encounter in putrefaction, that are intensely cultivated in the odoriferous glands of the skunk and civet. A relation that we may term dialectical becomes apparent. "Les extrêmes se touchent"—just as the spectrum exhibits, in the violet and red respectively, the terminal recurrence of a common colour, so here, the limits of olfaction, the stench and perfume, coincide, and the odour of corruption functions directly as an aphrodisiac. Does this fact stand alone as the lamentable idiosyncrasy of cats? Scarcely so—nor are we able ourselves altogether to disclaim their tastes. Albeit that there can be few of us here to whom the undiluted essence of civet affords delight, it is precisely to indole derivatives that perfumes owe their sweetness and allure. A perfume, it has been said, is a "diluted stink" (see the diagram above, p. 26. Witness, for example, the cloying sweetness of Jasmine (whose oil contains much scatole) which can become, through excessive production, in hot weather, definitely putrid in character. Conversely, witness how many bacterial decompositions which, if they ran their full course, would issue in bad smells, are, when partially inhibited, merely conducive to a pleasant fragrance. Again, for the same reasons, the extract of civet procures for itself a permanent place in the armoury of the manufacturing perfumer. It is interesting also to note how quantitative preferences in this regard vary with race and climate. As we proceed south, more and more indole must enter the composition of a perfume to afford the dying falls of an olfactory harmony; the extreme in this direction, I should imagine, being attained by the inhabitants of Somaliland, whose toilet, I have seen stated, does not fear to embrace the musk of crocodiles. All in all, then, the phenomenology of smell affords only mediocre arguments for the moralist and hygienist. Even the most sanctified odours owe a debt to corruption which they must find it hard to repay. Indeed, where it is lacking, sweetness, alarmed at so austere a cleanliness, is already on the wing. Shall we see, then, in the dialectic relations which Nature seems to establish not only between Birth and Death generally, but, in particular, between the very organs of excretion and those of generation, a bad joke or a good symbol . . . what Goethe would have called an "Urphänomen"? Well, maybe the two are not altogether incompatible, and Lucretius who, at the beginning of the *De Natura*, sublimely invokes Venus, towards the end of that masterpiece is found to indulge in some extremely spiteful, not to say malodorous comparisons. This, however, is scarcely our concern—what is here of importance being, simply, that we should recognize, as illustrated by the chemistry of perfume, the co-implicated participation of smell in the extreme terms of organic metamorphosis.'

186. MATING PRACTICES: MARRIAGE BY CAPTURE
See above, note 147, and below, note 194.

The atavistic savagery of the primeval lupine pack assuaging their bestial lust amidst an orgy of wolfish aggressiveness against the defenceless food-gatherers did not refrain from lacerating and even strangling the victims of aggression—and had no motive to do so, because the blind mating-instinct is by no means an inherited urge in man to reproduce his kind. (Dr. W. A. Brend, *op. cit.*, p. 185, has rightly emphasized this fact in his criticism of Mr. R. F. Harrod's assumption—shared by other authorities—that there exists an instinct of reproducing one's kind.) The fact that the Roman *Luperci* (below, p. 254, Appendix II) were still allowed, once a year, to chase the Roman matrons and beat them with leather thongs, shows the sort of tough behaviour of hunters and drovers corraling their booty which implanted in the female descendants of the victims of lupine aggression the paradoxical subconscious concatenation of the erotic urge with a desire to suffer violence, strong enough to overcome the natural desire to run away from the threatening ravisher. The 'folly' of the wer-wolves attacked both sexes (Judg. xix. 22)—indeed anything and everything living. 'Bestiality' in the technical sense of the word (Levit. xviii. 23 f.: xx. 15 f.), nowadays mainly practised by feeble-minded peasant lads, is said (Gen. vi. 12; 'all flesh has corrupted his way') to have been general in the antediluvian world. It is, indeed, plausible that cannibal wer-wolves devouring their own kind, because their predatory aggressive behaviour was untrammelled by reflexion about zoological 'class-distinctions', satisfied their libidinous urges with equal unconcern for the difference between 'intraspecific' and 'extraspecific' objects of their sexual appetites. (Cases of women carried off into the jungle by baboons and orang-utans are collected in the Rev. Dr. Mac-Culloch's *Childhood of Fiction*, p. 277.) Such mythological hybrid monsters as centaurs, goat-men, bull-men, etc., were not considered by the Babylonians (Berossos, frgm. 12 Schnabel, p. 254) and Greeks (Empedocles, frgms. 61 and 62 Diels) as creatures of human imagination and of ritual masquerade, but as the offspring of human beings mating with animals. Such myths as the story of Pasiphaë and the bull and of the bull-headed monster Minotaurus, born of this union, cannot very well be separated from the still observable phenomenon of therioanthropic delusion—men or women walking on all fours, trying to graze and imagining themselves transformed into bulls or cows or other sexually uninhibited animals (above, p. 163). Because of these indiscriminating sexual passions of the experimenting variety of *Palaeoanthropus* and because many a wolfish virago or 'harridan' (above, p. 159, note 116) of the Penthesilea type coursed with the pack, ready to put her canine teeth into the flesh of a captured male singled out for an erotic wrestle, a paradoxical longing for active as well as passive cruelty has been transmitted by sexual selection to members of both sexes descended from the aggressive lupine hunters and the submissive food-gatherers and food-growers. In all of them these 'tough', violent sex-experiences would be accompanied by a feeling of committing a grievous transgression of the ancestral laws of life and a 'bestial' sin of disobedience against the will of the gentler ancestral divinities dwelling in the protective grove of fruit-bearing trees (above note 177), deepened by the psychological depression following in the wake of such exhausting excesses—*omne animal post coitum triste*, as St. Augustine said in a disquisition about the *peccatum originale*—very truly indeed, if the sentence is referred to a mating of the atavistic lupine violence, devoid of all tenderness. It is this sin for which the sinners would try to atone by sacrifices, bloody immolations to divinities conceived in their own image as rejecting with contempt the vegetable offerings of the toiling serf of the soil (Gen. iv. 2 f.), accepting only slaughtered firstlings of their flocks or even first-born children of the human herd (Exod. xiii. 2) and gladly 'smelling the sweet savour of burnt-offerings' (Gen. viii. 21). While coyness and fear of gentle and uninhibited love-mating—such as Prof. Malinowski found among the Trobriand Islanders and described in a famous book (below, note 191), as the painter Gauguin met with it in Tahiti (below, note 191)—could not exist among the females of the undifferentiated herds of peaceful food-gatherers, any more than it does among those of the great apes, it stands to reason that these same females would dread and run away from the violent and reckless aggressions of the carnivorous and cannibal hunter in his wolf's pelt. The desperate flight of the maidens from these terrifying bridegrooms is idealized in the myth of the fleet-footed Arcadian Atalantê delayed by the temptation of the golden apples irresistible for females with the atavistic tastes of the fruitarian and her suitors. According to Callimachus (*Dian.*, 221 ff.) and Apollodorus (III, 9, 2) Atalantê was exposed by her father Mainalos ('the raving one', a male counterpart to the Maenades), son of wolfish Lykaon, son of the bear-hero Arkas, suckled and brought up by a she-bear. This feral child, radiantly beautiful, decides to yield only to the man who can run her down in a race—obviously the mythical *aition* or explanation of a mating-ritual, still surviving among certain African tribes, which led to an extremely useful sexual selection, only the fleetest runner being able to catch and mate with the fastest of the females (Marett, *op. cit.*, p. 163). According to

Apollodorus (*l.c.* and **XIII**, 3) Atalantê wrestled with Pêleus, the father of Achilles. It is obvious that among the rough bear-tribes of ancient Arcadia boys raced the maidens and wrestled with them as a prelude to mating or 'marriage by capture', a custom thought by J. F. McLennan (*Studies in Ancient History*, London, 1876–1896, cf. Lang and Atkinson, *Social Origins, Primal Law*, London, 1903), with better reasons than later anthropologists were willing to admit (W. H. R. Rivers, *Encyclop. of Rel. and Eth.*, VIII, p. 430, 21, 'Marriage by capture') to have been universal at some early stage in the evolution of mankind. These mixed races, wrestling and tumbling matches were re-vived in the matings of Hitler Youths with the members of the corresponding *Bund Deutscher Mädchen*.

187. Exogamic sexual intercourse would more often than not take on the shape of 'bride-robbing' and rape. It is therefore not surprising that the widespread 'original sin' tradition should lump together the reminiscences of the broken food-taboo and of the sexual insult upon the hunter's human booty.

188. THE BILI CULT

Cf. Count Byron de Prorok, *Dead Men Do Tell Tales*, London (Harrap), 1943, p. 72, a report about the secret *Bili* cult in the Yombi district of Africa; p. 72: 'the dancers advanced and receded to the savage rhythms. They were not only imitating, they were impersonating lions, tigers, leopards, hippos, elephants and smaller animals, even to their cries and roars and calls . . . and worked themselves into a state of fanatical frenzy. In front of the priest's close a row of virgins were lying motionless. Before the priest's tent a leopard's skin hung. From behind it he comes forth striped with white paint, wearing a hideous mask, otherwise naked. While the maidens on the ground are held powerless by four men, he possesses one after the other'. In order to perform this superhuman effort—analogous to that of Herakles, characterized by his costume as the lion-man of Greek antiquity, who deflowered the fifty daughters of Thespios in a single night (Diodor., IV, 29; Pausanias, IX, 27, 6; Tatian, *Adv. Graec.*, 21; Clem. Alex., *Protrept.*, II, 23; Arnob., IV, 26; Cosm. Hierosolym. *Ad. c. Gregor.* 3, 501, Migne, *P.G.*

XXXVIII, 405)—the *Bili*-priest is supposed to be drugged with an extract of plants producing intense satyriasis for hours on end.

189. JOHN BULL

Paul Haupt, *Journal of the American Oriental Society*, XXX, p. 17. Just as so many hunting tribes proudly called themselves 'Wolves', there must have been considerable remains of the original innocuous, vegetarian herds of early man, *Palaeoanthropus*, fancying himself ideologically as a peacefully grazing and chewing 'Taurian' or 'John Bull'. There were 'Taurians' on the northern coast of the Black Sea, this name being presumably the native appellation of the 'agricultural Scythians' (*Σκύθαι ἀγροτῆρες*) as distinct from the 'nomadic Scythians'. To judge from their heavy bovine type, accurately rendered by the Greek artists of the Ionian trading-towns on this coast, they were the ancestors of the bearded, sedate and hefty Russian *muzhik*. Red silhouette paintings of the post-glacial age on rocks of Southern Spain show men with bull-horns on their heads armed with a sort of boomerang, reprod. by Moritz Hörnes, *Urgeschichte der Kunst*, 2nd ed., Vienna, 1915, p. 155, fig. 2, who compared them with the bison-masks used by North American Indians in their dances imitating animals (*op. cit.*, p. 185). (See W. Deonna, 'Les masques quaternaires', *L'Anthropologie*, XXV, 1914, pp. 106 ff.). Mediterranean tribes wearing a helmet with bulls' horns sprouting from it—*i.e.* what the Greeks called a *ταυρείη κυνέη* or 'bullish dog's (cap)' (see below, p. 229, note 229) —are shown on Egyptian monuments. Bronze figures representing warriors with such helmets have been found in Sardinia. Evidently those men, called *Shardana* in the Egyptian sources, fancied themselves as bulls goring their aggressors with their horns.

'Lewis Baboon', 'Nicholas Frog' and all other zoological nicknames introduced in 1712 by Dr. John Arbuthnot into his now almost forgotten political allegory *Law is a bottomless Pit*, re-issued in 1727 as *The History of John Bull*, designed to ridicule the Duke of Marlborough, have sunk into oblivion. But 'John Bull' for the British 'caught the British imagination and has been in use ever since' (Burton Stevenson), because it does correspond to the ideology of the English (see W. L. Hanchant, 'John Bull: Who is he?', *The Leader*, 19 May 1945, pp. 11–14). 'In John Bull the nation of shopkeepers could view their own likeness' (Lester M. Beattie, *John Arbuthnot*, London, 1935). See (Charles Morgan), *Menander's Mirror* (*Times Lit. Suppl.*, 21 Oct. 1944). ' "Unenglish" is a perilous word, those who use it . . . are too ready to assume that our race is exclusively bovine.' In a print '*Paddy on Horseback*' dated March 1779, by Gillray, England is symbolized as a bull. In a print '*John Bull triumphant*' of 1780, the bull is shown throwing the Spanish bullfighter into the air. Out of the defeated *torero's* pockets money is seen to fall—an allusion to the three million dollars of prizes captured in the recent war.

190. William Robertson Smith, *Kinship and Marriage in Ancient Arabia*, 2nd ed., p. 219. Cf. *Kababish*, sing. *Kabashi*, from *kbs*', 'sheep', and *Ma'aze*, from ' '*z*', 'goat', as tribal names of Syrian and Arabic clans, B. Moritz, *Abh. d. Göttinger Gesellschaft d. Wissensch.*, XVI, 2, 1916, p. 29, note 3. C. H. Becker, *Encyclop. of Islam*, I, 561, on the *Baqqara* or 'cattle-breeding' Beduins of the Sudan.

The Christian Church, seeing itself as a herd of sheep, led by the Good Shepherd, has inherited this symbolism from the Jews, who represented their people in a curious Apocalypse written about 130 B.C., now incorporated in the Ethiopian *Book of Enoch* and illustrated on the sarcophagus of Junius Bassus (Eisler, *Orph.-Dionys. Myst.*, p. 49, figs. 22 f.) as a herd of sheep surrounded and attacked by the pagan nations travestied as packs of wild animals and birds. The metaphor is, indeed, much older. Israel is described as 'these sheep' by David in II Samuel, as 'the sheep' which 'became meat to all the beasts of the field' in Ezekiel and as 'the sheep of God's pasture' in many of the Psalms. It is not, however, peculiar to the religious literature of the Jews which became the Scriptures of the Christian Church. It is implied in the political theory of all the old Oriental monarchies—Egyptians, Kaspians, Babylonians, Persians—who all described their king as the 'shepherd of men'— or, to speak with the Homeric Achaeans, as the 'shepherd of peoples' ($\pi o\iota\mu\acute{\eta}\nu\ \lambda\alpha\tilde{\omega}\nu$)—and propounded the ideal, passed on to the Greeks at the time of Alexander the Great, that the whole of humanity should live peacefully as 'one herd under one shepherd'.

191. *Sex and Repression in Savage Society*, London (Kegan Paul), 1927, p. 111; *The Father in Primitive Psychology; The Sexual Life of Savages in North West-Melanesia.*

192. *Letters to his Wife and Friends*, ed. Maurice Malingue, trans. by Henry J. Stenning, London (Saturn Press), 1948.

193. HUNGER AND AGGRESSION

Dr. F. S. Perls, *Ego, Hunter and Aggression*, London (Allen & Unwin), 1947, p. 116, has the immense merit of having called the attention of the psychoanalyst to hunger, the one of the two powers 'keeping life alive'—as Schiller said:

> *Einstweilen, bis den Bau der Welt Philosophie zusammenhält,*
> *Erhält sie das Getriebe durch Hunger und durch Liebe.*

In an age when milk-bottles and loaves of bread grew on the doorsteps and the rest of the groceries flowed out of delivery vans, neither Freud nor Adler nor Jung devoted any attention to the baby's and the toddler's aggressive reaction to hunger. We had to wait for Dr. Perls's book (p. 133) to realize that the wolf in Grimm's fairy tale was not in love with granny when he swallowed her, but simply hungry or rather famished.

194. DERIVATION OF THE WORD SABINE

The name *Sabinus* is plausibly derived from an Illyrian word *saba'* for an intoxicating beverage, in Illyrian *sabaium*, in Italian *zabbaione*. (See J. E. Harrison, *Prolegomena to the Study of Greek Religion*, Cambridge, 1922, p. 419, note 2; Forcellini de Witt, *Lat. Dict.*, s.v. 'sabaium', quoting St. Jerome's *Comm. in Isaiam*, ch. 19: 'quod genus potionis est ex frugibus aquaque confectum et vulgo in Daciae Pannoniaeque provinciae gentili barbaroque sermone appellatur sabaium' ['A kind of drink which is made out of fruits and water, and in Dacia and Pannonia is commonly called *sabaium*']. Ammianus Marcell., 26, 8, 2, says that the emperor Valens was nicknamed *sabaiarius*; 'est autem sabaia ex ordeo vel frumento in liquorem conversus paupertinus in Illyrico potus' ['Sabaia is a wretched drink made in Illyria out of barley or wheat.']. Accadian *subu* is a kind of wine, Hebrew *sobe'*, denomin. *saba'*, Aram. *seba'*, 'wine-bibber'; Arabic *siba'*, 'wine', denominative *saba'a*, 'import wine'; Aethiopian *shewa*, 'beer', Tigrena *shuwa'*, 'millet-beer' (Littmann, *Aksum Expedition*, IV, 1913, p. 6).

The Thracian god Dionysos, =*Dios-synsos*, 'son of Zeus', is called Σαβάζιος, his followers Σαβαχοί; Sanskrit *sāvā* means to 'press wine'. The word has been borrowed by the Semites, probably from the Illyrian Philistines in Syrian Palestine. See Eisler, *Orph.-Dion. Myst.*, p. 232, note 3. Dr. Louis Berman, *Food and Character*, London (Methuen), 1933, p. 158, discussing what he calls 'natural vegetarian and naturally carnivorous varieties of human beings' (see above, note 183), points out that flesh-eaters prefer stronger alcoholic drinks and in general alcohol to sugar, while vegetarians prefer sugar to alcohol. This would, of course, induce hunting tribes to fall upon the fruit-eaters during the grape-harvest and to enjoy the new must in the fermented state, while the fruitarians would eat the grapes and drink the must in its fresh state. Dr. Berman points out (*l.c.*) that the flesh-eaters have larger reproductive organs, therefore presumably stronger sexual urges. This accounts for the tradition about women being raped in the vineyards. Even today the grape-harvest is a time of great erotic licence in all wine-growing countries. According to Coleman, *Hindoo Mythology*, p. 321, the metamorphosis into were-tigers is believed to be due to frequent alcoholic intoxication. In modern terms, it is considered a symptom of *delirium tremens*.

195. See above, p. 133, note 111.

196. See Dr. Rendel Harris, *The Ascent of Olympus*, Manchester Univ. Press, 1917, *The Cult of Apollo*, pp. 36–55. The god has now been found as *Apollionosh* on cuneiform tablets of the Hittite archives (E. O. Forrer, *Revue Hittite*, 1931, pp. 141 ff.

197. ARTEMIS AND ACTAEON
See above, p. 157, end of note 116. To the story of merciless,

wolfish Artemis *Λυκειῆ* who transforms Actaeon into a stag (the reader will remember the stag horns worn by the cuckold) and orders him to be torn to pieces by her 'bitches', because he, the voyeur or Peeping Tom, has seen her in her bath, nude, that is without the wolf's (or bear's) pelt; compare the story of the troubadour Pierre Vidal who fell in love with the lady known as *La Louve* (the she-wolf) of Penaultier, had himself sewn into a wolf's pelt and was chased away by her dogs and huntsmen (Raynouard, *Poésies des Troubadours*, V, p. 338, quoted by Bourquelot, *Mém. d. l. Soc. des Antiq. de France, Nouv. Série*, IX, p. 229, note 2). A similar story is told by Suetonius (*Nero* 29) of the emperor Nero, who had himself sewn into the pelt of a wild beast, caged and released, when he would proceed to attack the privy parts of men and women bound to stakes and finally allow himself to be 'slain' by his secretary, freedman and wedded 'wife' Doryphoros. Even as *La Louve de Penaultier*, Queen Isabel of Bavaria, wife of Edward II, the mother of Charles VII of France, whom she declared to be a bastard, was called *La Louve Bavaroise*.

> *She-wolf of France—with unrelenting fangs*
> *That tear'st the bowels of thy mangled mate*
> (Gray, *The Bard*).

In both cases 'la louve' is the equivalent of Roman *lupa*, Greek *λυκῆ*, 'harlot' (above, p. 155, note 116). The counterpart to this Provençal story is in the first book of Longus' novel *Daphnis and Chloë* (I, 21, p. 42, Edmonds), where the wicked shepherd Dorkôn (=the 'spyer', from *δέρκομαι*, 'look sharply', 'the voyeur' or 'peeping Tom') who dresses himself in a wolf's pelt before he tries to rape Chloë.

See above, p. 109, note 98, p. 148, note 116.

198. *Epist.*, I, II, 27. According to Pliny, *Nat. Hist.*, XIX, 52: 'the garden is the poor man's slaughter-house' (*macellum*).

199. See Robert Koch's description of the inhabitants of Sesse island in the Victoria Nyanza who 'live exclusively on bananas available all the year round so that they need no storage-huts. Each family needs a grove of four to five hundred banana plants

and lives in a hut in the middle of it. All the cattle is owned by the chiefs and constitutes a sort of "capital" (*pecunia*). Even they rarely slaughter one of them or a goat' (quoted after Moritz Hörnes, *op. cit.*, I, p. 489).

200. HUNTING, PRIMITIVE AND MODERN

Sociologists rarely realize that the stratified society, beginning in prehistoric times and leading to the establishment of mixed farming and to ploughing by means of yoked cattle in settlements grouped around fortified enclosures, is the result of the subjugation of a primitive matriarchal, frugivorous and agricultural, hoeing and dibbling population by hunters and drovers, not as yet really cattle-breeding tribes. The government of this stratified society remains in the hands of these herdsmen-hunters, first exclusively and then mainly. In order to grasp the relevant facts it is necessary to study the books on the history of hunting, such as Comte de Chabot's *La Chasse à travers les âges*, Paris, 1898; Kurt Lindner, *Die Jagd im frühen Mittelalter*, Berlin (de Gruyter), 1940, etc. Sacheverell Sitwell's delightful book *The Hunters and the Hunted*, London (Macmillan), 1947, ch. XIII, p. 79 ff., has a marvellous description of the *Chasse Royale de Louis Quinze*, the stylized stag-hunting with hounds, still practised in this country too. See p. 86 on the 'curée chaude', the ceremonial equivalent of the primitive Dionysian tearing asunder of the quarry; on p. 57 he discusses Lucas Cranach's picture of the 'mimic war'[1] against the stags, conducted from the two hunting castles Morizburg and Hartenfels. The careful contemporary statistics show that the two prince-electors Johann Georg I and II of Saxony killed with their hounds and huntsmen between them in the seventy years from 1611 to 1688 110,530 deer and 52,400 wild boars, besides many wolves and bears. Toudouce, *lieutenant de la vénérie* of Prince Condé de Chantilly, killed in thirty-one years 924,717 birds, and animals (Comte de Chabot, *op. cit.*, p. 216). Virginia

[1] William Somerville (1675–1742), *The Chase*:

> . . . *the chase, the sport of kings,*
> *Image of war, without its guilt.*

Cf. the Assyrian and Egyptian representations of the king as the great hunter and lion-killer.

Woolf, *Three Guineas*, London (Hogarth Press), 1938, p. 265, note 3, quotes from the Duke of Portland's *Men, Women and Things*, p. 251: 'The number of animals killed in England for sport during the past century must be beyond computation. 1212 head of game is given as the average of a day's shooting at Chatsworth in 1909 (most of these animals were bred, reared and sometimes imported for shooting. It is not the case that a superabundance of wild animals needed to be kept down so as to protect agriculture from depredations. Game breeding is a form of food-production just like cattle breeding, only far more expensive).' With this cf. Macaulay's *Diary, ed. cit.*, p. 537 (2 March 1850): 'I have been reading a book called *Les Gentils-hommes Chasseurs*. The old régime would have been a fine thing if the world had been made only for gentlemen and if gentlemen had been made only for hunting.' Also G. Bernard Shaw, *Heartbreak House* (Preface dated July 1919), Act III, p. 171 of Tauchnitz ed.: '*Lady Utterword:* "There are only two classes in good society in England: the equestrian classes and the neurotic classes. It isn't mere convention: everybody can see that the people who hunt are the right people and the people who don't are the wrong ones." *Capt. Shotover:* "There is some truth in this. My ship made a man of me and a ship is the horse of the sea." '

Actually, this is the whole truth and nothing but the truth. Admirals and captains, on leave or retired, ride in every one of the famous hunts. The hunters and robbers, the fishermen and pirates are conquerors who have subdued the 'finders' (collectors) and fruitgrowers all over the world. As to the mentality of the great hunting and until lately, governing clans in this country, see Sir Osbert Sitwell, *The Scarlet Tree*, London (Macmillan), 1946, p. 175 (concerning the horsy crowd at Londesborough and Blankney): 'But though (p. 176) in their fashion they were most kind, yet if during the day-time a spare moment not already occupied with slaughter occurred, it, too, must necessarily be devoted at once to killing; otherwise they would consider they had wasted their time. No small creature on four feet, no feathered thing with wings as it ran over the snow, was safe in it, neither the fox—but that was a lengthy business and very ritualistic—nor hare shrieking its soul out like a human being, nor pheasants designed so splendidly for a brief autumn,

nor partridges more discreetly clothed than those who shot them,
nor the dark long-beaked birds of the marshes, snipe and wood-
cock, nor the ducks . . ., none of these could hope for much
mercy, while as for rabbits, they were collected by the attend-
ants, put in sacks and emptied out of them at a moment when
there was no other killing to be had, so that the tweed-clad
hordes of men and the women, many of whom accompanied
them, could set their dogs on these confused bolting creatures
and knock them on the head with sticks . . . Should those amusements fail, ratting could always be improvised through cellars
or in lofts. Yet if the leaders of the Horde appeared to be con-
sumed by some divine fury against the fowls of the air and the
soft furry beings of the wild creation, perhaps in their own
minds they compensated for it by their fantastic devotion to
horses, their insane passion for dogs; the horses constituting, as
it were, the gods, the dogs the angels or patron-saints.—The
men of the Golden Horde were almost as kind to children as to
horses and dogs—though naturally they regarded them with
less reverence—but to any male of the species who did not run
true to type, they could show an equal cruelty in many directions.' Also the frank confession in Nancy Mitford's *The Pursuit
of Love*, London (Hamish Hamilton), 1945, 1946, 1947, p. 25:
' . . . more than anything in the world they loved hunting. It
was in their blood and bones and in my blood and bones and
nothing could eradicate it, though we knew it for a kind of
original sin' (see above, p. 51). 'For three hours that day I
forgot everything, except my body and my pony's body . . . I
forgot everything, I could hardly have told you my name.
That must be the great hold that hunting has over people,
especially stupid people. It enforces an absolute concentration,
both mental and physical'. Obviously, this concentration is
brought about by the resonance of the 'archetypal' unconscious
of these hunters born and bred.—To abolish 'blood-sports' by
legislation in this country may be possible. But the short-
sighted sentimentalists who advocate it do not realize with
what a terrific force the suppressed energies would break out
elsewhere. Besides, here, too, apply the words of Dean Inge,
Outspoken Essays, First Series, pp. 42 f.: 'It is useless for the
sheep to pass resolutions in favour of vegetarianism, while the

wolf remains of a different opinion.' (*ibid.*, p. 121, 'The Curse of War'): 'Hunting, fishing and shooting are still the chosen amusements of the leisured class. We are fond of playing at occupations which for our ancestors were the serious business of life.'

201. While this lecture was being prepared for publication, *Picture Post* of 11 June 1949 published a short notice '*Tree-worshippers*' (*l.c.*, p. 23: 'Certain students found . . . a leafy island called le Chaton in the Seine' (Département). 'Here the devotees plan week-end hikes . . . by aerial routes from tree to tree. They climb, scramble and swing themselves along these routes, often forty yards or more up in the air. Their proficiency is such that professional acrobats who made bets that they could beat them in a race along the aerial course . . . finished as bad and sulky losers . . . the police-prefect of the Seine-et-Oise district has joined their ranks in the tree-tops.') One of the captions of the accompanying photographs reads 'The favoured game's not Mothers and Fathers but Tarzan and Maureen.' Considering what *jouer papa-maman* means in French argot, I should think both archetypal games are still the fashion. Another caption says: 'It is like stealing thunder from a chimp.' It is more like the 'reconstruction of the gibbon' dreamt of by Prof. C. G. Jung's patient (below, note 205).

202. Dr. Jolan Jacoby, *The Psychology of C. G. Jung*, London, *s.a.* (preface dated 1939), p. 46.

203. *Two Essays on Analytical Psychology*, London (Baillière, Tindall & Cox), 1928, p. 71, note 1: 'I have often been asked whence come these archetypes or primordial images . . . It seems to me that their origin can be explained in no other way than by regarding them as the deposits of the often-repeated experiences of humanity . . . Therefore we may assume that archetypes are the often-repeated impressions of subjective reactions. Obviously this hypothesis merely pushes the problem further back without solving it. Nothing prevents us, however, from assuming that certain archetypes are already present in animals; that they are involved in the peculiarities of the living

organism itself and are therefore immediate expressions of life whose nature cannot be further explained.' *Psychologie und Alchemie*, Zürich (Rascher), 1944, pp. 77 ff.

These dreams were first discussed in Prof. Jung's lecture 'Traumsymbole des Individuationsprozesses' at Ascona, 1935 (*Eranos-Jahrbuch* 1935), Zürich (Rheinverlag) 1936, pp. 1–133). They are available in English in his book *The Integration of the Personality*, London (Kegan Paul), 1940, ch. IV, pp. 96–204, quoted in the following notes with '(Engl.)' before the page-number.

204. *Op. cit.*, p. 177 (Engl. p. 143).

205. *Op. cit.*, p. 185 (Engl. p. 146).

206. *Op. cit.*, p. 79 (Engl. p. 102).

207. Cf. Dr. Otto Fenichel, *The Psychoanalytic Theory of Neurosis*, London (Kegan Paul), 1945, p. 419: 'A schizophrenic episode began with a patient's despair over the fact that a new hat did not fit. Analysis revealed that the patient felt different when he wore this hat; he believed that the shape of his head was altered by the hat. The body image of his head was changed. The exaggerated reaction to the hat was a distorted expression of the patient's fear that something was wrong with his head.'

208. *Op. cit.*, p. 81 (Engl. p. 103).

209. *Op. cit.*, p. 81 f. (Engl. p. 103).

210. *Op. cit.*, p. 82 (Engl. p. 104).

211. *Op. cit.*, p. 132 (Engl. p. 124).

212. *Eranos-Jahrbuch*, 1935, p. 101 (Engl. p. 174).

213. CANNIBALISM AND WEREWOLFISM IN TIME OF FAMINE
Among the Sei'ar in Hadramaut part of the tribe could change into ravening werewolves, others into falcons and

vultures in times of drought (W. Robertson Smith, *Religion of the Semites*, 4th ed., p. 88; cf. above, note 123). Times of drought mean times of hunger. It is hunger which produces aggression (see Dr. Perls, above, note 193) and it is hunger that turned the original peaceful hominids of the woods into carnivorous and even cannibal beasts. Cannibalism has been resorted to in our times by shipwrecked sailors adrift in a boat on the high seas, tortured by thirst and hunger; witness Capt. Marryat sailor's yarn in *Poor Jack* of a boatload of men and one woman, their ship sunk far from shore; famine and thirst finally prevail and one sailor, watched with horror, but unhindered by his fellows, cuts the woman's throat and drinks her blood, 'holding the dying victim in his arms almost as if he loved her'; and then, as the author makes plain enough, they all set to and ate her. Cannibalism (Richard Andree, *Die Anthropophagie*, Leipzig, 1882; MacCulloch, *Encyclop. of Rel. and Eth.*, vol. III, pp. 194–209, col. 2; especially p. 196, §6, II, No. 1, 'cannibalism from hunger') has again been resorted to by starved Japanese troops in World War II. (*The Times*, 27 April 1945, quoting dispatches written from Finisterre Ranges, New Guinea, in February 1945, cabled by *The Times* correspondent from Sydney. Also *The Times*, 15 Sept. 1945, cable from Melbourne about the report of a Chinese interpreter boarding the Australian frigate *Diamantina* off Nauru: 'The Japanese practised cannibalism, killing and eating their own people and the Chinese when their food supplies ran out, augmenting this diet with fish caught in the surrounding waters. Over 300 Japanese died of starvation.'

The most 'archetypal' case of cannibalism I know, a real throwback to the life and diet of *Pithecanthropus pekinensis* and a historic counterpart to the man-eating 'ogre' (*i.e.* 'Hungarian' of the period of the Central Asian invasions) of the fairy-tales, is that of Sawney Beane, recorded in C. Whitehead's *Lives and Exploits of English Highwaymen, Pirates and Robbers*, London (Bull & Churton), 1883, I, p. 26 (Germ. trans., Leipzig, 1884, quoted by Iwan Bloch, *Sex Life in England, Past and Present*, London (Francis Aldor), 1938, p. 461). This man, born in East Lothian in the time of James I as the son of an honest hedger and ditcher, withdrew with an 'idle and profligate woman' into a cave on the sea-coast in the wilds of Galloway. She lived with him for twenty-five years in this hiding-place and produced eight sons and six daughters, who in turn begat eighteen grandsons and fourteen grand-daughters. The whole 'great family' lived as cannibals on the flesh of human beings whom they ambushed or lured into the cave, murdered and dismembered, cooked, roasted, and pickled like dried beef. When these cave-men were at last arrested the cave was full of salted and dried human meat dangling from the roof.

214. *Op. cit.*, p. 129 (Engl. p. 1).

215. *Op. cit.*, p. 97.

216. *Op. cit.*, p. 93.

217. Reprod. Eisler, *Orph-Dionys. Myst.*, pl. XXIII, fig. 136, expl. p. 377, note 2, pp. 378 ff.; cf. Eisler, 'Peace-loving Nations and War-making States', *Hibbert Journ.*, XLIII, No. 2, Jan. 1945, p. 127, on the Ethiopian *Book of Enoch* (*c.* 130 B.C.), representing Israel as a herd of sheep attacked by wild animals, *i.e.* by the pagan nations, on Israel called 'these sheep' by David (II Sam. xxiv. 17, cf. I Kings xxii. 17); 'the sheep of God's pastures' in Psalms 95, 7; 100, 3; etc.

218. *Op. cit.*, p. 88.

219. Eisler, *Gazette des Beaux Arts*, 1936, p. 59, fig. 1. The same explanation had already been found by Dr. W. Creizenach, 'Kleine Beitr. zur Deutung ital. Kunstwerke,' *Rep. f. Kunstwiss.*, 1898, p. 58. Emile Zola said, with profound intuition of this figure in his novel *Rome*: 'Quelle douleur sans nom, quelle honte affreuse, quelle abandon execrable cachait-elle ainsi?'

220. *Op. cit.*, p. 152.

221. Eisler, *Weltenmantel u. Himmelszelt*, Munich (O. Beck), 1910, I, p. 125, fig. 31.

222. See Alex. Hrdlička, *Children who run on all fours and Other Animal-like Behaviour in the Human Child*, New York (McGraw Hill), 1931, reviewed in *Nature*, 13 August 1932, pp. 220 ff.; especially p. 222 on some children exhibiting a remarkable prehensility of the toes, using them to pick up a pencil from the ground or to climb trees.

223. Matt. iv. 6.

224. JOSEPHUS ON VERTIGO

Flavius Josephus, *Antiq. Jud.*, XV, §412, who describes from his own experience this giddy urge felt by anyone who looked down from the high battlements of the Temple of Jerusalem into the Tyropoeon valley. Simon Magus (Ps.-Clementine *Homilies*, II, 23, ed. Migne, *P.G.*, II, 92) declared of himself: 'If I were to throw myself head foremost from a high mountain, I would be carried down unharmed.' This idea—a day-dream similar to the nocturnal flying dreams and Tarzan-like trapeze-swinging illusions—derives from the archetypal racial recollections of *Homo simius*, who knew that it is better to jump forward from a swaying tree branch and to catch another during the jump than to fall passively in a vertical drop to the ground.

225. THE LADY IN THE FUR TODAY

We can still see, walking about the streets and through the parks of our big cities on any hot summer day, the sadist 'Lady in the Fur', now with the added charm for the masochist of blood-red varnished, needle-pointed nails, looking as if she had just indulged in an omophagic orgy of tearing live animals to pieces and were now ready to scratch and pinch any male trying to make love to her with those same cruel claws and to mingle his blood with that of her previous victims. There is, at this season of the year, no rational justification whatever for the wearing of such a hot and heavy garment, but rather every reason to discard it—except the subconscious archetypal urge to appear as a superb aggressive beast of prey offering the 'lover's pinch' and scratch rather than as the hunter's defenceless quarry bent on alluring the 'wolf' rather than the sheep, who adorns herself with pretty flowers and fruit, printed on

light veils woven of flax-fibre or cotton-fluff, or bound on to
straw- or reed-plaited head-coverings, preferred by the opposite
type. This is not meant to imply that the two kinds of darlings
have any clear idea in their conscious minds of why they dress
as they do. But they 'know it in their bones'. They see to it that
the fox's or marten's head with the canine teeth blinking
brightly in the open maw remains attached to the pelt they
sport. They wear their furs as proudly as they walk shyly and
meekly when adorned with leaves, flowers and fruit, printed or
embroidered upon their transparent gowns fit for nymphs
chased by lascivious satyrs. As to the nails varnished so as to
look bloodstained, they are said to have been invented by
Creole women anxious to hide under the opaque colour the
tell-tale dark crescent betraying an admixture of Negro blood.
But this purpose could have been as well achieved by the silver
or gold varnish that imitates the precious-metal nail-sheaths
worn by Orientals, who prove by the length of their nails that
they have never worked with their hands.

226. Black-figured Attic vase-paintings after Gaston Vorberg,
Über das Geschlechtsleben im Altertum, Stuttgart (Julius Pittmann),
pls. 1 and 2.

227. THE 'WOLF' AND WOMAN TODAY
Don Iddon's *Diary, Daily Mail*, 4 Sept. 1946: 'Definition of a
wolf: A big dame hunter or a vulture without culture' (from a
collection of American wise-cracks). James Agate, *Ego 8*, London (Harrap), 1946, p. 108, May 5, prints as *Cocasseries* No. 14
from the *Saturday Review*, New York, Personal column, the
following: 'Talented, deep female, tired of disillusionment and
lycanthropic maledom, would sincerely appreciate correspond-
ence with educated man' . . . The *Sunday Express* of 9 March
1947 had a very witty '*Letter from a Wolf*' by Nathaniel Gubbins
remonstrating against the term 'wolf' being 'applied with growing frequency to any male of the human species who pursues
woman for a purpose too obvious to be described here.' It ends:
'If any wolf behaved like man he would be torn to pieces.'
Prof. Paul Maas thinks that the jocular expression may have
originated among university students sufficiently learned to

know Plato's *Phaedrus*, 241 d: ὥς λύκοι ἄρν᾽ ἀγαπῶσ᾽ ὥς παῖδα φιλοῦσιν ἐράσται ['as the wolf loves the sheep, thus lovers kiss a boy']. In the Norse *Förnaldar soegar*, III, pp. 560 f., the king's daughter Ingeborg dreams that two wolves attack her. The dream refers to the two wild *berserker* Sotni and Snakollr.

Among the uncatalogued Japanese erotic woodcuts of the Oriental Department of the British Museum is a colour-print by Utamaro, poorly reproduced in monochrome in the anonymous book *Japanische Erotik*, Munich (Piper & Co.), 1907 (?), pl. 21. It shows a girl crouching on an island and looking down into the sea, which here as elsewhere symbolizes the subconscious mind. Under the water she sees herself, seized and outraged by two male demons. In the same collection is a colour-print by Hokusai from the rare book *Kinoye Komatasi*, illustrating the dream of an Awaby diver girl imagining herself being outraged under water by polypi.

228. Paula Schlier, 'Geburt der Dichtung' (*'Birth of Poetry'*), *Der Brenner*, 17e Folge, Innsbruck, 1948, pp. 9–16.

229. HERNE THE HUNTER AND OTHER HORNED HUNTERS
The reader will remember Sir John Falstaff disguised as 'Herne the Hunter', 'with a buck's head on' in Shakespeare's *Merry Wives of Windsor*, V, 5, hailed by Mrs. Ford as 'my deer, my male deer'. He replies 'my doe . . . divide me like a brib'd buck, each a haunch': 'I will keep my sides to myself, my shoulders for the fellow of this walk, and my horns I bequeath your husbands. Am I a woodman, ha? Speak I like Herne the Hunter?' And, further on, Master Ford's words: 'Who's a cuckold now? . . . Falstaff's a knave, a cuckoldy knave, here are his horns', etc. On Actaeon in the stag's skin with the stag's antlers see Eisler, *Orph.-Dionys. Myst.*, p. 260, note 1. Actaeon is a figure of the Bacchic orgies. In Corinth he is said to have been torn by the clan calling themselves the Βαχχιαδες and mourned by the Corinthian people (Plutarch, *Amat. narr.*, 2; Schol. Apoll. Rhod., IV, 12, 12; Alex. Aetol. *ap.* Parthen., 24; Meinecke, *Anal. Alex.*, 219). The motive of the crime is erotic. As the Benjaminite 'wolves' in Judges xix. 22 f. 'beset the house round about, beat at the door and spake to the master of the house

. . . saying: Bring forth the man that came into thine house that
we may know him . . . and the man, the master of the house,
went out to them and said . . . Do not so wickedly, do not commit this folly'. . . so the Bakkhiades, one of whom fell in love
with Actaeon, arrange a nocturnal revelry (κῶμος) and enter
the house of Actaeon's parents to carry him away. The parents
resist and in the fight the boy is rent asunder. According to
Stesichorus, quoted by Pausanias IX, 2, 3, Actaeon is punished
for desiring to espouse Semelê (=Thracian zemelo, 'the earth',
Slav. zemlya), the mother of Dionysus, whom Zeus loves.
According to Hyginus, Fab., 180, and Nonnos, Dionysiaka, V,
301, Actaeon was lacerated by the dogs because he had
attempted to rape the goddess Artemis (see also Diodor., IV,
81, 4). The name 'Αϰταιῶν is derived from Greek ἀϰτή, 'bruised
grain' or 'corn' in general, and Actaeon's passion belongs to
the cycle of 'John Barleycorn's' sufferings (Eisler, op. cit., p. 260,
and p. xx to p. 260, note 1; G. W. Elderkin, Kantharos, Princeton, 1924, pp. 19 and 41; also Eisler, op. cit., p. 236, on 'the
passion of the corn'). The metamorphosis into a stag is brought
about by donning a stag's pelt with the head and antlers
attached to it (Pausanias, X, 30, 5, on Polygnotus's painting;
cf. the bas-relief on the metope of Selinus; Arch. Zeit., 1883,
p. 239; Benndorf, Metopen von Selinunt, pl. VII, Roscher, Mythol.
Lexikon, vol. I, pp. 215 f. Pollux, IV, 141, describes the Actaeon
mask in his catalogue of stage-properties. Sir F. G. Kenyon in
H. von Herwerden's Album Gratulatorium, Trajecti ad Rhenum,
1902, pp. 137 ff., has published an epic fragment concerning a
man disguised as a stag, slain and eaten (A. Ludwich, Berl.
Philol. Wochenschrift, 3 Jan. 1903, pp. 27 ff.; A. B. Cook, Journ.
Hellen. Studies, XIV, 1894, pp. 133 ff.; Zeus, I, p. 67, note 3,
and p. 674). In Syracuse the cattle-drovers (βούϰολοι) entered
the town in procession wearing on their heads stag-antlers
wreathed in green, as the antlers are often seen after the stags
have been crashing through the thick of the woods or rubbing
their antlers against the trees (ηὔρησις τῶν βουϰολιϰῶν), schol.
Theocrit. Diomed., III, 787, 17 K; Probus in Verg.; Bucol.
comm., p. 2, 8 K; Servius, Praef. in Bucol. ap. Isid., Origg., I, 28,
16; Schol. Bern., Jahrb. f. Philol., Suppl. IV, 741, 51 ff., Hagen;
Marx, Ber. d. sächs. Gesellsch. d. Wiss., ph.-h. Kl., LVIII, 1906,

pp. 101 ff.; Maass, *Österr. Jahreshefte*, X, 1907, pp. 113 ff.; Radermacher, *Sitz. Ber. Wien. Akad.*, ph.-h. Kl. CLXXVII, 1918, 3. Abh., pp. 114 f.; Nilsson, *Arch. f. Relig. Wiss.*, XX, p. 78, 3 ff.; Fedor Schneider, *ibid.*, XX, pp. 89 ff. Medieval processions of men with antlered stag-heads (*cervulum facere*) are attested all over Europe in the sources discussed by the above-quoted authors and Eisler, *op. cit.*, p. 260, note 2. Indian and Siamese parallels are discussed by Jean Przyluski, 'Les hommes-cerf', *Journ. Asiat.*, 1929, pp. 326 f., 343. On Tibetan masked dancers with stags' heads see a report from Lhasa 'from our special correspondent', date-lined 'Lhasa, 11 Feb. 1940' in *The Times* of the following day.

Medieval mummers with animal masks—a stag's, a rabbit's and wolf's head accompanied by a musician—are painted in the lower margin of the Bodleian MS. 264 (reprod. by M. R. James, *The Romance of Alexander*, a collotype facsimile, Oxford Univ. Press, 1931, pl. 21 v°, descr. p. 14).

A report with a photograph of the Horn-Dance on Wakes Monday in the Staffordshire village of Abbots Bromley is printed in *The Times*, 7 Sept. 1936 (see Christina Hole, *English Folklore*, London, 1940, p. 136, fig. 42). Cf. Violet Alford, *Antiquity*, VII, 1933, pp. 203–209, and Prof. Vuia's account of the ... stag-dancers who still delight the conservative Rumanian peasants in Henry Baerlein, *The Romanian Scene explained by writers in English and other People*, reviewed in *The Times Lit. Suppl.* of 2 March 1946. The reviewer mentions analogous survivals in the Welsh Mairi Llwyd and the Abbots Bromley stag-dancers. The men masquerading as stags are originally camouflaged stag-hunters. They expiate the killing of the stags in an annual ceremony by killing, rending and devouring one member of their own gang. See Eisler, *op. cit.*, on a number of similar magical expiatory customs of 'hunting the hunter', 'fishing the fisher', 'threshing and hoeing the thresher and hoer', etc., all intended to assuage the bad conscience of the killer.

The victim in the stag-mask is deified and becomes a forest or hunter god with antlers, such as the Celtic 'horned' god Cernunnus represented on an altar found under the apse of Notre Dame of Paris, now in the Cluny Museum (No. 3; Orelli 1993; Murat 1066, 5; H. d'Arbois de Jubainville, *Le cycle mythol. Irlandais*, p. 385; G. Grupp, *Kultur der alten Kelten u. Germanen*, Munich, 1905, p. 164), called *Jupiter Cernenus* on a Dacian wax-table of Budapest (*Corp. Inscr. Lat.* III, p. 925), or the Teutonic antler-crowned god on the silver bowl from Gundestrup in Denmark (*ibid.*, p. 288). According to Thomas Barns, *Encyclop. of Rel. and Eth.*, XII, p. 453, col. a, it is the divinity which survives as

> *Herne the Hunter,*
> *sometime a keeper here in Windsor Forest,*
> *who doth all the winter time, at still midnight*
> *walk round about an oak with great ragg'd horns;*
> *and there he blasts the trees and takes the cattle*
> *and makes milk-kine yield blood and shakes a chain*
> *In a most hideous and dreadful manner*
> (Shakespeare, *Merry Wives of Windsor*, IV, iv, 29).

He seems to have been impersonated by one Richard 'Horn', a poacher of the time of Henry VIII (see above, p. 173, about the 'Wilde Hunt' and the medieval poachers' gangs).

230. A relevant bit of English folklore has fortunately been preserved for us in Rosamund Lehmann's charming book *The Gypsy Baby*, London (Collins), 1946, p. 27. Isabel, the author's nurserymaid, says to a naughty cottage-child: 'Don't you know what happens to little girls who bite? They get turned into nasty little dogs, they do. Don't you ever do such a shocking thing ever again' (cf. above, p. 82, note 23). So now we know how 'bitches' come into existence.

231. See Ernest Simmel, *The Psychology of a potential Lust-murderer*, a Paper read in the Psycho-Analytical Study Group of Los Angeles, 1939.

232. SADISM AND MASOCHISM IN MODERN SOCIETY
J. C. Powys says in his *Autobiography*, London (John Lane), 1934, p. 137, very frankly: ... 'my indurate sadistic vice was always seething in the background of my nerves. I recollect wandering alone on more than one occasion over hill and dale near Sherborne looking for something to tear to pieces.' The

only real crime he committed under this urge was the cruel destruction of a nest full of unfledged little yellow-hammers. But he wrote and published *A Glastonbury Romance*, which tells the life of a sadist, as he longed to live it. With J. C. Powys's one sadistic crime cf. the following reminiscence of Charles Darwin, *Life and Letters*, London (John Murray), 1887, p. 30: 'When at Maer' (the house of his uncle Josiah Wedgwood) 'I was told I could kill worms with salt and water, and from that day have never spitted a living worm though at the expense, probably, of some loss of success (in angling). Once as a little boy I acted cruelly. I beat a puppy, I believe simply from enjoying the sense of power' (cf. Bain, *The Emotions and the Will*, p. 195, on 'the pleasure of power in its coarse and brutal form'). The beating could not have been severe, for the puppy did not howl, of which I feel sure as the spot was near the house. This act lay heavily on my conscience, as is shown by my remembering the exact spot where the crime was committed . . . my love of dogs was a passion. I was adept in robbing their love from their masters.' Even more valuable as a real *document humain* is Lynkeus, *Phantasien eines Realisten*, Dresden and Leipzig (Reissner), 1899, part II, pp. 116 ff., 'Ein Gottesurteil' ('The Ordeal'). The author, Joseph Popper, a famous civil engineer and philosopher, whose monument in the Vienna City Hall Park was removed by the Nazis in 1938, once told me that the following words are taken, very nearly *verbatim*, from the actual written confession of a well-known scientist, hanged for his crime, personally known to both of us—to me by sight only—and never suspected before this breakdown of any abnormal tendencies by any of his friends and acquaintances. The end of the short story—the 'ordeal' which gives the title to this famous masterpiece—is, of course, entirely invented.

'A man of ripe age, slender build and with features expressing a high degree of intelligence was walking on an early summer morning through the countryside. He had left far behind him the little town from which he had started on a clear moonlit night, walked over several low hills and was now about to reach the edge of a fir-grove.

'After being awake most of the night, the warm morning mist, the aromatic smell of the fir-tree resin and the gentle exercise of walking in the fresh air put him into a most pleasant mood, which developed very soon into a highly stimulated sexual excitement. He was entirely filled with an erotic urge, but, as far as he could see, there was no female being anywhere.

'While he continued to walk through the grove, his excited fancy raised before his imagination the illusive memories of all the beautiful women he would have liked to encounter here; all those he had ever seen or heard of; tender young ones, vivid and longing, or robust ones—all of them were thus wafted before his eyes.

'The erotic tension of his nerves had become almost unbearable, when an old woman suddenly stepped forward from among the trees, carrying a wooden basket upon her back. Her sudden appearance hit the man like a lightning stroke; his heart beat so violently that he could not speak to the woman, but merely stood still, waiting for her to approach. She understood him immediately, and a sly, lustful glance shot out from her hypocritically averted eyes. It set him at once a-tremble. Immediately afterwards she feigned indifference, wished him a good morning and pretended to walk past him and away. The man, however, seized the wooden basket she carried and dragged it violently from her back. "What is it you want of me?", she said. But he was too excited to speak, could utter only a few hoarse sounds, and, without starting any negotiations, grasped the woman around the body, threw her on to the grass and himself upon her. Full of a nervous feeling of potency he was incapable of assuaging his urge even in the most violent sexual activity. In consequence of the convulsive movements of his whole body, all through which he felt consciously superior to the woman, a peculiar sort of lust awoke in him which appeared to be the natural continuation and climax of the preceding sensation. "Here", he thought, "I am quite alone with this person. Nobody sees me, the whole of nature is still dark and misty; it must be a prodigious experience to take this life. Nobody cares, anyhow, for this old woman; also nobody will ever know who did it. It would be a thousand pities, not to yield now to the urge of Nature. For it is Nature herself who urges me on to it.[1] Happen what may, a moment like this

[1] Cf. above, p. 71, note 4.

cannot occur again. No, one does not live twice through such an instant" . . . "Woman, I'll kill you!" To which she replied laughing: "That as well as all this?" "Yes", he said. "Indeed it must be done, nothing else will do"; and with these words more and more urges welled up within him. She was still laughing, but he began to grin in a peculiar way and to press her throat. "Get off me," she said, "you will really kill me", to which he replied "but that's just what I want to do." While he compressed her neck he observed her features with intense curiosity. The old woman showed first a pained, then an imploring, then a reproachful and finally a resigned expression, looking unflinchingly into the man's eyes. This persistent look irritated him more and more. Finally, she lay there, throttled, a corpse.

'While the man went on observing her, his previous sensations and urges vanished; after a few moments he found it impossible to imagine what he must have been feeling only a few seconds before. Continuing to look at the corpse, he saw his own deed with growing amazement and horror. Meanwhile the sun had risen, the mist had dispersed, nature became clear and serene and he suddenly felt himself amidst human society again. He was aware of its commands and conscious of its threats. After a moment's reflection, he left the corpse where it lay and continued on his way in feverish excitement.

'Soon after, the body was found by peasants who had passed on the road and noticed the strange townsman walking away from the fir-grove and, naturally, connected him with the murder. They carried the dead woman into the next village, borrowed horses, rode after him, overtook and arrested him. Locked up with the corpse in the local slaughter-house he sat through a sleepless night. He saw the dead woman lying before him in the dim light of the lamp illuminating the room. He could not look away from the face that had seemed so insignificant while the woman was alive, but now in death assumed a strange and wider significance. It seemed inconceivable to him that he should have been the murderer of this woman. All that had happened appeared to have been but a nightmare. While he looked again and again at the corpse and became more and more conscious of his deed, he was seized by such profound remorse that he began to cry for self-pity and compassion for all mankind. "And is such a thing possible?" he said to himself. "Was a man like myself capable of such a deed? I am considered good-natured, wherever I go, and indeed I think I am. I have more intelligence and knowledge than thousands of other people, and yet—a fresh summer morning, a little scent of resin, was enough to drive me to this gruesome and vile action in the wood. What is man? A mixture of everything. Not only do kindness, humanity, scholarship and many other qualities I was rather proud of dwell in me, but also the vilest, most bestial lust and murderous cruelty are lurking in me and only wait for an occasion to emerge." He felt plunged into a sadness so profound that he could look at himself with complete detachment. He knew that his life was forfeit and that his guilt would be proved. He recognized that what would be done to him was as fatally inevitable as the deed he had committed. "A terrible force hitherto unknown to me", he concluded, "has urged me on; it has overcome all my reason and all my morale; with all my thoughts and all my remorse I cannot get away from this thing, the hard, inexorable, terrible facts. May they then take their course, as they have begun".'

I do not think it is possible to describe more clearly and more truthfully the sudden break-through of the archetypal werewolf personality emerging from the depth of the ancestral unconscious mind.

The man pleaded guilty; did not allow his lawyer to plead any attenuating circumstances or to dwell on his blameless, indeed meritorious, antecedents; agreed with the opinion of the experts that he had been conscious all through of what he was doing, remembered every detail and was by no means insane. No taint of insanity was discovered in his ancestry. He had never been seriously ill and never had any accidents in his life. He refused to appeal to the mercy of the Emperor, who had asked for a special report on the case. He went to confession, received the sacraments of his church and died in perfect resignation. Both the judge and the chaplain who had to be present at the execution broke down and had to be cared for by the prison doctor who certified the death of the executed murderer and who subsequently gave these details to Joseph Popper.

It is certain that the murderer wanted to die, and would

probably have been driven to suicide if he had been imprisoned for life as a criminal lunatic. However desirable the abolition of capital punishment may be in the moral interest of society and its organs now forced to co-operate in social actions contrary to fundamental ethical principles, it cannot contribute anything to the solution of the problem of how to protect potential victims against the assaults of individuals more or less suddenly over-whelmed by subconscious lycanthropy. The chances of curing a potential murderer of his sadistic propensities are negligible, because the affected individual does not feel abnormal but superior to other men, and therefore does not seek the aid of the psychoanalyst. After a crime has been committed the psychia-trist is confronted with the futile problem of stating whether persons of this kind are 'insane' and 'irresponsible' or not. 'No sex-murderer has as yet been analysed' (Dr. Otto Fenichel, *op. cit.* note 152, p. 356). If he were, no analytic treatment could effect a cure that could guarantee society against a relapse of the patient into his former dangerous state of latent lycan-thropy. The only effective protection of the normal majority of the population against the sadist is to facilitate or, at the very least, not to obstruct his contacts with masochists longing for the painful treatment he would inflict upon them. The crowds of women, elegantly dressed as well as in rags, queueing for admission to the small court-room where Neville Heath was tried, were entirely made up of persons who fervently desired —consciously or subconsciously—to be victimized by the hand-some killer. They were one and all willing to risk death in the adventure, but confident, not unreasonably, that they would be able to manage the affair so as to avoid paying the ultimate penalty. It is pathetic to read in Havelock Ellis, *Studies in the Psychology of Sex*, New York (Random House), 1936, III, part 2, pp. 180 ff., in the confessions of 'Florrie', about the difficulties she had to overcome before she could at last find a man who gave her the thrashing she longed for, while at the same time, as likely as not, dozens of normal women were helplessly groan-ing under the tortures inflicted upon them by cruel husbands or lovers unwisely chosen or accepted by females devoid of what the French so wisely call *l'intelligence du cœur*. Thousands of wives keep on nagging their husbands in the conscious or subconscious hope of provoking them to give them a good hiding, the very thing they will not do, because they are not that sort of person and have, moreover, been brought up to believe wife-beating the most despicable thing a man can do. Is there any reason why these women should not get what they are craving for and find the release they desire? If only the editorial watch-dogs who supervise the advertisements in the "personal" columns of the daily Press could see their way to winking at offers to sell, demands to buy or to exchange against lamb-skins untanned wolf-pelts or hides—a commodity not dealt in regularly now-adays by the *bona fide* fur-trade—they could do more towards saving the lives of helpless girls, now snatched from hospital wards or killed in dark lanes or in abandoned air-raid shelters, than all the police officers on patrol duty, confronted with an impossible task. *Volenti non fit injuria.* If one could feel sure that none but masochists would ever suffer violence from sadists, the problem would be reduced to its proper proportions among the assortment of ills to which mankind is heir.

It is hardly necessary to say that, while so-called 'blood-sports' may well be considered a 'lesser evil' and a compara-tively harmless 'abreaction' of inherited lupinomaniac disposi-tions, this tolerant verdict should not be extended to the caning licence still enjoyed by the *plagosus Orbilius* and his prefects in charge of most public schools. They are systematically develop-ing latent potentialities of both sadism and masochism and handing down from generation to generation what the French call *le vice anglais.*

Magnus Hirschfeld, *Sexual Anomalies and Perversions*, London, (Torch Publishing Co.) *s.a.* (1937?), p. 363, quotes from Thos. Shadwell, the Virtuoso, the story of one Mr. Snarl who comes to a bawdy house to be flagellated. Asked by the girl how he came to develop this craving, he answers: 'I became so used to it at Westminster School that I cannot give it up' (cf. Iwan Bloch, *Sex-Life in England, Past and Present*, London (Francis Aldor), 1938, pp. 320–386, on flagellomania).

Hirschfeld, *op. cit.*, p. 362, quotes Lord Byron as writing:

> *O ye who teach the ingenious youth of nations,*
> *Holland, France, England, Germany and Spain,*

I pray ye, flog them upon all occasions.
It mends their morals, never mind the pain.

(see *ibid.* on Dr. Parr, the flagellant headmaster of Westminster School and his special rod-maker, a man cut down from the gallows; p. 363 on both Milton and Dr. Johnson having been flogged in public as schoolboys).

It is aggravating to have still to read in *The Times* reports of headmasters' speeches publicly and unashamedly declaring that without the master's right to cane, 'a single lout might be able to tyrannize and demoralize a whole school', when it is evident that a sufficient dose of the continental *carcer* (C. G. Coulton, *Fourscore Years, An Autobiography*, Cambridge Univ. Press, 1943, pp. 42 f.)—solitary confinement over the week-end and in a bare room furnished with a hard chair and table, with only a slice of dry bread, a jug of water and a book of serious reading from which a digest is to be made—will break the resistance of any 'lout', especially when it is preceded and followed by a reasonable 'heart-to-heart talk'. Caning and birching is demoralizing for him who administers as well as for him who suffers the punishment. The first effect of the demoralization is the lasting incapacity of the birchers and caners as well as of the birched and caned even to understand how disgraceful it is to go on tolerating such a system, on the plea that it is recommended in a book (*Prov.* xiii. 24) believed only by the ignorant to have been written by King Solomon and only by the Fundamentalists to be 'verbally inspired'.

Dr. Millais Culpin (*op. cit.* below, note 233, p. 131) says: 'The victim of a sadistic or masochistic impulse may turn from that impulse in horror, or may gloat over any reference to it, and in either case publicity is an evil. That being so, I propose to avoid any discussion about corporal punishment in schools, except to say that incidents connected with it come up again and again in the history of patients where sex instinct has followed some abnormal path.'

Ample evidence concerning domestic and scholastic flagellation can, however, be found in E. L. Voynich, *Jack Raymond*, London, 1901.

(News item, *Sunday Express*, 22 May 1949: 'Boys of Nelson

College, New Zealand, voted for the head prefect's right to cane')!

233. NUDISM

Dr. Millais Culpin, *Mental Abnormality, Facts and Theories*, London (Hutchinson), *s.a.* (1948), p. 119: 'In spite of the remaining taboo upon nakedness, nudist camps exist where, I am credibly informed, children and adolescents accept the situation without embarrassment and even discuss quite freely how far it is necessary for them to conceal their participation when they return to ordinary life.' As to the embarrassment—which disappears rapidly, of course, through the acquirement of the habit—a very pertinent observation of the Cardinal de Bernis is quoted from his 'Quattre Saisons' by Pidanzat de Mairobert in the *Espion Anglois*, London (Adamson), X, 1737, p. 204: 'L'embarras de paraître nue fait l'attrait de la nudité.' As soon as the embarrassment has disappeared, the sexual attraction of nudity becomes evanescent. The lack of the erotic element in nudism has been rightly emphasized by Jacques Chabanne, *Mitropa*, Paris (George Valois), 1932, pp. 90 ff., who describes a nudist club celebration of thousands of members in the Luna Park of Berlin in the years just before the dawn of the Third Reich. The German nudist movement (*Nacktheitsbewegung*) is mentioned as early as 1912 in E. A. Crawley's article 'Dress and Nudity' in the *Encyclop. of Rel. and Eth.*, V, p. 61 b. William Herbert Sheldon, *The Varieties of Human Physique*, New York (Harper), 1940, p. 220, speaks of the 'wave of interfamilial nudity following the general dissemination of psycho-analytical doctrine' in the U.S.A. A nudist movement among early Christians—sectarians named *Adamiani*—is described by Epiphanius (*Encyclop. of Rel. and Eth.*, XI, p. 320 b). They worshipped naked in the public baths, professing scrupulously to maintain their virginity. The sect seems to have survived in the Eastern Church. The late Prof. Konrad Grass of Dorpat (Tartu) catalogued as still existing in 1915 a Russian sect of 'Adamites' who endeavoured to 'get rid of all shame' which they considered a consequence of the Fall. They attended their divine services in the nude and went naked in their own houses. Westermarck, *Human Marriage*, 2nd ed., London, 1894,

p. 118, reports that Papuan men glory in their nudity and consider clothing fit only for women.

234. THE PURGING OF FEAR AND PITY

The term καθάρσις (='purification'), *viz.* from certain affects
and passions, is best known from the discussions of Aristotle's
definition of the aims of tragedy in his *Poetics*, 1449, b 28; (best
discussion in Theodor von Gomperz's *Introduction* to his German
translation of the work, Leipzig (Veit), 1897. The book contains an appendix, *Wahrheit und Irrtum in der Katharsistheorie des
Aristoteles*, by Alfred Baron von Berger, then director of the
famous Imperial Burgtheater of Vienna, which quotes, on p. 80,
note 1, the then new *Studien über Hysterie* by Drs. Josef Breuer
and Sigmund Freud, and tries to elucidate Aristotle by reference
to the new technique of psycho-analysis. Aristotle found the
term καθάρσις in Plato, *Phaedo*, 67 c, where it is explained as the
'widest possible separation of the soul from the body' (τό χορίζειν
ὅτι μάλιστα ἀπὸ τοῦ σώματος τῆν ψυχῆν). The nearly synonymous
term, καθαρμός, in the plural καθαρμοί, 'purging', is first found as
the title of a poem by the mystical philosopher Epimenides of
Crete and another by Empedocles (Diels, *Vorsokr.*, 2nd ed.,
p. 496, frgm. 10, and p. 205, frgs. 112–153 a). All the three
great tragic poets know and use the word. Euripides, *Bakkh.*,
72 ff., praises the specific purifications practised in the Bacchic
mysteries. They were specifically aimed at liberating the initiate
from λύσσα, the bestial lycanthropic mania. As reconstructed in
Eisler, *Orph.-Dionys. Myst.*, chs. 32 and 33, pp. 281–298, they
aimed at divesting the human soul of its perversions, represented
by the mask of the predatory animal, first put on for the purpose
of 'indulging in madness in the right way' (Plato's ὀρθῶς
μανῆναι). The orgy of tearing living animals to pieces and
devouring the raw flesh and indulging in complete erotic
licence is followed by a rite of divesting oneself of the animal
travesty and adopting henceforth the abstemious, chaste, ascetic
and holy vegetarian life of the Orphic initiate, exemplified by
Hippolytus in Euripides' *Phaedra*. Faces made up with clay,
soot and similar material (see above, p. 120) are 'scraped clean'
(ἀπομάττειν), and the whole body is ceremonially washed. All
the human vices are represented either as animal spirits obsess-

ing the mind and inhabiting the human heart, which have to be driven out, or as animal masks covering the real human face created in the image of the god, which have to be thrown off to restore the original innocence before the Fall.

Translated into modern terms, it would mean propagandizing ethical vegetarianism of the kind discussed above, pp. 195 ff. by making the neophytes participate actively, in a state of drunkenness, in the actual primitive process of chasing and killing a live animal and devouring the warm, bleeding flesh, after they have been dressed up as wolves or lynxes or panthers after the manner of the 'Isâwîyya (above, pp. 120 ff.); when they have woken up with a hangover from their intoxication, tired out by the physical exertion of their wild debauches, they would be stripped of their bestial accoutrements, given a bath and made to take a vow of abstinence, radical vegetarianism and perpetual chastity. I daresay that this procedure—which we might yet see revived by one of the queer religious sects springing up on the other side of the Atlantic—might have a more profound and lasting effect than mere verbal exhortation and preaching to the converted, which is so unlikely to affect those most in need of a conversion to the ideals of non-violent, peaceful co-operation. There have been celebrations among the Russian *Khlysty* of rites making the individual recipients of inspiration from the Holy Ghost realize their own bestial nature by crying out in various animal voices (Eisler, *Arch. f. Relig. Wiss.*, vol. XXVII, 1929, pp. 172 f., note 1). But there is no evidence of this practice having had any influence on Generalissimo Stalin, seen by Lord Moran to doodle red wolves on his blotting-paper while listening to the arguments of his Western allies.

235. JEALOUSY MURDERS

News item (*Star*, 2 June 1949, p. 3): 'Killer of Girl is hanged. Dennis Neville, 22, a glazier's labourer, of Manor-row, West Town, Dewsbury, was executed at Armley Prison, Leeds, today for the murder of 21-year-old Marian Poskitt, a weaver of Low-road, Dewsbury. Miss Poskitt was found strangled in a Dewsbury cricket field. At the trial at Leeds two doctors called for the defence said Neville had schizophrenia—"split personality"—but the prison medical officer said he thought Neville knew what he was doing. The jury rejected a submission that *provocation by the girl* justified a finding of manslaughter.'

The same *caveat mulier!* applies, of course, with equal force to the numerous cases when a man kills a woman whom he cannot 'possess', so that 'nobody else should possess her'. In these cases, too, the victim is generally guilty of having led on the murderer up to a point, beyond which she was never willing to go ('I do love you, but not that way'). It should be generally known that this is a more dangerous game than playing with fire. It is, however, only because the possessive attitude in sexual relations is so largely shared by judges and jurymen that murders of this particularly vile and objectionable kind are so often romanticized and more easily condoned than the sadistic crime, committed in the course of the sex-act itself, as described above, pp. 232–5, in note 232.

No doubt whatever should be left in the minds of juries and judges as to the archetypal character of all murders committed for motives of jealousy. Juries acquitting in cases of *crime passionnel* absolve because they feel so strongly that they themselves in the same situation might act in the same way. Since most of the frugivorous Primates are jealous fighters for, and many are jealous killers of their females, the possessive murderer of 'unfaithful' or unyielding women cannot be classified as a lupinomaniac. But murderers of this kind are more dangerous because more numerous than real sadistic lycanthropes. The murder of the Medea type—revenge against the 'unfaithful' lover or husband—is not an archetypal, but a sophisticated crime, as Euripides shows quite clearly, although he characterizes his heroine as, in a sense, a primitive, uncivilized, un-Hellenic barbarian. Juries and male judges show no undue leniency in such cases, because they are aware of how easily they could find themselves in the place of the murdered victim.

236. The paper 'Man into Wolf', originally published in the *Hibbert Journal*, XLIV, No. 2, 1946, was one of the initial chapters of a *Sociology of War and Peace* which the author has not completed.

237. HYPERTRICHOSIS

I had, in my young days, a great friend with a face of uncommon, classic beauty, a Greek scholar of no mean achievement, held in great esteem by all who knew him, who gave me
the shock of my life when he came to stay in my parents' house
on the Attersee and I saw him undressing at the shore for a
swim, his head and neck of a youthful Dionysos emerging from
a pelt as thick and black as that of a bear. Even the upper parts
of his feet were thickly covered with hair. I hasten to add that
he was the gentlest person one could wish to meet, and yet was
decorated for conspicuous bravery as an Austrian infantry captain in the First World War.

Another uncommonly hairy individual was Restif de la
Bretonne (1734-1806), described by Helmina von Chezy, who
met him in the drawing-room of Fanny de Beauharnais, an
aunt of the Empress Joséphine. He was fond of walking about
in a labourer's dress with his hairy chest and arms exposed
(Otto Flake, *op. cit.* note 1 above, p. 199).

238. Dr. Edward Glover, Director of Scientific Research of
the London Institute of Psycho-analysis, was, I believe, the first
to publish a book on *War, Sadism and Pacifism* (London, 1933)
in which he says 'to put it crudely: so long as the humblest civil
servant is an unconscious sadist and suffers from unconscious
guilt, the country is not safe from war'. This is, surely, putting
it a little too crudely. It is to be taken with no smaller a grain
of salt than Mr. Nathaniel Gubbins' (of the *Sunday Express*)
epithet 'Mr. Bloodsucker' for the taxgatherer (see Dr. Brend,
op. cit., p. 88). World-peace will certainly not be brought any
nearer by psycho-analysing civil servants, humble or exalted.

239. WAR AND THE DUEL

The Latin grammarian Festus derives the word *bellum*, 'war',
from *duellium*, 'duel'. This may be the true etymology. Homer
represents the war of the Achaean thalassocracy against the
Trojans, levying toll from the ships passing through the straits
into the Black Sea to trade with gold-producing Kolkhis, as a
series of duels fought against the ravisher of fair Helen. In the
fairy tales the hero fights for the hand of the princess, and in the

romans de chevallerie the heavily-armoured knights on horseback are supposed to fight for the favours of their gracious ladies. This fiction was maintained alive until at last Cervantes managed to kill, by the ridicule he poured on Don Quixote de la Mancha and his 'noble' Doña Dulcinea del Toboso, the romantic glorification of, in the main, very realistic and materialistic robbing and plundering expeditions aimed at capturing as many as possible of the leading robbers on the other side and holding them up to ransom. See for the ethnological background of the problem Leo Frobenius, *Menschenjagd und Zweikampf* ('Manhunting and Duelling'), Jena, 1914; also Gerald Heard, *Man the Master*, London (Faber), 1942, p. 288: 'Even today war combines two elements in it. One is the duel. This is the humanized development of animals' sexual fights, the only fighting which nature permits within the species.' ('Nature permits' is, of course, a mythological way of describing the facts simply as they are.) 'The fighting itself, the more it is studied, the more it shows itself to be far more a test of strength and endurance, of courage and will than of murderous and treacherous violence' . . . 'outstanding physiological weapons— horns though deadly against another attacking species such as the carnivores—lock against each other, cancel out as weapons in the sex-duel and so permit strength to be displayed with minimal damage. Further, it is the signal of the female that indicates whether the victor has really won, i.e. whether she will accept him. The conquered rival is frequently permitted to retire once he has been vanquished' (p. 239). 'Factors of the sex-duel are still mixed up in the practice of war. All the "virtues of war" spring from the instincts of the sex-duel. The other aspect of war has no virtues, no rules.' 'War today sheds its last tie with the duel.'—This explains why all the more technically perfected arms killing at a distance and by non-human, impersonal power harnessed through cunning, from the bow and arrow to the atomic bomb, have always been criticized by the technically less advanced party as cowardly tricks unworthy of a brave man. See also Bertrand Russell, *Why Men Fight. A Method of Abolishing the International Duel*, New York (Century Co.), 1916. In the English edition the characteristic term 'international duel' for war has been replaced

by the indifferent title *Principles of Social Reconstruction* (Allen &
Unwin), 1916, now in its 10th edition. Neither Gerald Heard
nor Bertrand Russell have witnessed the bestial mass-rapes
committed by the victorious Red Army in Austria and Germany, allegedly *en revanche* for the undoubtedly equally
gruesome sex-crimes committed by the Nazi hordes in Russia
and the Ukraine. Otherwise they would have realized that even
modern armies fight to preserve their own women-folk from
the werewolf-behaviour of the barbarian invader.

240. See Eisler, 'Religion for the Age of Reason', *Hibbert
Journal*, XLV, No. 4, p. 337. 'In-nocence' is meant in the sense
of the basic principle *'primum non nocere'* in the Hippocratic oath
of the physician.

APPENDIX I

PROF. JUNG'S 'ARCHETYPES' AND NEO-LAMARCKISM

The first to recognize the existence of a superindividual, ancestral layer in our memories, common to all mankind as a zoological species, an *Artgedächtnis*, preserving a reminiscence of ancestral experiences, ideas such as are encountered all over the world in the myths, legends and folklore of all ages, was not Prof. C. G. Jung but Goethe's friend, the physician and scientist C. G. Carus (born Leipzig, 3 Jan. 1789; d. Dresden, 28 July 1869; from 1815 Director of the Dresden Medical and Surgical Academy, from 1827 physician-in-ordinary to the king of Saxony; lectured on psychology after 1831) in his books *Psyche, zur Entwicklungsgeschichte der Seele*, Leipzig, 1846 (repr. Leipzig, 1898, in Kröner's *Taschenausgaben*; new ed. by Klages and Prinzhorn, 1926) and *Psychologie der Geschichte der Seele in der Reihenfolge der Tierwelt*, Leipzig, 1866. Cf. Bernouilli, *Die Psychologie von C. G. Carus*, Basel, 1925; Hans Kern, *Die Philosophie des C. G. Carus*, Leipzig, 1925.

Nietzsche used to speak in this context of an *Artmelodie* (melody common to the species). See R. A. S. Macalister's note on p. x. of R. R. Schmidt's *The Dawn of the Human Mind, a Study of Palaeolithic Man*. Jung himself (*Eranos-Jahrbuch*, Zürich Rheinverlag), 1934, p. 181, acknowledges his indebtedness to Lévy-Bruhl, *Les fonctions mentales dans les sociétés inférieures*, Paris, 1922, pp. 27 ff., who speaks in this context of *représentations collectives*. In a certain phase of his thought Freud too operated with the concept of racial memory (see Heinz Hartmann and Ernst Kris, 'Die genetische Betrachtungsweise in der Psychoanalyse', *Psyche*, Jg. III, Heidelberg, 1949, pp. 11 f.

At the time when Jung wrote the words quoted above (p. 105,

247

note 89) from his *Psychological Types*, London, 1923, ch. X, No. 8, most biologists were, and some still are, under the influence of August Weismann († 1914) and his theory of the seminal plasma. They therefore inclined *a priori* to deny the inheritance of acquired characteristics, such as Jungian 'archetypes' would necessarily have to be. Jung was aware of the difficulty, and carefully formulated his theory so as to guard it against this sort of objection:

'I do not by any means assert the inheritance of ideas, but only of the possibilities or germs of ideas, something markedly different' (*Two Essays*, etc., p. 67). These 'germs' or 'possibilities' could only be conceived as a sort of inherited 'engrams' on the micro-structure, of the supra-granular cortex. See Jung's note 1 on p. 104 *op. cit.*: 'In his philosophical dissertation on Leibniz' theory of the unconscious H. Ganz has used the *engram* theory of Semon[1] as an explanation of the collective unconscious. The concept of the collective unconscious advanced by me coincides in essentials with Semon's concept of the phylogenetic *mnēmē*.'

Semon's theory was originally stated by the great physiologist Ewald Hering in 1870 in a paper read before the Imperial Academy of Sciences at Vienna, *On Memory as the Universal Function of Organized Matter*. 'Wherever there is life with growth and development, there memory must be predicated, since each new process is the outcome of the old and implies its retention. Memory is a faculty not only of our conscious states, but also, and much more so, of our unconscious ones . . . Our ideas do not exist continuously as ideas; what is continuous is the special disposition of nerve substance in virtue of which this substance gives out to-day the same sound which it gave yesterday, if it is properly struck . . . The reproductions of organic processes, brought about by means of the nervous system, enter but partly within the domain of consciousness, remaining unperceived in other and not less important respects . . . The memory of the so-called sympathetic ganglionic system is no less rich than that of the brain and spinal marrow . . . A muscle becomes stronger the more we use it . . . After each individual action it becomes more capable, more disposed towards the same kind of work, and has a greater aptitude for repetition of the same organic

[1] *The Mnēmē*, trans. by L. Semon, London (Allen & Unwin), 1921.

processes. It gains also in weight, for it assimilates more matter than when constantly at rest. We have here . . . the same power of reproduction which we encountered when we were dealing with nerve substance . . . This growth and multiplication of cells is only a special phase of those manifold functions which characterize organized matter . . . Reproduction of perform-ance, therefore, manifests itself to us as reproduction of the cells themselves, as may be seen most plainly in the case of plants, whose chief work consists in growth, whereas with animal organisms other faculties greatly preponderate.' Hering states the doctrine of the heredity of acquired characteristics with great simplicity. 'We have ample evidence of the fact that characteristics of an organism may descend to offspring which the organism did not inherit, but which it acquired owing to the special circumstances under which it lived. . . . What is the descent of special peculiarities but a reproduction on the part of organized matter of processes in which it once took part as a germ in the germ-containing organs of its parent, and of which it seems still to retain a recollection that reappears when time and occasion serve?' For Hering the marvels of instinct are but the marvels of habit handed on from generation to generation. 'He who marvels at the skill with which the spider weaves her web should bear in mind that she did not learn her art all on a sudden, but that innumerable generations of spiders acquired it toilsomely and step by step.' Samuel Butler, in *Life and Habit* (1877), set forth the same doctrine, although he was at that time ignorant of Hering's paper. In a later book, *Unconscious Memory*, he incorporated a translation of the German lecture. At the present day a similar view of memory is presented by such biologists as Francis Darwin, R. Semon, and H. S. Jen-nings. It should be noticed that in such a biological doctrine of memory there is no necessary reference to consciousness.

Since then Dr. E. W. MacBride, F.R.S., Professor of Zoology at the Imperial College of Science, London, and biographer of T. H. Huxley, has defended a Neo-Lamarckism that would supply a solid evolutionist basis for Jung's theory. In an illus-trated lecture of 5 June 1931 to the Royal Institution of Great Britain, entitled *Habit—the Driving Force of Evolution*, of which I treasure an offprint autographed by the author, he discusses

APPENDIX I

Dührken's experiments with the ordinary cabbage white butter-fly *Pieris brassicae*, modifying the colour of the pupae by rearing the caterpillars under orange light and observing for five years the effects of this procedure on all the following generations, as well as Heslop Harrison's repetition of this experiment on the allied species of the turnip white *Pieris napi*. Most instructive in our context are Heslop Harrison's experiments with the gall-fly *Pontania salicis*, which normally lays its eggs on a particular species of willow (*Salix Andersoni*). By forcing them to lay their eggs on another species of willow, *Salix rubri*, he caused a heavy mortality among the next generation of gall-flies, but the sur-vivors established themselves on *Salix rubri* and their offspring continued to lay their eggs on *Salix rubri*, even after *Salix Ander-soni* had been made available again to this local race of *Pontania salicis*. This is clearly a case of an acquired habit becoming hereditary and establishing a new 'biological race' with differ-ent feeding habits. Metalnikoff established in six generations a hereditary immunity of the caterpillars of the *Galleria* moth from infection by the cholera bacillus. The process is exactly the same 'natural selection' by which the Jews. of the European ghettoes have acquired a certain immunity from tuberculosis, not shared by Yemenite, Abyssinian and Moroccan Jews who had lived under the open sky and not in dark overcrowded dwellings. Similar cases have been discussed by Dr. Thorpe in his article 'Biological Races in Insects', *Biological Review*, vol. V. After Prof. MacBride had propounded his Neo-Lamarckian theory at the Norwich meeting of the Zoological Section of the British Association in 1935, he was criticized by Dr. Julian Huxley in his presidential address to the Blackpool meeting of the British Association in 1936 (see letters in *The Times*, 19 Sept. by Prof. MacBride, and 22 Sept. by Dr. Julian Huxley, who also published a little book on the subject in 1937). In *Nature*, 2 July 1932, p. 26, Prof. J. B. S. Haldane attacked Prof. MacBride, who replied in the issue of 23 July (*Nature*, 1932, p. 900, quoting Dührken, *Grundriss der Entwicklungsmechanik*, and expressed (p. 901) the hope that in the end my much-maligned compatriots Kammerer and Přzibram would be vindicated. In 1943, Prof. Frederick Wood Jones, *Habit and Heritage*, London (Kegan Paul), published further indubitable evidence concerning the hereditary transmission of anatomic variations in the foot skeleton of certain primitives due to their habitual squatting position.

Fortunately, it is not necessary for me to take sides in the quarrel between Neo-Lamarckism and Darwinian-Mendelian selectionism which has now become a major political issue in the U.S.S.R. (*Soviet Monitor* issued by the Tass Agency, 27 Aug. 1948, discussed by Prof. Eric Ashby, 'Science without Freedom?', in *The Listener*, 4 Nov. 1948, pp. 677 f.; *id.*, anonymously, the same text as 'Soviet Biology', *The Times*, 6 Nov., p. 5, cols. 6 f.; also John Langdon Davies, *Russia Puts Back the Clock*, with a foreword by Sir Henry Dale, O.M., F.R.S., London (Gollancz), 1949; reviewed by Bertrand Russell, 'Stalin declares War on Science', *Evening Standard*, 7 Sept. 1949, p. 9). On the problem itself the reader may consult Dr. P. S. Hudson's (Director of the Imperial Bureau of Plant Genetics, Cambridge) book *The New Genetics in the Soviet Union*, Imperial Agricultural Bureau, Penglays, Aberystwyth, 1946, and his article 'How New Crops are Found' in *The Countryman*, XXXIV, No. 2, Autumn 1946, p. 45: 'The Russian investigators take their ideas mainly from T. D. Lysenko, well-known originator of the principle of vernalization, who grew winter wheat plants under abnormally warm conditions and found that the progeny behaved mainly as spring forms. From this he argued that, by suitable training, the hereditary nature of a plant or animal could be radically changed without recourse to hybridization. Other instances of this were quoted from the work of the now famous Russian fruit-breeder, the late I. V. Michurin, who, among other things, advocated the use of "mentors", claiming that a young hybrid, by having grafted on to it, in its early growth stages, a scion of an old-established variety, acquired many of the desirable characters of the old variety. Finally, great importance is attached by the Michurin-Lysenko school to vegetative hybrids produced by grafting. Most vegetative hybrids in the past have proved to be merely individuals with mixed tissue, where no true fusion of the hereditary elements has occurred, but the Russian school refer to the work of Darwin and bring forth a large body of new evidence from which they confidently affirm that vegetative hybrids can not only be produced, but behave in inheritance

251

in exactly the same way as true sexual hybrids. All this leads the Russians to conclude that the hereditary constitution of a plant or animal is not fixed, as supposed by other geneticists, but is subject to modification under the direct influence of the environment, much in the way assumed by Darwin when he formulated his theory of the origin of species. The difference between the two schools of thought is fundamental: the orthodox geneticists believe that the genes, and all that goes with them, are unchangeable, except by some profound process known as mutation, which occurs at random and is not capable of being regulated or directed by man. The Russian school, on the other hand, believe that no difference exists between the reproductive tissue and the ordinary body tissue, and that any changes exerted on the latter by environmental influences are transmitted to the offspring; they believe, moreover, that these changes can be directed and controlled and made to go in whatever direction the experimenter desires.

'There is another subject on which emphasis has been placed by Lysenko and his school; the benefit to be gained from crossbreeding, and the loss of vigour that is usually associated with close breeding, a principle which again was a favourite topic in Darwin's writing. In pursuance of this principle, crossing has been practised not only between species and between varieties, but between individual plants within an agricultural variety which, judged by mere morphological standards, was homogeneous. Quite material improvements in yielding capacity, quality and other features have been claimed from this procedure. The anthers or male organs are removed from one set of plants, which are left free to be pollinated by any other plants that happen to be growing in their vicinity in the field; in this way their capacity for selective fertilization is exercised to the full. The method was first called by Lysenko "marriage for love", but this designation seems to have been dropped in the more recent Russian literature on the subject.

'Yield increases such as those described by the Russians have been obtained by workers who have repeated the experiments in the U.S.A. and elsewhere, though few geneticists outside the Soviet Union are prepared to agree with the theoretical explanation put forward by the Russian school. In some of

Lysenko's other experiments, notably those on graft hybrids, the results themselves have been called in question, since there is some doubt as to the validity of his experimental technique. Nevertheless, there is much food for thought in the experiments of this Russian school. While it is clear that the results call for careful re-examination and verification, the viewpoints of the more orthodox geneticists are undergoing considerable modification too. It seems more than probable that the two schools of thought, which today seem so much in conflict, will prove, on further examination, to have some ground in common.'

It is, therefore, quite sufficient for me to insist on the fact that the hereditary transmission of certain acquired characteristics is proved beyond the possibility of doubt. Nor is there any need for me to state my own very definite views about how this transmission can be understood. That the facts, as even laymen can observe them, appear to be most mysterious, can be best illustrated by the following quotation from Montaigne's *Essays*, I, ch. 22: 'Quel monstre est-ce que cette goutte de sémence de quoy nous sommes produicts qui porte en soy les impressions, non de la forme corporelle seulement, mais des pensements et inclinations de nos pères? Où loge-t-elle, ce nombre infini de formes? et comment porte-t-elle ces resemblances d'un progrèz si tesméraire et si déréglé que l'arrière petit-fils respondra à son bis-aïeul, le nepveu à l'oncle? Les communes imaginations . . . infusés à notre âme par la sémence de nos pères? . . .'

To this question, there is—although this assertion may sound preposterous—a complete answer from the point of view not of biology, but of Eleatic ontology and the complete geometrization of the universe by modern relativity-theory. But it would, obviously, not be advisable to attempt at the end of such a far-flung disquisition, even an outline of the epistemological theory which the present writer has tried to explain in his Oxford lectures as Wykeham Professor of Philosophy in 1941.

APPENDIX II

THE ROMAN *LUPERCI* AND THE *LUPERCALIA* RITUAL OF BEATING WOMEN WITH LEATHER STRAPS

CONTEMPORARY PARALLELS

The exact meaning of the name *Luperci*, mentioned above, p. 134, note 111, is not certainly known. This is not surprising, since *lupus*, 'wolf', itself is not a genuine Latin word, but borrowed from the Sabine dialect (Osthoff, *Indogerm. Forsch.*, IV, 278; Ernout-Meillet, *Dictionn. étym. Lat.*, p. 539; Walde-Hoffmann, *Lat. Etym. Wörterb.*, Heidelberg, 1938, p. 836). According to Varro (quoted by Arnobius, IV, 3), the 'harsh she-wolf' (*lupa non mitis*) who suckled Romulus and Remus was called as a goddess 'Luperca dea' (Lactantius, *Inst.*, I, 20, 3 'Romuli nutrix Lupa honoribus est affecta divinis'; ['The she-wolf who nursed Romulus is given divine honours']. Jordan (*Kritische Beiträge*, pp. 164 f.) has compared this name or word *luperca* with *noverca*, 'step-mother'—from *nova*, 'new'—the only other Latin word with this -*erc*- suffix. Since the she-wolf *lup-erca* evidently 'acts' as a step-mother or 'new' mother to the abandoned twins, this comparison is certainly apt. The possibility cannot be denied that early Latin or Sabine may have had a word corresponding to Greek ἔργον, ἐργάζω, old Teutonic *werk*, *werah*, Saxon *werk*. In this case *nov-erca*, 'step-mother', would be *nov-erca* (*mater*), 'one who acts as a new mother', *lup-erca* would be one who acts as a *lupa*, that is 'plays the harlot', and *lup-ercus* —also as a proper name of the god *Lupercus*—would be the exact counterpart of Greek Λυκο-όργος or Λυκο-έργος, Λυκ-οῦργος 'who acts as a wolf' or 'behaves as a wolf', that is the werewolf. As to the meaning 'act', cf. *orgia* for the ritual actions in the mysteries. The traditional explanation of *lupercus* and λυκοῦργος, which takes the suffix to be derived from *arceo*, 'hold at bay', 'avert', (Ernout-Meillet, *Dict. étym. Lat.*, 2nd ed., Paris, 1939, following Deubner and denying the connection with *noverca*), Latin *arceo*, Greek ἔργω, ἐργάω, would not explain *noverca* at all. The same argument can be opposed to the theory that *luperci* means *lupi hirci*, 'shaggy wolves' (Vetter, *Glotta*, vol. XV, 1926, p. 7, cf. Sabine *fircus*, 'goat', Oscan *hirpus*, 'wolf'; rejected by Walde, *Lat. Etym. Wörterbuch*, Heidelberg, 1910, p. 447), for surely a *noverca* cannot mean 'a new shaggy' mother? Otto, *Philologus*, vol. 72, pp. 161 ff., and Altheim, *Römische Religionsgeschichte*, vol. II, pp. 71 f. and 82, explain *luperci* as 'the wolf-like', suffix as in *noverca*. But is a stepmother 'new-like'?

For the same reason, it is not likely that *luperci* means the 'goat-wolves' (*hircus* = 'goat', lit. 'the shaggy one', that is 'the goat-killing wolves'), like the French word '*loup-cerviers*', 'wolf-attacking (even) stags' for the lynx (Sal. Reinach, *Orpheus*, Paris (Picard), 1909, p. 147; Deubner, *Arch. f. Relig. Wiss.*, XIV, p. 305). Clearly a *noverca* or 'stepmother' can hardly mean a 'new she-goat', as it were a she-goat to whose udders the orphaned child is laid. The proposed equation of *lupercus* and λυκοῦργος 'working', 'acting as a wolf', would accord very well with the sacrificial killing of a goat which the *Luperci* perform annually at the *Lupercalia* festival on 15 February (Plutarch, *Rom.*, 21; Varro, *Ling. Lat.*, V, 85; Ovid, *Fasti*, II, 267–452; Val. Max., II, 2, 9; Serv., *Aen.*, VIII, 343). They also sacrifice a dog (Plutarch, *l.c.*; *Quaest. Rom.*, 68, 111), as wolves will kill the watchful protector of a herd of goats in their attack. Having sacrificed one (Ovid, *l.c.* 361) or several (Plutarch, *l.c.*) she-goats, they touched the foreheads of two noble-born children with a bloodstained knife, wiping the blood off with wool dipped in milk, the two youths being expected to laugh at the end of the ceremony. This rite—thoroughly misinterpreted by scholars unacquainted with the customs of modern hunting folk (see the literature given in Marbach's articles *Lupercal, Lupercalia, Luperci, Lupercus*, Pauly-Wissowa-Kroll, *Realenzyklop.*, vol. XIII, 2, 1927, cols. 1815–1839)—is, of course, the still practised 'blooding' of novices, 'in at the kill' for the first time, mentioned, for instance, in David Garnett's novel *Lady into Fox*.

It is this blooding rite—a magic and apotropaic anticipation of the sanguinary revenge the other members of the killed animal's kin might otherwise feel compelled to take—that explains the word λυκαῖμιας, 'wolf-blooded' (from λύκος, 'wolf', and αἷμα, 'blood'), found in a new fragment of Alcaeus (*Oxyrh. Papyr.*, XVIII, London, 1941, ed. E. Lobel, C. H. Roberts and E. P. Wegener, No. 2105, col. II, 17). In Hesychius' *Lexicon* λυκαῖμιας, corrupted to the meaningless λυκαιχλιας, is explained as λυκοβρότος, from λύκος, 'wolf ', and βρότος, the Homeric word (*Iliad*, VII, 425 *et al.*; *Odyss.*, XXIV, 189) for 'coagulated blood', βροτόομαι, 'I am smeared with blood'. In this context, the 'wolf-blooded' person is supposed to be a solitary outlaw, a lycanthrope. The white milk of childish innocence is used to remove the bloodstain and, symbolically, the 'guilt' connected with it. The young have 'to laugh it all off' so as to show they are not afraid of blood. After this the *Luperci*, mostly young people, stark naked, gird themselves with the skins of the slaughtered goats ('make themselves a garment of skin'). They then run in this half-naked state around the old Palatine (*i.e.* pale-dwelling) town, beating those they meet in the streets, especially women, with leather straps or tongues cut from the skins of the sacrificed victims, 'for fun and in a lascivious way' (Livy, I, 5: *'per ludum et lasciviam'*; Valer. Maxim. II, 2, 9; Nicol, Damasc., *Vita Caesaris*, 21: Cicero, *Philippicae*, II, 34, 87; III, 5, 12; XIII, 15, 31; Cass. Dio, XLV, 30; Pope Gelasius, *Coll. Avellana*, ed. Günther, 453 ff.). The genteel scholars who have so far tried to explain this ritual survival of an atavist, wolfish chase, which, in a very literal sense, 'made game' of the hunted women and men, could hardly be expected to understand what was 'lascivious' about the behaviour of this 'fera sodalitas ... germanorum lupercorum' ... 'coitio silvestris instituta ante quam humanitas atque leges' ('this bestial pack of real goat-wolves' whose 'savage gang was brought together before humane life and laws were known'; Cicero, *Pro Caelio*, 26) or about a rite intended, as Livy says gravely (*l.c.*), 'not in order to prevent sickness, but infertility of the women' ('nec propter morbos inhibendos institutas ... sed propter sterilitatem mulierum ... exhibenda'). We have now been taught the hard way what such things mean, by men in whose minds this primeval lupine bestiality has welled up again from archetypic depths. The following *verbatim* account has been obtained from one of their victims, now a respected member of one of the learned professions in this country: 'When the German occupation authorities closed down the Czech University of Prague, a considerable number of students, girls and boys, went in an orderly procession to the entrance doors, rhythmically shouting their demands that the doors should be re-opened so that they could continue their studies. After this had been going on for some minutes, a flying squad (*Rollkommando*) of S.S. men drove up in lorries, surrounded the students and drove them through the doors which had suddenly been opened from the inside by other SS. guards. The students were herded into the largest lecture-hall with blows and kicks. Then they were told to strip completely. When nobody obeyed, the SS. commander in charge shouted that if they did not obey at once, their clothes would be "recklessly" (*rücksichtslos*) ripped from their bodies. They would all realize that clothes were hard to come by, also they would need them to go home. They would probably not enjoy walking home in what rags and tatters they would be able to keep on their backs. Again nobody obeyed. Orders were then shouted "rip down the rags" (*Fetzen runterreissen!*). Those standing in front—among them the witness who dictated this report—were then set upon by the young blackguards who began forcibly to tear down their clothes. At this sight most of the other victims, terrorized beyond endurance and wanting to save their precious clothes from destruction, started to undress and to fold their things neatly into bundles which they kept in their hands. When the order had thus been carried out the doors were opened and the prisoners were told they "could go", indeed "run out", "girls first". In rows on both sides of the door stood S.S. men who had taken off their own leather belts weighted with the regulation metal buckles. The stripped victims had to run the gauntlet between them, while they were savagely beaten up with these belts and pursued with relentless blows through the long, empty, resounding passages of the house—into the arms of other S.S. men posted at the end of the run to stop the girls. They were then strung up by their arms, each one on the back of one of the "soldiers", held by others if they tried to kick, beaten more savagely and finally raped by their assailants, who took turns in these atrocities. After that, all the students who had taken part in the demonstrations were brought to a concentration camp. The witness escaped by hiding during the final uproar under a staircase in a small dark recess, where the University cleaners kept their pails and brushes, and by creeping after nightfall through a small window of the now empty and deserted University building into the street. Since a number of S.S. men, especially of the higher ranks, were themselves former university students, it might be argued that they had read some of the texts about the *luperci* chasing and beating the Roman women with leather straps "per ludum et lasciviam". But it does not seem to be necessary to resort to such a far-fetched explanation to understand the lupinomane repristination by men whom "absolute power had corrupted absolutely" of what was once a habitual practice of the "Wild Hunt" of their werewolf ancestors giving chase to the helpless "little women of the woods" ' (see above, note 110).

Self-righteous readers tempted to react to this horrible document with the usual argument 'it could not happen here', are invited to consult the photographs which appear in *Life*, International Edition, 29 Sept. 1947. They show American Legionaries amusing themselves in New York, some of the toughs among the members using the occasion of some parade or festivity to administer shocks to women encountered in the street by means of electrically charged canes and to squirt water from 'grease-guns' on women's legs 'made up with sun-tan'. *En revanche* a 'lady' can be seen giving 'a robust kick in the pants' to a 'trapped legionnaire'. Here are the modern *luperci* and the horse-play acted *per ludus et lasciviam*, with the plain-clothes policeman looking on tolerantly—for a time. What would happen if the civilian control were suddenly removed and 'absolute power' conceded to men of this type?

APPENDIX III

THE FLAGELLATION OF WOMEN IN THE DIONYSIAN MYSTERIES

In 1909 a *triclinium* of a Roman house was discovered near Pompeii in the *fondo Gargiulo* of the Villa Item, also known as the *villa dei misteri*. The room was decorated with frescoes showing life-size figures (see *Notizie dei Scavi*, 1910, p. 139: *Journ. Rom. Studies*, 1913, III, p. 157; *Memorie d. R. Acad. di archaeol.*, Naples, 1914, III, p. 39; *Revue Archéol.*, 1915, II, 329; 1921, II, p. 425; Cagnat-Chapot, II, p. 59; *Rev. Études Anc.*, 1917, p. 172). My old friend, the late Salomon Reinach (*Répertoire de Peintures Grecques et Romaines*, Paris (Leroux), 1929, p. 115), whom the great ladies of Paris that one used to meet in his Sunday drawing-rooms called 'Salomon le candide' because of his ingenuous attitude to all sex problems, says: 'On a écrit des insanités au sujet de 7–8 (prétendue flagellation rituelle)', presumably referring to Theod. Reick, *Probleme der Religionspsychologie*, Vienna (Deuticke), 1919, pp. 69 ff. Although he himself mentions in his paper 'La flagellation rituelle', *Anthropologie*, 1904, pp. 47–54, repr. in his *Cultes, Mythes et Religions*, I, Paris (Leroux), 1922, pp. 173–183, on p. 180 the crucial passage in Pausanias (VIII, 23, 1), he has not seen the connexion of it with the frescoes of the Villa Item. According to this guide-book, written in the time of Marcus Aurelius, there was in the ancient Arcadian town, Alea, of which considerable ruins survive to this day, a temple of Dionysos, in whose honour a feast was celebrated every year, known as σκιερεῖα ('shade-booths'; cf. the σκιάς of ivy and grape-vines and other fruit-bearing boughs built for Dionysos, Athenaeus, V, 198 D: also Hesychius, s.v. σκιάς: 'the vine trained over trees (ἀναδένδρας) and the cupola-shaped shade-booth (σκιάδειον) under which

Dionysos is enthroned'). 'At the bidding of the Delphic oracle women were whipped on this occasion, as were the Spartan youths in the temple of Artemis Orthia.' It seems that the cult-legend of this ceremony is illustrated on the walls of the Villa Item. At the beginning of the series of pictures, there is a little boy reading a scroll to a group of women who had been listening to the music and chant of a lyre-playing Silenus and of a little satyr, playing the syrinx. Another boy plays with two of the kids (ἔριφοι), sacred to Dionysos, one of the women carries the sacred winnowing basket (λίκνον), another one, seated with her back to the spectator, seems to mix flour in a bowl with the water poured out by another woman, presumably kneading dough for the sacred pastry. At the opposite end, another little boy presents a writing tablet to a young man standing beside a young woman seated on a chair. The two look like a young married couple. I should say that the two boys—possibly winged Cupids—are delivering the message of the Delphic oracle to the assembly of initiates grouped round Dionysos, who is enthroned in their midst, holding his bride Ariadne in his right arm. On his left another Silenus with pointed ears holds a big round object—apparently an egg—in his hands, averting his face so as to turn his ear towards it. Two young boys, one of them holding a Dionysian mask, also appear to listen to some noise coming from the egg. On the right side of Dionysos and Ariadne, a kneeling woman holds the cloak of another woman who kneels and hides her face in the lap of a third sitting female. The kneeling woman is being severely whipped with what looks like an ox-thong or a cane by a winged female who can only be Iris, the messenger-maid of the gods. A Bacchic priestess holding the thyrsos-staff looks on impassively at the whipping, while another one beats cymbals to drown the sound of the moaning of the flagellated woman. At the other side of the room, a young female hurries into the room in such haste that her veil is blown from her face by the rush of the air. She holds up her hand with a gesture obviously intended to stop the procedure, as if she were to say: 'Enough of this!' The egg, in connexion with the god Dionysos, can hardly be aught else but the one that was produced by the incest of Thyestes (from θύω, 'sacrifice' and ἑστία, 'hearth', 'altar') and his sister Daitô (the 'banquet-preparer'). From it was born Enorchês, who built a temple to Dionysos (Tzetzes commenting on Lycophron, 212). The story, as illustrated in the Villa Item, can easily be reconstructed: Thyestes, the 'sacrificer' and his sister Daitô, the banquet-provider (cook) of the Dionysian θίασος, have committed incest. The large egg laid by Daitô was found ἐν ὄρχοῖς, in the rows of vines, in the vineyard (ὄρχος, a row of vines or fruit-trees; Hesiod, *Scut. Heracl.*, 296; Homer, *Odyssey*, VII, 127; XXIV, 341; Hesychius: ὄρχας, an enclosure (περίβολος), English 'orchard' =*orch-yard) by one of the Sileni and the Delphic oracle consulted about the prodigy. The priestess wrote, in answer to the question, that the egg was the result of incest and that all the women should be whipped to punish the crime of the unknown sinner. Iris is sent by the gods to flagellate them. While the execution is in process, Daitô rushes into the room, stops the beating and confesses that she is the guilty one who has given birth to the egg. The baby Enorchês is heard to cry in the egg, the egg is broken and the child given to the mother who brings up the hero. He atones for her fault by building a temple for Dionysos, who had hitherto dwelt in mere shade-booths (σκιερεῖα) in the vineyard rows.

If this reconstruction of the ἱερός λόγος, the 'sacred tale', explaining the ritual flagellation in the Dionysian orgies, is correct, the idea must have been to punish and expiate by whipping all women for the secret incestuous acts or thoughts indulged in by some of them, so that none should escape punishment, although her crime may not have been discovered. The procedure may be compared to the methods of 'Dr. Keate, a late Georgian headmaster of Eton, who was in the habit of caning boys quite indiscriminately, and on one day publicly flogged eighty without regard to their guilt or innocence. It was reported by W. E. Gladstone that, at an Etonian dinner, Keate was cheered with the wildest enthusiasm by a company which consisted almost entirely of men he had once mercilessly birched' [Doris Langley Moore, *The Vulgar Heart*, London, 1945, p. 233). No wonder, since the sadist gives to the masochists what they fervently desire. Since it is quite unlikely that any compulsion could have been applied, it can safely be assumed that the women initiates of Dionysos offered themselves voluntarily for their annual whipping.

APPENDIX III

Ferdinand Baron Reitzenstein, 'Der Kausalzusammenhang zwischen Geschlechtsverkehr und Empfängnis im Glauben und Brauch der Natur- und Kulturvölker', *Zeitschrift für Ethnologie*, 1909, pp. 671, 679, has shown that the flagellation of women with birches and tree-branches plays a great role in the puberty and initiation rites of women, practised by many people. In barbaric early Russia the severe whipping of the bride was frequently part of the marriage-ceremony (Anton Thomson, *Arch. f. Religions-Wissenschaft*, IX, 1906, pp. 397 ff.; Ernst Pfuhl, *ibid.*, XIV, 1911, p. 644). The same holds good of certain Teutonic tribes (Reitzenstein, *op. cit.*, p. 681; cp. above, p. 257, App. II, on the German black guards and the girl-students of Prague). Obviously the Thracian brides and, after the penetration of Dionysian cults into Greece, those of Argos and Arcadia were whipped in the sanctuary of the god as a preparation for their wifely duties and the process was repeated annually, allegedly as an expiation of possible undetected incestuous lapses in the privacy of their homes.

Pausanias was an author known to Renaissance humanists from the time that the first Greek manuscripts were brought by the earliest refugee scholars fleeing from Constantinople after the conquest of the imperial city by the Turks in 1453. There is little doubt that Italian scholars knew, and that their erotic imagination was fired by, the paragraph about the annual whipping of the Arcadian women at a Dionysian festival. Not knowing any of the details now revealed by the frescoes of the Villa Item, they could only conclude that the whipping was done by the usual acolytes of Dionysos, the Satyrs, so often represented in intimate erotic relations with the female votaries of the god. This is how Giulio Romano chose to visualize the scene when he was asked by one of his learned patrons to illustrate the passage in question. It is worth recording that his drawing, engraved by Marc Antonio Raimondi, represented the nude female victim of flagellation exactly in the position reported by the eyewitness of the Prague S.S. atrocities. Since this engraving is extremely rare and has never been reproduced, it is very unlikely that anyone of the Black Guard leaders responsible for the outrage ever saw it. What the conscious or subconscious motive of this arrangement may be I cannot say, unless it is the intention to minimize the erotic enjoyment which the satyr acting as a living whipping-post could derive from his participation in this sadistic ritual. But again, why should this be intended either by the leading sadist of the Prague orgy or by the unknown patron of Giulio Romano and Marc Antonio Raimondi?

Finally, it is worth mentioning that flagellation rites are practised with fanatical cruelty by the 'Isâwîyya, whose lycanthropic customs have been described above, notes 105–6, characteristically enough (Brunel, *op. cit.*, pp. 43 ff.) in connection with the fire rites, as practised by the *Hirpi Sorani*, the 'Wolves' of Mount Soracte (above, note 111) and their modern imitators. They dig 'un grand fossé dans lequel les disciples entretenaient un feu ardent destiné à engloutir les offrandes que les visiteurs apportaient'.

APPENDIX IV

A CLEAR CASE OF VAMPIRISM[1]

A clear case of vampirism had been tried while this lecture was being prepared for publication. John George Haigh, 'company director', of Onslow Park Hotel, South Kensington, London, was sentenced to death at Lewes on 9 July and executed on 15 August 1949. The accused, an inventor of considerable intelligence, confessed to having murdered nine people, including three strangers entirely unknown to him, by decoying them into a basement or store-room used by him for his work, shooting or clubbing them from behind. In every case he opened the jugular vein at the neck with a pen-knife, 'tapped' a glassful of the hot blood and drank it, then dissolved the bodies in sulphuric acid and disposed of their property for his own gain. He also drank his own urine, allegedly under the inspiration of a text of the Gospels which the press did not report, obviously John vii. 38, 'He that believeth on me, as the Scripture hath said, out of his belly shall flow rivers of living water' (the explanation of this text has been given by the present writer in his book *Jesous Basileus ou Basileusas*, Heidelberg Univ. Press, 1931, II, p. 287, note 7; the 'scripture' quoted is the second half of Isa. xxviii. 16, deleted by the Pharisees at the time of the quarrel about the feast of 'pouring out of water' in the course of the feast of Tabernacles).

At school Haigh was nicknamed 'Chink' because of the peculiar slant of his eyes, and may at that time have shown slight traces of Mongolism.[2] He had been brought up in the

[1] See the excellent report in *The Times* of 20 July 1949, p. 2, cols. 1–2, and the photographs in other contemporary newspapers.

[2] F. G. Crookshank, *The Mongol in our Midst*, 3rd ed., London (Kegan Paul), 1931, pp. 19 and 136. In view of a remark by the reviewer of the above-printed lecture in the *Lancet* of 12 July 1948 I should like to state that

literalist fundamentalism of ignorant Plymouth Brethren parents[1] in a fanatically religious atmosphere, where newspaper reading and listening to the wireless were forbidden, where the wrath and vengeance of God was held over his head as punishment for every trifling misdemeanour and where the belief in salvation through the drinking of the blood of the sacrificed Lamb of God was impressed upon him in the gruesome literal sense in which an African witch-doctor would understand this mystic doctrine. He then joined the Church of England and became a choir-boy and later assistant organist of Wakefield Cathedral, taking to a form of worship in which ritualism held a prominent place. At seventeen he won a 'divinity prize' with an essay on 'St. Peter in the Gospels and in the Acts' (judged to be a 'very praiseworthy effort'). The Harley Street psychiatrist Dr. Henry Yellowlees—who did not refer to either vampirism or to Jung's discovery of archetypal ideas (see above Appendix I)[2]—was told by the accused of a dream constantly recurrent at that period which he called 'the Dream of the bleeding Christ'. (No details were reported of this dream, but the reader will remember the frequent pictures showing the blood of Christ flowing from the spear-wound below the heart into the eucharistic cup from which it is drunk by some saint or ordinary communicant.)

'All along it was the question of blood that was troubling him

I knew nothing of the existence of this book until I read this notice. I have since then read it. Some of the author's statements—especially those on p. 462 concerning the alleged ape foetus then to be seen on Leonardo's 'Madonna of the Grotto' in the National Gallery, in reality accidental discolorations of the varnish removed in this year's (1949) cleaning of the picture—are quite fantastic. But it is conceivable that mongoloid features may be due to atavistic regression. Since it is certain that neither Haigh's school-fellows nor the journalists reporting the case knew of Dr. Crookshank's racialist theories, the fact of the multiple murderer's mongoloid appearance in his young days—not visible in his adult face—seems worth mentioning.

[1] See a portrait of the mother with the boy, *News of the World*, 24 July 1949.

[2] He diagnosed the case as one of 'pure paranoia'—whatever 'pure' may mean in this context—quoting Eugenio Tanzi's more than forty-years-old *Textbook of Mental Diseases*, Engl. trans. by W. Ford Robertson and T. C. Mackenzie, London (Rebman), 1908.

and he could not understand why he was told Christ was left to die slowly on the cross and was not killed at once' (in his later crimes he took care to kill his victims instantly and from behind so that there should be no unnecessary fear of death or suffering; incidentally, this case should be carefully meditated upon by those who repeat incessantly that a specifically Christian education is necessary for the development of human decency but who confuse what G. B. Shaw has opposed as 'Crosstianity' to Christianity, with the true *Imitatio Christi*).

The accused told the alienist that he had, at Wakefield, at the age of 16 or 17, a 'divine revelation' and was 'divinely guided' to interpret a verse in the Old Testament' (obviously Prov. v. 15, 'drink water out of thine own cistern and running waters out of thine own well'; cf. above, on John vii. 38) 'as an instruction to drink his own urine'. 'He had constantly followed this instruction to the day of the trial and was certainly doing it when the physician saw him' (another example of the pedagogic consequences of unguided solitary Bible-reading by Occidental children unfamiliar with the exuberance of Oriental metaphor not intended for sensitive and possibly neurotic readers of a critical age, rightly forbidden by the Roman Catholic Church).

A second 'revelation' was given to him in 1944 or 1945 by the appearance of 'the tree dream' which the psychiatrist appears to have made no attempt to explain to the judge or the jury. 'The dream was that he went out into a forest of crucifixes' (clearly a reminiscence of the many pictures, newspaper and other photographs of cemeteries of World Wars I and II with thousands of crucifixes marking the graves of the victims of human bestiality). These crucifixes 'turned gradually into trees with branches at right angles dripping with dew or rain. As he got near he saw it was blood dripping from the trees. One of the trees gradually assumed the shape of a man who held a bowl and collected blood from one of the trees. This tree got paler, and he himself felt that he was losing strength. Then the man, when the bowl was full, approached and invited him to drink it. At first he was unable to reach the man, who receded and the dream ended.' This dream was repeated six or seven nights in succession and during that time he was uneasy and distrait (in other words obsessed by his archetypic sacrificial magic ideas). 'After that the killings occurred and after one or two of them he dreamt again. Then the man did not recede from him and he was able to drink the blood.'

We are often told how much a classical education contributes to our humane understanding of our fellow-creatures. Yet none of the learned gentlemen who accused, defended or judged this religious maniac and who suggested to the jury that he might have invented his dreams because he 'elaborated' the account of his experiences from one session to the other—as if this were not the usual result of an anamnesis and psycho-analysis!—seems to have been helped to an understanding of this 'tree dream' by the faintest reminiscence of the bleeding tree in Ovid's eighth *Metamorphosis*:

> *Cuius ut in trunco fecit manus impia volnus*
> *Haud aliter fluxit, discussa cortice sanguis.*

['When the impious hand made a wound in its trunk, blood flowed from the broken bark.']

Nobody remembered from his Vergil (*Aen.*, III 26 ff.),

> *horrendum . . . dictu . . . mirabile monstrum*
> *nam quae prima solo ruptis radicibus arbos*
> *vellitur, huic atro liquuntur sanguine guttae*
> *et terram tabo maculant . . .*

['An awful portent, wonderful to tell. For from the first tree, which is torn from the ground with broken roots, drops of black blood trickle and stain the earth with gore.']

the awful portent of the tree torn up with his roots broken[1] which 'trickles with black blood and stains the earth with gore because these trees have grown up out of the unquiet grave of Polydorus, the bleeding tree who says with a piteous groan

> *nam Polydorus ego.*

'I am Polydorus. Here an iron harvest of spears covered my body and grew up into sharp javelins.']

[1] Blood flowing from the roots of a tree also in Afzelius, *Volkssagen und Volkslieder Schwedens*, Germ. transl. by Ungewitter, II, p. 308.

Even less could they be expected to know the child's question in Schiller's *Wilhelm Tell* (III, 3):

> *Vater, ists wahr, dass auf dem Berge dort*
> *Die Bäume bluten, wenn man einen Streich*
> *drauf führe mit der Axt?*

['Father, is it true that on that mountain yonder
The trees would bleed, if one did cut them with an axe's blade?']

Neither the lawyer nor the alienist is required to study anthropology. How should either of them know of such archetypal ideas as the belief that the alder tree bleeds when cut by the axe (Grimm, *Mythol.*, 2nd ed., quoting Meinert, *Kuhländchen*, p. 122; Mannhardt, *Baumkultus*, p. 35), that, indeed, all trees are believed to bleed when felled (*Aus der Oberpfalz*, II, 335; Mannhardt, *op. cit.*, p. 35, note 1) and that 'the tree feels the wound not less than a human being' (A. Peter, *Volkstümliches aus Österreichisch Schlesien*, Troppau, 1867, II, p. 30; Mannhardt, *ibid.*, note 2). They have not heard of the sacred larch-tree of Nauders in Tyrol, felled only in 1855, the trunk of which 'bled at the touch of the axe and from the branches of which blood was seen to drip' (Zingerle, *Sagen, Märchen und Gebräuche aus Tirol*, Innsbruck, 1859, pp. 109 ff. and 176).

For one who has seen the forest of crosses standing in the war-cemeteries, dripping with rain under the grey skies of Flanders and Northern France, it needs no great effort of imagination to think of these rain-drops as symbolizing the blood oozing from the tortured bodies of the men mouldering in their thousands, each one under the symbol of the *arbor infelix*[1] upon which the Son of Man hung in His supreme agony.

In the dream the tree which assumes the shape of a man collecting the blood of all the victims in a bowl which he offers as a drink is, of course, the Christ on the larger cross standing in the centre of the war-cemetery, somehow identified, as it were, with the human figure collecting the blood from the lance-wound of the Christ in the eucharistic chalice offered to the

[1] See the legal formula of judgement in the law-suit against Horatius (Livy, I, 26), 'arbori infelici' ['to a desiccated tree'] '*reste suspendito*' ['shall he be hanged by a rope'].

communicants. This tree[1] getting 'paler and he himself losing strength' is a transparent symbolization of the dreamer's vanishing 'strength through faith' which he passionately desires to recapture by drinking the blood of the sacrificial victim who died for the salvation of tortured humanity.

Then he has a motor accident which causes blood from a scalp-wound to flow into his mouth and gives him for the first time the intoxicating taste and *cruenta voluptas* of warm blood (above, note 24). This too he takes as a divine revelation and the recurrent dream as a 'divine guidance': he must 'drink the blood' to be saved.

Anyone who has read with an open and critical mind the distraught vapourings of Søren Kierkegaard on Abraham commanded to sacrifice Isaac and making ready, in blind obedience to his terrible god, to cut the throat of his son with a knife, will have no difficulty in reconstructing the interpretation which this alleged Old Testament prefiguration of the crucifixion—characteristically not mentioned in the three sittings the alienist had with the murderer—must have received in the obsessed mind of a man who justified the drinking of his own water from Prov. v. 15 (and John vii. 38). Only after his killings and the vampirist blood-drinkings did 'the man not recede from him and he was able to drink the blood' of salvation and recapture the firm faith in eternal life. (He said the killings were a third revelation and thought they might have to do with 'eternal life, but did not know how'. (He objected violently to his 'killings' being called 'murders'.) This lack of comprehension would not, of course, be too great a difficulty for the wishful thinking of the infantile mind of one who had been taught to believe even what seemed absurd to him, if he was to be saved.)

Men who cannot see the intense egotism of those who count the world well lost if only their own little souls survive death for ever, would think, with the alienist in charge, that the murderer's 'killings were entirely different from the other offences of dishonesty of which the prisoner had been convicted.' Yet, why should the religious maniac who sacrificed nine lives of

[1] See the Christ suspended on the 'tree of life', Eisler, *Orph-Dionys. Myst.*, p. 339, note 1, pl. XXI, fig. 122; cf. *ibid.*, p. 148, on the vine as the 'tree of life'.

strangers as well as of acquaintances to the 'salvation' of his wretched soul and to the strengthening of his primitive faith, not have appropriated with sly cunning the possessions of other victims to sustain the precious life of what he would have distinguished as his body from his soul? Why should maniacs *not* be actuated by motives of sordid profit? Because it is rational to strive for gain, does it follow that a man ceases to want wealth and an easy life when his mind begins to be obsessed by contorted religious ideas? Because English law—by the so-called Macnaughten rules—absurdly defines insanity as a state of mind in which a man does not know what he is doing or does not know that what he is doing is wrong, does it follow that a madman may not be perfectly aware of what he is doing and know that what he is doing is wrong? May not a madman say to himself in the words of Ovid

video meliora proboque, deteriora sequor

just like a sane person? The fact that the consciousness of a paranoiac is dominated by deep-rooted archetypal ideas does not mean that his power of logical reasoning is affected to the extent that he must act in an absurd and illogical manner in every other way. It does not mean that he is unconscious either of his actions or unaware of the social disapproval they are bound to incur—*if* he is found out. He may perfectly well know what he is doing, he may know that everybody else considers his actions criminal. His 'moral insanity' consists in his inability to resist the powerful impulses welling up from the subhuman atavist background of the individual mind and in the childish credulity which enables him to accept as 'divine revelations' justifying his behaviour the most absurd interpretations of misunderstood scriptural passages torn from their context.

There is no doubt that such individuals are extremely dangerous and must be permanently segregated. Otherwise, everything said above (pp. 49–50, and note 232, p. 236) applies with undiminished force to this clear case of vampirism complicated by religious mania.

INDEX

275

INDEX

INDEX

278

INDEX

Due